JASON COWLEY is a magazine editor, journalist and writer. He has been widely credited with transforming the fortunes of the *New Statesman*. According to the European Press Prize, 'Cowley has succeeded in revitalising the *New Statesman* . . . and giving it an edge and a relevance to current events it hasn't had for years.' In 2017, he was voted Editor of the Year - Current Affairs & Politics for the third time at the British Society of Magazine Editors Awards. He is the author of a memoir, *The Last Game*.

REACHING FOR UTOPIA

Making Sense of An Age of Upheaval

JASON COWLEY

SALT

CROMER

PUBLISHED BY SALT PUBLISHING 2018

2 4 6 8 10 9 7 5 3 1

Copyright © Jason Cowley 2018

Jason Cowley has asserted his right under the Copyright, Designs and
Patents Act 1988 to be identified as the author of this work.

First published in Great Britain in 2018 by
Salt Publishing Ltd
12 Norwich Road, Cromer, Norfolk NR27 0AX United Kingdom

www.saltpublishing.com

Salt Publishing Limited Reg. No. 5293401

A CIP catalogue record for this book is available from the British Library

ISBN 978 1 78463 152 9 (Hardback edition)
ISBN 978 1 78463 153 6 (Electronic edition)

Typeset in Neacademia by Salt Publishing

Printed and bound in Great Britain by Clays Ltd, Elcograf S.p.A

Salt Publishing Limited is committed to responsible forest management.
This book is made from Forest Stewardship Council™ certified paper.

For Edward

'The crisis consists precisely in the fact that the old is
dying and the new cannot be born; in this interregnum,
a great variety of morbid symptoms appear.'
ANTONIO GRAMSCI

'A map of the world that does not include
Utopia is not worth even glancing at.'
OSCAR WILDE

'Brexit means Brexit.'
THERESA MAY

CONTENTS

PART 3: LIVES AND LETTERS

INTRODUCTION: GETTING
THE BALANCE RIGHT

THERE'S NO DENYING that we are living through an
era of extraordinary politics. Old certainties are crumbling,
social trust has declined, and shocks keep happening, from the
election of Donald Trump as president of the United States, to
the vote for Brexit, to the no less astonishing triumph in France
of Emmanuel Macron, a former Rothschild banker who founded
his own movement and party and swept to power in 2017.

The *New Statesman* - where I have worked as editor since
autumn 2008 - began in 1913 as a weekly review of politics and
literature. So, it has existed for more than a century - through two
world wars - and yet by any measure the present era is remarkable:
Trump, Brexit, the Scottish independence referendum, the election
of Jeremy Corbyn as Labour leader and the rise of the radical left,
the crises in Europe, the rise and fall of Islamic State, a mini world
war in Syria, an unprecedented shift in power from the West to
the East - these are turbulent and volatile new times.

Our world is defined by entrenched wealth inequality, the
mass movement of people - including free movement within the
European Union - and astounding technological innovation and

disruption. Through globalisation and social networks, we've never been more connected to one another. And yet nationalism has returned with a vengeance, and we have entered a dangerous new age of great power rivalry, with China ascendant and Russia re-emerging to challenge America's faltering leadership of the West. It could be that we're returning to a state of affairs closer to the late nineteenth century, when Germany, Tsarist Russia and the United States were contesting Great Britain's imperial hegemony.

Many of our present anxieties and woes have their origins in the financial crisis of 2007–08. Since then, living standards for many in the West have declined (while soaring for the top one per cent) and wages have been stagnant. At the same time, globalisation has lifted hundreds of millions of people out of poverty in India and China; remarkable growth has reduced global extreme poverty from sixty per cent in the 1970s to less than ten per cent.

But these same forces have created new economic insecurities in the West. The decline of stable, well-paid work means that, for the first time, most of those living in poverty are employed.

Meanwhile, since the financial crash, Europe has been further destabilised by the eurozone crisis, the Greece crisis and the refugee crisis. The latest and most demanding disturbance to the balance of power is, of course, Brexit. No country has ever left the EU: but that is the epic task Britain has set itself. Our European partners are dismayed. Of the present leaders, perhaps only Macron has a vision for European reform.

❧

In Britain, we have lived through two distinct political and economic eras since the end of the Second World War. The first, from 1941 to 1979, was broadly the period of the social democratic welfare capitalist consensus, which ended when Margaret Thatcher won the 1979 general election.

The second – the so-called neoliberal era – was characterised by far-reaching free market transformation: the privatisation of nationalised industries; the rolling back of the interventionist state; tax cuts and deregulation; the liberalisation and opening up of the City of London (through the abolition of capital and exchange controls, the 'Big Bang', and so on); and the emergence of the new globalised economic order.

The left initially misunderstood Thatcherism, dismissing it as a transient phenomenon. But it became clear that it was something quite different: a counter-hegemonic project. The Thatcherites aspired not merely to alter the way the economy was run, but to reshape common sense. 'Economics are the method: the object is to change the soul,' Margaret Thatcher said.

But Thatcher's economic liberalism, paradoxically, undermined her social conservatism. Or as David Marquand put it in the *New Statesman* in 2009: 'The greatest irony of the Thatcher crusade is that its economics pulled against its ethics.' The society that emerged was not what the Thatcherites had intended.

In time, the conviction that there was no alternative to free-market triumphalism hardened into dogma, an ideological statement of faith. We moved from having a market economy to being a market society, as the Harvard philosopher Michael Sandel said to me.

The financial crisis of 2007–08 marked another turning point. New conjunctures are incubators of the new: but a new political and economic settlement, a new consensus, is waiting to be born. In their different ways, the Corbynites and the Brexiteers are both competing for supremacy as liberal centrists are marginalised. It could be that the next British general election will be a contest between Corbynism and Brexitism. Whatever happens, this feels like an age in passing, what Antonio Gramsci called an interregnum.

∗

The pieces in this book were all written under the pressure of deadlines and have been revised or edited for publication: some cuts have been made, some have been restored. And I have written postscripts where it was necessary to take account of events: a referendum, a snap general election. I hope they share a family resemblance: when I am writing about politics I am writing about culture, and vice versa.

As a journalist, I am fascinated by the people in power attempting to create the history of our era, as well as those who document it. Reading through these pieces I notice that themes recur and interconnect: Englishness and English identity; the future of the British Union; the class system; the failures of centre-left social democracy and the rise of populism; the end of political eras; nostalgia and memory; the politics of the common good; how to write convincingly about the defining particulars of the present moment.

When I interview prime ministers or party leaders (these encounters have been negotiated and have strict time limits), I'm not seeking to trap them into making a gaffe, nor am I chasing a quick headline (though headlines are always appreciated). But I do want to know what they know. How and why do they do it? What motivates them to seek power, beyond personal ambition, to go on and endure, even in the deepest crisis? Do they have a method? And, crucially, what distinguishes a successful politician – Blair, Farage, Salmond, Corbyn – from someone who fails, such as Ed Miliband?

I also enjoy writing about football, for some of the same reasons that attract me to politics: both are an intensely competitive, results-driven business and the key protagonists, or 'players', are constantly being tested and evaluated in the white heat of the public arena. There's a rhythm to each season, and fixed annual set-piece events: a cup final or party conference speech. And, of course, stuff keeps happening, which means there's continuous speculation and the excitement of anticipation – what are the trends, who's up, who's down, who's winning and losing? And why?

Writing about politics and editing a political and literary magazine have made me less rather than more partisan: my politics are sceptical and the shocks of recent times have made me much warier of prediction. And I think liberals, in particular, should reflect on why they have suffered so many setbacks.

Yet, in spite of the darkening of the hour, we cannot lose faith in liberalism, democracy and the rule of law. Yes, we have discovered that freedom and toleration cannot be taken for granted, but this means that we must all the more vigorously defend them, just as we should cherish common institutions such as the NHS and BBC, which help create the ties that bind the multinational British state together.

Having spoken to and interviewed many senior politicians, it's clear to me that our democratically elected leaders must show greater humility. They ought to be more honest and have more realistic expectations about what politics can achieve. They should stop over-promising and acting as if all of the world's problems are soluble. They should be guided by empiricism not ideology. Politics is a competition between partial truths, which is why reason and evidence are so important. Incremental improvements and progress are possible, but not inevitable. What is gained can just as easily be lost – but what is lost can also be regained.

One should accept the complexity of the world and the limits of our understanding. Moderation is desirable, especially in this age of extremes. In the words of the American commentator David Brooks, 'Being a moderate does not mean picking something mushy in the middle, but picking out the strong policies at either end, because politics is essentially about balance, getting the balance right.'

For the political philosopher and *New Statesman* writer John Gray, 'politics is the pursuit of a succession of temporary remedies to recurring human evils'. That may be too dark but the subtext is this: liberal societies cannot depend on history for their survival. The assumption that markets and democracy are mutually reinforcing was always an illusion. China and Russia have not evolved to become liberal democracies. Economic liberalisation has not led to political liberalisation.

In fact, ours is increasingly becoming an age of crony capitalism, buttressed by authoritarianism and nationalism – think Putin's Russia, Trump's America, Erdoğan's Turkey, Xi Jingping's China, Modi's India. Or the illiberal democracies of eastern Europe. Or the Gulf autocracies. Macron is a liberal optimist; there aren't many like him.

Moderation, scepticism, caution, decency, empathy, humility, order, security, moral wisdom, social responsibility, the common good, the protective state: these should be some of the watch words and phrases of any new political dispensation or settlement that emerges out of this age of upheaval. One can only hope. Meanwhile, the long interregnum goes on.

PART 1

REACHING FOR UTOPIA

NEW TOWN BLUES

THE THREE MEN had been drinking for several hours by the time they arrived at The Stow shopping centre in Harlow. It was approaching midnight on a warm bank holiday weekend towards the end of August. Arkadiusz Jozwik and his two companions – the men were Polish and lived and worked locally in the troubled Essex town – were hungry and tired. Jozwik bought a pizza from a takeaway and sat on a wall to eat it. It was then that he and his companions noticed a group of teenagers nearby, some of them on bikes. The boys, and they were boys, aged fifteen and sixteen, approached and there was a confrontation. The men became loud and antagonistic, and, as each group goaded the other, one of the boys slipped out of the pack and sneaked up behind Jozwik, landing to the back of his head what would later be described in court as his 'Superman punch'.

Jozwik fell – perhaps partly because he was drunk, perhaps partly because he was off balance – and hit his head hard on the pavement, after which the boys panicked and fled. Jozwik was unconscious and blood leaked from his ears as he was taken by ambulance to the town's Princess Alexandra Hospital, from where he was transferred to Addenbrooke's in Cambridge.

The next day Essex police described the attack as 'brutal' and called it a 'potential hate crime' – the suggestion being that Jozwik was assaulted because he was heard speaking Polish. Which alerted the media that what had happened on the night of Saturday 27 August 2016 at The Stow shopping centre was more sinister than a routine late-night altercation that had gone seriously wrong. It was a hate crime, a political crime.

This was the febrile summer of the European referendum, when the air was rancid with accusation and counter-accusation and England had never seemed more divided between those who wanted the United Kingdom to continue as a member of the European Union and those who wanted out; between 'Remainers' and 'Leavers'. Like hundreds of thousands of other Poles who had moved to Britain in the years after former communist states from Eastern Europe joined the EU, Jozwik, who was single, believed life in England offered opportunities that his home country could not. In 2012 he followed his mother, a widow, to Essex because he did not want to be alone in Poland. He lived with her in Harlow, where he found work in a sausage factory.

The day after the attack in The Stow, six youths were arrested on suspicion of attempted murder. Then, on 29 August, Arkadiusz Jozwik – Arek to friends and family – died in hospital, having never regained consciousness. He was forty years old and had suffered a brain injury and a fractured skull.

No one has established the exact motivation for the attack – a witness reported that Jozwik racially abused one of the boys, who was black or mixed race – but whatever the motive, the impact of the punch that felled Jozwik was felt around the world: the *New York Times* incorrectly reported, for instance, that he was 'repeatedly pummelled and kicked by a group of boys and girls'. And soon it was being called the 'Brexit Murder'.

Every district in Essex voted Leave in the referendum of 23 June 2016 (the pro-Brexit vote in Harlow, which has high unemployment and areas of deprivation, was sixty-eight per cent compared with the national average of fifty-two per cent). After Jozwik's death, the Polish president, Andrzej Duda, wrote to religious leaders in Britain requesting their assistance in preventing further attacks on Polish nationals, and the Polish ambassador to Britain was taken on a tour of Harlow. Around the same time, Polish police officers were sent from Warsaw to patrol the area around The Stow, and the Polish community organised a solidarity march in the town.

'We Europeans can never accept Polish workers being beaten up, harassed or even murdered in the streets of Essex,' the president of the European Commission, Jean-Claude Juncker, said in an annual state of the union address on 14 September.

The subtext of Juncker's intervention was this: the death of Arkadiusz Jozwik was a manifestation of the xenophobic forces unleashed by the Brexit referendum, and Harlow and its people were implicated.

Sometimes I dream about Harlow. I was born in what was then called the new town, at home, in a rented maisonette above a parade of shops, with just a midwife to keep watch on my mother as my father waited anxiously with my four-year-old sister in another room. I was educated at various state schools in the town and lived there for the first eighteen years of my life.

In these dreams of Harlow, I am who I am now – middle-aged, a husband and father – but I'm invariably back in the house in the quiet cul-de-sac where we lived as a family of five from 1972 to 1983 and where I spent most of my childhood and adolescence before my parents, unsettled by what they considered to be the inexorable decline of the town, moved to Hertfordshire. My father, lucid and calm as he ever was, is alive in these dreams, and I have a sense of having the conversations that his sudden death from a heart attack at the age of fifty-six never allowed us to have.

There was a time, when I first began working in London in my mid-twenties, that I never wanted to be reminded of where I grew up. I could scarcely admit that I was an Essex man, Harlow-born.

There was a blockage. A desire to forget or escape. It was as if I was embarrassed about something I couldn't quite articulate, something bound up with the gradations of the English class system and people's perceptions of Harlow as a failed town, as 'Chav Town'.

Located at the junction of First Avenue and Howard Way, The Stow opened in the early 1950s as the first of the town's neighbourhood shopping centres. But, as with so many of Harlow's public and civic spaces, it has been neglected. I know The Stow well. Our family dentist had his surgery there and, when I was in primary school, after each visit to see him, my mother would treat me to a hot sausage roll or sugar-encrusted jam doughnut from Dorringtons, a family bakery which today still occupies the same space in the two-tier shopping centre, close to where Arkadiusz Jozwik was punched, fell and hit his head.

When I returned to The Stow last April, drawn back by interest in the 'Brexit Murder', I was shocked at how run-down it was. In the pedestrian-only precinct, pound and charity shops – the RSPCA and Salvation Army occupied what were once prime sites – and scrappy fast-food joints proliferated. There was a tattoo and body-piercing shop. A Thai massage parlour was adjacent to an undertaker, a nice juxtaposition of sex and death that would have amused Freud. The Essex Skipper – the original pubs in the town were named after butterflies or moths, just as some of the roads were later renamed after left-wing political heroes: Mandela Avenue, Allende Avenue and so on – was shabby and unwelcoming.

It was an unseasonably warm afternoon yet the area seemed

desolate. When I returned to my car three young men were sitting on a wall next to it. One of them introduced himself by saying, 'Good car!' He spoke heavily accented English. He and his friends turned out to be Romanians and when I asked what life was like for Eastern Europeans in the town they weren't interested in telling me. So I asked if they worked. They said they did not. How long had they been here? Not long. They had believed they were coming to a new town. But, they said, Harlow wasn't new: it looked old.

My parents arrived in Harlow in 1959 when there were fewer than six thousand people there (today the population is eighty-six thousand and rising). They were from east London and had been child wartime evacuees, an experience of separation and dislocation my mother found especially upsetting. Their education was interrupted by the war and they both left school at fifteen, my father (who passed up a scholarship to study engineering) to work as an apprentice shirt cutter and my mother as an assistant in a City of London law firm. They met at a dance at Manor Hall, Chigwell, Essex, and were married in 1958. A few months later they moved to Harlow - my mother's eldest sister had already settled there - searching for new opportunities in the nascent new town.

The 1946 New Towns Act created eight towns, the purpose of which was to provide decent housing for 340,000 'surplus' or 'bombed-out' Londoners - after more than a million houses were destroyed or damaged in the capital during the Second World War. Most of them were already small country towns - Hemel, Stevenage, Hatfield, Welwyn - that would be extended or built around. But Harlow in rural west Essex would be completely new - sixty per cent of the land was compulsorily purchased from one owner, Commander Godfrey Arkwright, the head of an old Essex hunting and landowning family - and the first arrivals there considered themselves pioneers, marking out new territory.

The original village of Harlow (renamed Old Harlow) is mentioned in the Domesday Book. This and other long-established settlements – Potter Street, Parndon, Netteswell, Tye Green, Latton, Churchgate Street – were subsumed by the chief architect-planner, Frederick Gibberd, into his urban masterplan: built on and around, developed, expanded, but not erased or demolished. It was essential for Gibberd that Harlow combined town and country, the urban and rural: he wanted open countryside inside and surrounding the town. He wanted to create 'a fine contrast between the work of man and the work of God'. The valley of the River Stort formed the northern boundary and, as Gibberd wrote, 'small hamlets and fine woods [were] interspersed throughout the area'.

My parents were delighted by how rural Harlow was when they arrived: the town was being built around them, self-contained neighbourhood by neighbourhood. For the first time in his life my father suffered from hay fever, which blighted his summers but mysteriously disappeared whenever he returned for any length of time to the city or travelled overseas.

For my parents, moving to Harlow was a form of escape: away from the bomb sites and ruined Victorian buildings and streets of east London towards, they believed, a more optimistic future. From the old to the new. Lord Reith, the first director general of the BBC, was chairman of the New Towns Committee. For Reith, these towns were 'essays in civilisation', and he wanted the people in them to have 'a happy and gracious way of life'.

The emphasis in Harlow in the early years was always on the new – on new hope, new beginnings and on the vitality of youth. Don't look back. Never look back. Yet, in the 1960s, there were reports of a phenomenon that became known as 'new town blues'

– the experience of dislocation and isolation felt by those who were struggling to adapt, or who simply mourned the loss of the communities from which they'd been deracinated.

But I knew nowhere else. By the time I was born, Harlow was known as 'pram town' because of all the young couples starting families there, and the birth rate was three times higher than the national average. Henry Moore, whose house and studio were in the nearby Hertfordshire hamlet of Perry Green, was invited to create a public sculpture that symbolised the radiant promise of the new town.

Today, Moore's *The Harlow Family Group* is situated in the expansive entrance area to the town's civic centre. A man and woman sit side by side, proud and upright. The man's right arm is wrapped protectively around the woman and she is holding a young child. At its unveiling outside St Mary-at-Latton Church, Mark Hall, in 1956, Sir Kenneth Clark, then chairman of the Arts Council of Great Britain, called Moore's 2.5 metre high and 1.5 ton sculpture a symbol of a 'new humanitarian civilisation' that had emerged out of the devastation of the Second World War.

The Harlow Family Group was one of many notable pieces by Barbara Hepworth, Leon Underwood, Ralph Brown, Elisabeth Frink, Gerda Rubinstein, Auguste Rodin, Karel Vogel and others bought and commissioned by the Harlow Arts Trust, which was set up in 1953 and supported by philanthropists and the town corporation. It was paternalistic, this desire to create public art for ordinary working people, but the motivation was pure. 'So often sculpture is a sort of cultural concession that has little relevance to the real life of a town but, in [this] case, it has become an integral part of Harlow,' Frederick Gibberd said in 1964. He wanted Harlow to be 'home to the finest works of art, as in Florence and other splendid cities'.

This was an era – hard to believe now – when London was de-populating. Before he was married my father, the only child of a bus driver, lived in a terraced house in Forest Gate, which, as the name suggests, is where the East End thins out and nudges up against Epping Forest. The family home had a small garden and outside lavatory. My father was a talented boy and a gifted cricketer, and he and his mother were frustrated by the life that was being mapped out for him (his father, Frank, who boxed recreationally in the East End pubs, was a quiet, kindly, unambitious man). He did not want to follow his father onto the buses or work in the docks as some of his ancestors had. Nor did he want to emigrate to Australia, like one of his uncles. My father was culturally aspirational. Encouraged by his fiercely protective, austere, red-haired mother (she used to wear a brooch displaying a photograph of her son, whom she called 'everyone's favourite'), he dressed smartly, read poetry, listened to jazz and bought the *Observer* every Sunday for the books and arts reviews. He liked the theatre and was enchanted by Hollywood. He adored the Marx Brothers and W. C. Fields. The East End of his late adolescence was not today's vibrant, polyglot, multi-ethnic realm of hipster bars, tech start-ups, barista masterclasses, Balti curry houses, craft-beer festivals, Tinder and Grindr hook-ups, and astronomical property prices: it was parochial, impoverished and diminished. He wanted out.

Yet something happened to my father in middle age, a period when his good career in what he always called the 'rag trade' seemed to drift and stall, and he became increasingly nostalgic and introspective. He began to brood on the old world he'd left behind as a young man – the sense of community he'd known, the neighbourliness. Perhaps very belatedly he, too, was suffering from new town blues. He listened repeatedly to music from the 1940s, especially the popular songs of Al Bowlly, the southern African crooner killed by a German parachute bomb that exploded outside his London flat in 1941. 'Oh no, he's going on about the war years again,' we used to tease. He showed me some of the poems he wrote, always set in the East End during the early 1940s or just at the end of the war. One was called 'Don't Cheer Us Girls We're British', an ironic slogan he'd seen written on a jeep carrying troops along a road close to where he lived.

My father was a war child. The first day of the Blitz, 7 September 1940 – 'Black Saturday' – a day of clear blue skies, coincided with his sixth birthday. He was so traumatised by the experience of the assault on the docklands and nearby neighbourhoods – he recalled burning buildings and an apocalyptic red glow in the sky – that he lost his voice. His father, the bus driver, refused to leave the house during subsequent intense bombing raids. My father and his mother would hurry to an air-raid shelter whenever they heard the sirens warning of an imminent Luftwaffe attack; but Frank would try his luck above ground, even as nearby houses and buildings were being destroyed.

Towards the end of his life, my father spoke often about how the depredations but also the intensity of a child's experience of the home front, and indeed of the urgency of wartime more generally, united the people around him: there was a commonality of purpose, a conviction that if they could endure, if they could get through the worst, the future would be better. Which is why Harlow seemed so attractive to him.

War and the wartime command economy (Labour leader Clement Attlee officially became Churchill's deputy prime minister in the coalition government in February 1942, though he was the effective deputy as Lord Privy Seal from May 1940) created the conditions for socialism and a new settlement in Britain. Without the war, the Labour Party would not have swept to power in 1945. 'The revolution in England has already begun,' H. G. Wells said on 22 May 1940 when Attlee introduced the Emergency Powers

Defence Bill in the House of Commons and sandbags went up across Westminster. For Orwell, who admired the patriotism of the working class, the 'English revolution' gathered momentum with the epic retreat from Dunkirk. 'Like all else in England, it happens in a sleepy, unwilling way, but it is happening,' Orwell wrote. 'The war has speeded it up, but it has also increased, and desperately, the necessity for speed.'

To grow up in Harlow was to be on the front line of the English revolution. More than this, you were a cog in a grand social and political experiment. I understand this now, but back then I was just living. My friends and I were children of the welfare state. The social transformations and central planning of the immediate post-war period, as the new Labour government set about building what Attlee called a 'New Jerusalem', had created thrilling possibilities for us. The National Health Service was established; the National Insurance Act abolished the hated means test for welfare provision; essential industries such as the railways and mining were nationalised; the Town and Country Planning Act was passed, opening the way for mass housebuilding and the re-development of huge tracts of land; Britain's independent nuclear deterrent was commissioned; the gap between rich and poor narrowed.

This was a very British revolution, and a pragmatic experiment with socialism: the state was powerful but not all-powerful. It was not a vindictive exercise in destruction but one of creation: about a new social contract between the state and the individual to enhance the common good. The monarchy, the landowning families and the ancient public schools (Attlee was a proud Haileyburian) were untouched. Individual freedom and the great British institutions were cherished. The cost of war had impoverished the nation, left it with a ruinous trade deficit and ended Britain's imperial hegemony. But these were new times. Progressive change was not only possible, it was believed to be necessary. As Attlee recognised, the British people 'wanted a new start'. They had suffered and they had endured. Now, he said, they were 'looking towards the future'.

Our lives as children were socially engineered and it seemed everything we needed was provided by the state: housing, education, health care, libraries, recreational and sports facilities. There were playschemes where we gathered to play or take part in organised games during the holidays. The town had a network of cycle tracks, among the most extensive in the country, which connected all neighbourhoods to the town centre, the High, which was built on the highest settlement, and to the two main industrial areas, Temple Fields and the Pinnacles. In 1961, a multi-purpose sports centre, the first of its kind in Britain, was opened. It was funded by local people through voluntary contributions via their rates (my aunt was proud to be one of the enthusiastic contributors).

One friend has since described the experience of growing up in the town in the sixties and seventies as 'East Germany without the Stasi'. Those of us born and raised there were referred to as 'citizens of the future'. Rural spaces (the so-called green wedges of the master plan, one of which became the magnificent town park, with its skating rink, bandstand, nine-hole pitch and putt golf course and animal centre) and planned recreation areas for children were meant to encourage us to lead healthy, active lives and to play out safely. In the words of a 1958 public information film about Harlow, 'If these boys and girls don't grow up to face successfully the problems of their day, it will not be the fault of the architects and planners who helped to give them a start.'

What I didn't realise then – of course, I saw but I did not see

– was that Harlow was, in effect, a monoculture. The original aspiration was to create a 'classless' society but, growing up there, it felt mostly as if you were living in a one-class town – that was, working class. There was a small middle-class intelligentsia, who participated in Labour Party politics, in the local drama, literary and film societies and who gathered around the Playhouse, which had opened in 1971 for live theatre, films and exhibitions. My father, whose interests were cultural rather than political, was part of this scene.

But, on the whole, nearly everyone I met was white working class. Out of the two hundred and fifty or so children in my year at secondary school – a huge non-selective, mixed-ability comprehensive, opened in 1959 and enlarged in 1972, one of eight in the town – I remember one boy whose family was Hong Kong Chinese (he ended up running an Oriental restaurant in Germany) and two girls whose parents were Indian. Everyone else was white. My classmates' parents had, for the most part, come from the East End or the poorer parts of north London, such as Edmonton or Walthamstow, and many worked in the town's factories and manufacturing plants – the International Telephone and Telegraph Corporation (which by the end of the 1970s employed eight thousand people), the Cossor Group, Revertex Chemicals, Johnson Matthey Metals, Schreiber, Pitney Bowes, United Glass.

These companies had their own social clubs and sports teams, even boys' football teams, which I played against in the recreational league for Newtown Spartak, a name more redolent of the Soviet Union.

Before the introduction of Margaret Thatcher's Right to Buy scheme, which enabled tenants to buy their council house at a large discount, most of the houses in the town were owned by the town corporation. (Even today, a third of the housing stock is council-owned.) Yet from 1972 we owned our house, and lived on one of the few private developments, or executive estates as they were known. This set us apart somewhat. This and the fact that my father did not work locally but commuted to London, driving there in his Alfa Romeo rather than take the train. Because he worked in the rag trade – designing, range-building, merchandising – he wore fashionable, often flamboyant clothes, and he travelled incessantly – to India, Hong Kong, the United States, South Korea, France, Switzerland, Italy, Germany.

My father had studied at night school and was unusually articulate – 'posh' my friends called him. But he wasn't posh: he simply did not speak with the local accent, which today we call 'Estuary English', the dialect associated with people living in and around London, especially those close to the River Thames and its estuary. My mother called it 'sub-cockney', distinguishing it from the accent of her father, a hard-working and thrifty carpenter who was born, as she liked to remind us, 'within the sound of the Bow Bells' (the bells of St Mary-le-Bow church, Cheapside), a badge of honour worn by true cockneys.

Daily life at my secondary school was a process of negotiation and adaptation: I could not speak there as freely and candidly as I did at home. At home, if I spoke as I did at school, my mother would chasten me for my glottal stops and h-dropping. At school, if I spoke as I did at home, I would have been mocked as 'posh', a grave insult. If some of my classmates visited our book-cluttered house, I used to hide my father's magazines – the *New Statesman*, the *Listener*, *i-D*, *City Limits* – and newspapers because he did not read the *Sun* or the *Mirror*, like their fathers. I was frustrated that he did not conform to Harlow norms, even though the conformity I wished upon him would have been a betrayal of all that he wanted, who he was, his great expectations. Sometimes when he was out I'd open his wardrobe and be overwhelmed by the warm, seductive smell of his clothes. I was especially fascinated by his two-colour shoes and exotic shirts and bright ties. Why did he dress so unlike my classmates' fathers, some of whom wore donkey jackets and DM boots to work?

There was little sense, in the five years I spent at comprehensive school (I left at the age of sixteen to do A levels at Harlow College), that we were being prepared for university. I once mentioned, on a whim, that I'd like to study law without knowing what that would have entailed. I was told by a teacher that law was for 'private-school boys', as if that was the end of the matter. *It was useful to get that learnt.* Most weeks it was a case of getting through and getting by. Woodwork, metalwork, motor vehicle studies and home economics were among the subjects taught. I was hopeless at all of them.

The headmaster was dictatorial and belligerent. Short, stocky and bald headed, he did not so much walk as strut angrily. He was missing a finger from one of his hands and we fantasised about how he might have lost it. If he'd once had ideals – I discovered decades later that he was a committed communist – they didn't seem to inform his style of leadership. The only time I saw him show any emotion other than rage was when, with passionate intensity, he recited in assembly Wilfred Owen's protest poem 'Dulcet et Decorum Est'. Whenever he strutted into the dining hall at lunchtime I looked down as a chill settled over the room, as if the large windows that overlooked the playground had been thrown open on a winter's day. The ritual was unchanging: the headmaster would shout, rap a coin furiously on one of the tables before shunting several of them across the floor, as if there was some perfect alignment into which he was for ever trying to force them.

My secondary school was not dysfunctional – I never witnessed shocking violence in the classroom or complete loss of control by a teacher – but it was mediocre. And there was an absence of joy: a joy in learning and intellectual discovery.

One of my closest friends joined the Inter-City Firm (ICF), the hardcore firm of West Ham hooligans, and was sent to prison after being implicated in an ICF rampage on a cross-Channel ferry. The late 1970s and early 1980s was a period of profound social unrest: football hooliganism, industrial strikes, inner-city race riots, the rise of the skinhead movement and the neo-fascists of the National Front. There seemed to be a psychological connection between the aggression and violence some of us experienced in our daily lives – fights in the playground or in the streets or on the terraces at football matches – and what was happening in wider society as the post-war political and economic consensus crumbled. With the election of Margaret Thatcher in 1979, Britain was entering another period of revolutionary – or perhaps, more accurately, counter-revolutionary – change.

Utopia means nowhere or no place. Harlow is often called a nowhere zone or left-behind town, which you pass through on the way to somewhere else. *News from Nowhere* was the title of William Morris's futuristic novel about a socialist Utopia. There was only bad news from Harlow following Arkadiusz Jozwik's death in the summer of 2016. The suggestion in much of the initial reporting of the so-called Brexit Murder was that in reaching for Utopia, the town's pioneers and planners had ended up creating the opposite of what was intended: a dystopia.

On 31 July 2017, I went to Chelmsford Crown Court to hear Judge Patricia Lynch deliver her verdict on the Jozwik case. Before proceedings began, I sat in a tatty reception area outside the courtroom directly opposite to where the teenage defendant's family waited. Almost a year had passed since Arkadiusz Jozwik had died, and the defendant was now sixteen. His family – including his mother and grandmother – were suspicious of my interest and did not want to be interviewed when I approached them. The youth just looked at me blankly. I gave the family my contact details and asked if they would call me, but they never did. I followed up with several phone calls to their solicitor in Old Harlow. But the family had chosen silence.

That afternoon I spoke to the defendant's uncle as he smoked a cigarette in the sunshine outside the court building. He was in his twenties, had a sleeve of tattoos on one arm and expressed bewilderment about what had happened at The Stow. Inside, his nephew wore a white shirt several sizes too big, a loosely knotted thick dark tie and plain black trousers. He was short, had a wavy fringe and a wispy moustache. He seemed lost and, at times, even bored as he sat in the box, watched anxiously by his mother. She had a heavy cold, though it was high summer, and I noticed her nails were bitten down to stubs.

The mother looked sadly unsurprised as her son was convicted by a jury of the manslaughter of Arkadiusz Jozwik. Jenny Hopkins, Chief Crown Prosecutor, said she was satisfied that there had been no intent by the youth to kill Jozwik. It was not a racist attack or hate crime, as had been widely reported. 'We decided therefore that the correct charge was one of manslaughter,' she said. 'Manslaughter is the unlawful killing of another person with an intention to do some harm, or the foresight that some physical harm may result.' The court was told the youth put 'the full force of his body into the punch' and he must have been aware 'when he punched Mr Jozwik in this way that some harm was likely to be caused'.

The Chief Prosecutor continued, 'This was a senseless assault and with that one punch, which was over in seconds, the youth was responsible for Mr Jozwik losing his life and causing unimaginable anguish to Mr Jozwik's family and friends.'

The judge announced that sentencing would take place on Friday 8 September. By this time, the media were losing interest in the case. This was no 'Brexit Murder'.

❧

One rainy morning just before Christmas, I went to see the head of Harlow Council, an animated Labour councillor called Jon Clempner. He was angry at how, in his view, Essex police had mishandled the case, allowing the fires of rumour and allegation to rage out of control. (Clempner resigned as leader in January 2018.) 'The police knew within twenty-four hours that it was not a racist attack or a murder. But they did not close down the speculation until it was too late,' he told me as we drank tea. His office was in the civic centre overlooking the Water Gardens, which were originally designed by Frederick Gibberd as a series of parallel terraces and have since been reconfigured and truncated. From the wide, high window, I looked out across the Water Gardens, over a car park, cycle track, some woodland and nearby fields. Beyond these fields I could see in the far distance the housing estate where my grandfather came to live after he retired, so that he could be closer to his son, who would die before him.

Something was missing, however: the high-rise modernist town hall, once considered to be Harlow's most important building in its most important space, the civic square. Designed by Gibberd and opened by Clement Attlee in 1960, it was demolished in the mid-2000s as part of the first phase of the redevelopment of the semi-derelict town centre. A huge Asda supermarket now dominated the space where the town hall once stood in imposing isolation, like a monumental watchtower.

One afternoon, many years ago, while on a school trip to the High when I still lived in the town, some friends and I detached ourselves from the group and slipped illicitly into the town hall. Local rumour had it that there was a nuclear bunker in the basement and we wanted to find it. But, instead, we took the lift up to the observation tower, where we found ourselves quite alone.

We looked out across the surrounding landscape. There, laid out before us, were the cool, clean geometric patterns of the town in which we lived, with its centrally planned network of roads and avenues, its schools and factories and council estates and green wedges. We remained in the observation tower until it was almost dark, watching in wonder as the lights in the distant houses below were switched on, one by one, their amber shimmer illuminating the grid-like structures on which the town was built. And then the houses seemed to melt away and I tried to imagine what it must have been like here before the new town came, the rural tranquility and the emptiness, the very absence of people.

It's taken me a long time to recalibrate the experience of growing up in Harlow. Most of the children I knew, some clever and gifted, never considered for a moment that university was a possibility for them and they contentedly left full-time education as soon as they could. Who knows what became of them.

Like most of my peers, I very nearly didn't make it to university. I rebelled at Harlow College, switching subjects and missing or repeatedly turning up late for classes, before eventually dropping out. In my late teens, after signing on the dole, restlessly bored, in love with someone who was in love with someone else, and in need of money, I found a job as a clerk at the Electricity Council at Millbank in London. I couldn't afford the train fare so commuted on a coach from my parents' house, a journey that took two or three hours on some days because of traffic congestion. And then I had to do it again in the evening. But it was during those coach journeys that I began reading seriously for the first time.

After six months working as a clerk in a labyrinthine public-sector bureaucracy, I decided to cram-study A levels. In other words, I gave myself nine months to change my life. A benevolent senior manager at the Electricity Council allowed me 'day release'

from the office every Friday to return to Harlow College, where I'd
been such a poor student and mocked as a 'dilettante' by my tutor.
This time, I would study politics, in which I had an intensifying
interest. I also enrolled to study for an A level in English literature
at a Thursday-evening night class at a comprehensive school in
Old Harlow. Here I came under the influence of a man called
David Huband, who was wise, soft-voiced and bearded, and the
kind of inspirational teacher I'd never encountered before, the *one*
teacher we all need to meet. As one of the local intelligentsia, he
knew people who knew my father and he took an interest in me.
He must have sensed that I was in trouble, existentially alarmed
and adrift.

The three hours I spent in his company every Thursday
evening, from seven to ten, changed how I thought about the
world, and those nine months, from September 1985 to May 1986,
working at the council, reading while on the coach and studying at
weekends at Harlow library or at home, were transformative. I told
virtually no one I was studying because I feared failure and the
continuing humiliation of life as a clerk. In late May and June, as
the football World Cup played out in Mexico, I took my A levels.
At the end of the summer I left for university: in one bound, I
believed I was finally free from Harlow and all its associations,
never looking back. Forward, forward, forward.

On 8 September 2017, a sixteen-year-old Harlow resident was
sentenced to three and a half years in a young offender institution
for the manslaughter of Arkadiusz Jozwik. Passing sentence, Judge
Patricia Lynch said that Jozwik had been a 'perfectly decent, well-
loved man in his prime'. He would be mourned by his family. As
the judge spoke you could hear people in the courtroom weeping.
'A year has passed since Arek died but every day I miss him as
much,' Ewa Jozwik, his mother, said in a statement read out in

court. 'There are moments I don't want to live any more.' She was present for the sentencing and wept continuously.

For the defence, Patrick Upward said that the youth, who once again wore a white shirt and black tie as he sat in the defendant box, felt 'remorse' at what had happened – he nodded when he heard this – and made reference to his troubled family background and the serious illness of his father. The court heard that he had two previous convictions, one for threatening behaviour, yet was 'not far removed from being a youngster of good character despite those difficulties'. But, in her final address, Judge Lynch said that the defendant had fled the shopping centre after the attack and done 'nothing for the welfare of the deceased'. When the sentence was announced, the youth – who resembled more than ever a lost boy – waved meekly at his family and stumbled slightly as he left the box. His mother, crying now, shouted, 'I love you.' She and other family members hurried out of the courtroom and could be heard weeping in the corridor.

It was raining as Ewa Jozwik left the court building in Chelmsford. Asked by waiting reporters outside, several from Polish television stations, if she believed the sentence was fair, she shook her head in a forlorn gesture of frustration or defeat. 'All the time I can see in my mind the moment I saw him lying motionless in the hospital bed connected to the life-support machine,' she said of her dead son. 'I wanted him to wake up badly.'

Arkadiusz Jozwik is buried in Harlow and the inscription on his gravestone is: *you were a dream, now you are a memory.*

Reflecting on the case, I felt only sorrow – for Jozwik, of course, and those who loved him, but also for the incarcerated youth, 'not far removed from being a youngster of good character', and his family. I felt sorrow, too, for Harlow, which in the immediate aftermath of Jozwik's death, as the town was flooded with reporters from around the world, and Polish police patrolled

The Stow shopping centre, had come to symbolise all that was perceived to be rotten in England. The vote for Brexit had revealed a fractious and fractured country. Harlow, a once-utopian settlement, was one of the 'left behind' towns, with a disenchanted and xenophobic population. Though only a short thirty-minute train ride from the stupendous wealth and diversity of one of the world's most globalised cities, it had been locked out from prosperity, as if part of another country altogether.

One recent afternoon I went on a bike ride around Harlow: the cycle tracks, though more rutted and uneven than before, remain among the glories of the town. I enjoyed being back on a brisk cold day. I know few people there nowadays and visit only very occasionally to see my mother's eldest sister, who is ninety. She has lived in the same modest terraced house for more than five decades, a short walk from the first school I attended as an infant. Yet, in recent years, rather than go straight home after visiting my aunt, I've found myself driving around estates I once knew so well, along roads still familiar, past fields where I used to play. Once I pulled up outside the church where I was an altar boy – until playing Sunday-morning football liberated me from the unloved ritual.

I'm not sure what I'm looking for. I once even retraced my morning walk to secondary school, which involved making my way along a narrow alleyway that ran between the gardens of two houses at the end of which teenage smokers would wait intimidatingly. For amusement or out of boredom they kicked holes in the wooden garden fences and, though they were only one hundred metres or so from the school gates, there were never any teachers around to caution them.

The school closed long ago and is now a business centre, yet, in my imagination, especially since our young son started full-time education four years ago, I can't stop wandering its corridors. On that return visit, as I stood in a car park that had once been our playground, it was as if I could hear the thrilling sound of children's voices all around and, in my chest, I felt the burning sensation of long-dormant frustration and regrets.

Harlow celebrated its seventieth anniversary in 2017 and there are palpable signs of renewal: ten thousand new homes will be built as part of the Gilston Park development as the town expands north of the main train station; Public Health England is building a new science and research campus there that will create thousands of new jobs; an Enterprise Zone is attracting inward investment; the town centre, so boisterous and vibrant, especially on market days, when I was a boy, is set to be redeveloped and will, at last, become fully residential. Harlow is fortuitously situated between London and Cambridge on the M11 corridor. It need not be left behind.

In common with most of the other post-war new towns, Harlow declined, especially after the remit of the Development Corporation ended, because of a lack of capital investment and of the failure to renew its housing estates and its infrastructure. Many of the large factories and manufacturing plants also closed or relocated, creating unemployment and lack of opportunity and aspiration in the young. As early as 1953, the *New Statesman* warned that, without greater investment, the new towns would bear 'for the rest of their life the marks of early malnutrition'. It was a prescient observation.

From the beginning, there were flaws in Frederick Gibberd's master plan, most significantly making the town centre non-residential, as well as segregating the residential and industrial areas. Town centres thrive when people live and work in them. Some of the council estates, such as Bishopsfield, which was close to where we lived and was known locally as 'the Kasbah' because of its oppressively narrow alleyways, were ideological experiments in modernist design. Less consideration was given to what it was like to live on these brutalist estates, some of which had to be pulled down in later decades because they were built using inadequate materials and failed to meet the government's 'decent homes' standard. Plus, Gibberd did not plan for the preponderance of motor cars, and today many of the small front gardens in the estates have been concreted over to provide space for them.

As an energetic, sports-obsessed boy, so much of what I relished back then – the swimming pool, the sports centre, the playschemes, the pitch and putt in the park, the town hall – was allowed to decay and was then demolished. But perhaps the truth is that the second generation who were born in Harlow and had no experience of wartime or life elsewhere did not believe in the town as their parents had. For them, it just happened to be where they lived, nothing more or less. The children of the idealistic middle class did not, on the whole, stay there: as soon as they could they moved on and out. They moved to London, an inversion of their parents' original journey.

My father liked to remind us that we owed our opportunities as citizens of the future to the idealism of the war generation. But progress isn't inevitable. There's no guarantee that things will keep getting better, that the arc of history bends towards enlightenment. History isn't linear but, I think, contingent and discontinuous, even cyclical. Ron Bill, an associate of my mother who worked for the Harlow Development Corporation, once told me that he and his colleagues had reached for Utopia. 'The town attracted progressives, community-minded people,' he said. 'Frederick Gibberd was an example of such a person. That first wave of people who came to the town in the Fifties and Sixties – many of them socialists and communists – they wanted to build something. The trouble is, there wasn't a second wave equal to the first.'

If I once thought I disliked the town or was embarrassed by it, I no longer feel that way. I'm grateful the wartime generation reached for Utopia. My father and mother did the right thing by leaving London when they did. It's worth remembering that Utopia also means good place. Somewhere along the way Harlow ceased to be special and it ceased to be new. But it is not nowhere or no place. It is where I was born and grew up. It is my home town.

(2018)

THE GOLDEN GENERATION

I N THE SUMMER of 2000 I was commissioned by *Harper's Bazaar* magazine to write about the gilded young special advisers who were working for Tony Blair and Gordon Brown or gathering around them, or who were close to Peter Mandelson. I understood that most of them wanted to be MPs. I did not know them personally, but I knew a lot about them – about how they lived, worked and socialised. Some of them lived together – indeed, even slept together. They were intelligent: all had been educated at Oxford or Cambridge, and some had known each other from student days. They were well connected, competitive, football-loving metropolitans, liberal, and good Europeans. They were fascinated by American politics (some of them had done graduate research at US universities or had worked on campaigns for the Democrats). They'd studied closely how Bill Clinton and his advisers had remade the Democrats – through triangulation, message discipline, media mastery – as a centrist, optimistic, pro-capitalist, election-winning force.

Older Labour MPs naturally resented these 'Young Turks'. More, they envied them. John Prescott called them 'teeny boppers'; others called them 'faceless wonders' and much worse. They were considered cliquey, superior in manner, even conspiratorial. They were likened to the classics students in Donna Tartt's bestselling novel *Secret History*, who are punished ultimately for believing in the myth of their own intellectual superiority. Blair and Brown worked the Young Turks hard but believed in them, just as they in turn believed in themselves.

It was obvious that this group expected one day to be running not only the Labour Party, but the country. They had a sense of purpose and mission, as well as self-righteousness. They were the best and the brightest of their political generation and comparisons were made between them and the young policymakers who had worked for John F. Kennedy and then Lyndon Johnson in the 1960s.

Today their names are familiar: David Miliband, Ed Miliband, Ed Balls, James Purnell, Andy Burnham. There were others among the group whose names are less familiar, such as Peter Hyman and Liz Lloyd, who both worked in the Downing Street Policy Unit. (Hyman later set up a successful free school.)

Balls and David Miliband were considered the brightest of the group, and Balls, in particular, was admired at the Treasury for his formidable intellectual powers.

'Ed was really exceptional,' a former politician who knew him back then told me. 'In terms of managing the Treasury, he was the most brilliant sort of aide-de-camp. That's not a pejorative expression: I mean Gordon Brown needed that sort of intellectual grip and energy, and the thuggishness as well – you know, to turn the Treasury into an instrument for Gordon. Probably only Nigel Lawson in our lifetime had a similar mastery of that department. And Ed was absolutely fundamental to that in all kinds of ways. He's not a great visionary and thinker, but he's got huge intellectual grip.'

Back in 2000, I called this group Labour's Golden Generation, and *Harper's*, in the Photoshopped illustration accompanying my piece, brought them all together in a mock football line-up. We dressed them in the shirts of the Demon Eyes football team, for which some of them played and which was named after the notorious Conservative 1997 election campaign poster. Conceived by M&C Saatchi, the poster depicted a demonic Tony Blair, his burning red eyes staring out from a black background, above the slogan 'New Labour, New Danger'.

Although I did not write about them for *Harper's* because they were already MPs, Yvette Cooper and Douglas Alexander were part of the Golden Generation as well. Cooper was only twenty-eight when she won the safe seat of Pontefract and Castleford at the 1997 general election. She married Balls the following year, having met him when they shared an office as advisers.

Alexander became an MP in November 1997, at a by-election. He was thirty. Together with Jim Murphy, Alexander (who, before entering parliament, had worked for Gordon Brown as a speech-writer) ran David Miliband's campaign for the Labour leadership in 2010. Neither would ever again be trusted by Ed Miliband, who won that contest, which pitted the Golden Generation against one another. Burnham was also a leadership contender in 2010 and so was Balls.

There were others, in and around the core group, who burned brightly and burned out (Derek Draper), or who peeled off early to work in PR, consulting or television (Benjamin Wegg-Prosser, Tim Allan), or who never sought elected office (Liz Lloyd, Mark Leonard, and Spencer Livermore, who was a long-time Brown favourite).

'The emergence of these bright young things is largely down to Tony Blair,' Derek Draper, a former adviser to Mandelson who became a lobbyist and then a psychotherapist, once told me. 'He was the first Labour leader to pluck young Oxbridge graduates out of nowhere and put them in charge of his office. This put people's backs up. It even put my back up, and I was one of the young insiders myself. "Where have they been in the party?" I kept asking.'

Naturally, some in the group were in the orbit of Brown at the Treasury (Balls, Ed Miliband) and some were in Blair's (David Miliband, Purnell). Blair and Brown both became MPs in 1983 and, in the aftermath of the Labour split two years earlier, they experienced the party's devastating loss to Margaret Thatcher under the leadership of Michael Foot. Blair and Brown were formed by these early setbacks and they felt that there was no option but to combine tactical ruthlessness with strategic vision as they set about reforming the Labour Party, dragging it across the hardest ground to where they believed it had to be. The death of John Smith in May 1994 accelerated the process, but it would have happened anyway.

Blair and Brown had different protégés, but they shared a sense of mission: to create New Labour.

They picked out people – clever, presentable, driven young people – who they believed would carry on their legacy when the time came. Along the way, older, gifted politicians – such as Alan Milburn, who was a difficult man but, having grown up on a council estate, had an interesting personal story, or Estelle Morris, who was a good minister but suffered a loss of confidence – were squeezed out or gave up altogether.

We were witnessing the beginnings of a party being hollowed out and of a deepening disconnection between Labour MPs and their core supporters, which, in time, would empower the SNP in Scotland and create an opportunity for UKIP and the populist right in England.

'I can give you a whole cadre of these people who weren't the Oxbridge elite, the special advisers and all of the rest of it,' one former MP told me, 'but they were politicians and they did have a sense of what voters wanted and they had a way of communicating with voters that these guys [the young MPs and special advisers] never did. Just never did. And as a result, it was a profound misunderstanding of what democratic politics was about. It's not a seminar.'

Call it vanity, call it hubris, but whatever you call it, the foundations of the mansion built by Blair and Brown were neither deep nor strong. Under pressure and in adversity, it began to crumble and then, after the 2015 election defeat, it collapsed, and now Jeremy Corbyn and his followers are roaming through the ruins, creating a new party of anti-austerity radicals.

&

I'm not sure quite what divided the Blairites and Brownites politically, in retrospect. Perhaps the Brownites were more Eurosceptic, more numerate and economically literate, and were always resolute in their opposition to British membership of the eurozone. The Blairites were more internationalist, perhaps (though Brown was a convinced Atlanticist), liberal cosmopolitans who were idealists in matters of foreign policy. Blair's April 1999 Chicago speech remains one of the defining texts of liberal interventionism. Justifying the NATO intervention against Serbian aggression in Kosovo, he defended Western 'values' and made the 'moral' case for getting 'actively involved in other people's conflicts', which meant intervening militarily against despotism when and where necessary. (When David Miliband ran for the leadership of the party in 2010, he defended the Iraq War. His younger brother, who was not an MP at the time of the invasion because he was at Harvard, claimed to have been against it from the beginning.)

But, in essence, though there was much personal rivalry

between the two camps, they were united in believing in the New Labour project. 'Fundamentally, there wasn't a big ideological gulf between Blair and Brown,' Ed Balls told me. 'There wasn't even, really, a big policy divide – in 1997, Tony was the Eurosceptic rather than Gordon. Things changed in terms of how he saw himself as a leader, but I don't think he ever really wanted to join the single currency. He just really wanted to look like he wanted to join the single currency because he thought that that was important for Britain, and [for] his standing as PM at that time.'

When the main opposition party is so weak, as the Conservatives were in the late 1990s, Balls said, 'The prism of politics becomes the succession within the governing party,' hence the obsession with the rivalry between Blairites and Brownites.

'When it came to the crunch, Tony so often backed Gordon that it used to drive him mad,' Balls told me. 'There was a not ideological divide on the private sector in the health service, or markets and the health service. But what happened was "Gordon is anti-reform" became a rallying cry for those who were trying to prevent him defeating Tony. So I think it was much more of a political thing, rather than about policy and ideology.'

Marginal differences, then. Certainly none of the Golden Generation doubted that the left had been vanquished inside Labour and beyond it. The parliamentary Bennites in the Socialist Campaign Group – Jeremy Corbyn, John McDonnell, Diane Abbott and the rest – were considered cranks. They offered no threat. They should not be respected.

Moreover, the Conservatives were in retreat, decisively beaten in 1997, as they would be again under the leadership of William Hague in 2001. Blair and Brown were contemptuous of the Tories, even when David Cameron and George Osborne, modernisers who had studied Blair carefully, took control of the party. They simply didn't take them seriously because they considered them beneath taking seriously.

The Golden Generation, along with Blair and Brown, believed, too, that devolution would settle the Scottish national question. Devolution would 'kill Scottish nationalism stone dead', boasted the future Labour defence secretary George Robertson in 1995. In the 1997 general election, Labour won fifty-six of the seventy-two seats in Scotland; the Tories won none. Scotland belonged to Labour, or so the party believed.

⚜

By 2000 everything appeared set fair for the Golden Generation. Nothing, it seemed, could stop them from dominating public life for as long as they wished. Apart from one another, as it turned out. In the event, they never quite made it, not in the way they would have wished, even if some of them had ministerial careers. The painful truth was that before any one of them reached the age of fifty, it was too late, already too late: the best of their political careers was in the past.

Consider where they are today:

ED BALLS, who longed to be chancellor and ran for the Labour leadership in 2010, has left politics after losing his seat at the 2015 election. He enjoyed a kind of celebrity by appearing as a contestant on the BBC's *Strictly Come Dancing*. In his memoir *Speaking Out*, he writes nostalgically about his early years at the Treasury working closely with Brown. That was his time – and he was not yet thirty.

JAMES PURNELL is the head of BBC Radio, having quit politics in despair in June 2009. On abruptly resigning as work and pensions secretary, he called for Gordon Brown 'to stand aside to give Labour a fighting chance of winning the next election'. He hoped, perhaps believed, his resignation would lead to a cabinet rebellion against Brown and that David Miliband would become prime minister. But no one followed Purnell over the top and he was shot down in no-man's-land. When I met him not long after his resignation, he seemed liberated. 'The way we do politics in this country is infantile,' he said.

DAVID MILIBAND, who resigned from parliament in 2013, is based in New York as the head of the International Rescue Committee, having had his political career destroyed by his brother. 'Had Ed not stood against him, none of this would have happened,' a senior Labour figure said to me, referring to the 2015 general election defeat, the capture of the party by the radical left and Brexit. It is difficult to see a way back for David in British politics, should he even wish to return.

ANDY BURNHAM, having twice stood to be leader of the party, left Westminster to become the first mayor of Greater Manchester. Burnham's second run for the leadership in 2015, when, despite being the early front-runner and favourite, he was defeated by the 100–1 outsider, Jeremy Corbyn, was a sad failure. He posed as the anti-Westminster candidate, the People's Andy, the boy who would burst what he called the 'Westminster bubble', but he did not seem to know his own mind or what he wanted for the country. By the end of the campaign his pledges and promises were received with derision.

DOUGLAS ALEXANDER, who was shadow foreign secretary under Ed Miliband and Labour's 2015 election co-ordinator, was perhaps the most obsessive US politics watcher of all that generation. He was credited with bringing David Axelrod, the American political strategist, to work on Labour's 2015 campaign. Articulate and personable, he humiliatingly lost his Paisley and Renfrewshire South seat to a twenty-year-old student, Mhairi

Black of the Scottish National Party. Alexander has said very little about Labour's defeat and its collapse in Scotland, and now advises Bono of U2.

ED MILIBAND and YVETTE COOPER, who ran for the leadership in 2015, remain as MPs, but each in a different way is struggling to recover from defeat and to find purposeful self-definition. Miliband is resented by the Corbyn-sceptics in the Parliamentary Labour Party. Not only did he lead Labour to an election defeat in propitious circumstances, he introduced the new rules by which the party elects its leader, opening the way for the Corbyn insurgency. Many of those who served in the Blair and Brown cabinets resented Miliband's reluctance when he was leader to defend the record of those governments. 'I thought there had been enough of an opening up of debate under Ed Miliband that if Jeremy was on the ballot paper we would do quite well,' Jon Lansman, a close adviser of the Labour leader and chair of the pro-Corbyn Momentum group, said. In 2016, Miliband called for Corbyn to resign.

⁂

I put it to Ed Balls that the Golden Generation failed. How else to account for the rise of Corbyn and the collapse in support for moderate social democracy among party members and activists?

'It might be that every generation has their time, and as it happened for our generation, it has happened to Cameron and Osborne,' he said by way of a reply. 'And it may be that politics has become more – well, your shelf life goes down. It's harder to regenerate politically, when you think of how long people like [Harold] Wilson or Denis Healey managed to be around. Maybe that's harder these days. It may be that we made a mistake, and we should talk about that. It may be that, because we were people who succeeded early, and therefore became identified with the mainstream, we became casualties – on both sides of politics – when the centre ground gets rejected for the extremes . . . I don't think we ever got complacent.'

Balls found the 2010 election defeat especially painful: after all, he had known only success. 'We'd been in government for thirteen years . . . But when you go out of government in those circumstances, it feels like something that's not going to be short-lived or temporary. There are some people who wait all their lives to get to a senior position in the civil service, or in government, or get into the cabinet, and they get it in their sixties. But because it happened for me on my thirtieth birthday, and the cabinet in my early forties, maybe you have a sense that your time may have been at an earlier stage. I definitely felt that in 2010.'

Eddie Morgan has worked for the BBC and ITV as an editor and producer. He was close to Cooper and Purnell in the late 1980s when he read philosophy, politics and economics at Balliol College, Oxford (where they overlapped with Boris Johnson) and he worked alongside the Golden Generation in the early 2000s when he was Labour assistant general secretary. 'How foolish that now all looks,' he said, reflecting on the Blair-Brown conflict – the so-called TBGBs. 'Talk about the narcissism of small differences! They really were a golden generation, weren't they? Yet even back then I was struck by how uncollegiate it was. Everyone had their baronial fiefdoms. There was not a lot of glue between them.'

This might explain why no one emerged as the natural leader of the group, as David Cameron did among the younger Tory modernisers, and four of them – Balls, Burnham and the two Milibands – went up against each other in the 2010 Labour leadership contest.

For Eddie Morgan and his friends, working for the Labour

Party offered thrilling opportunities. 'After the ERM debacle [Britain was humiliatingly forced to withdraw the pound sterling from the European Exchange Rate Mechanism in September 1992], the Tories were on the way out. They'd been in power too long. The feeling was that they were weak and indeed wicked. The future was ours. If you'd become an MP, like Blair and Brown, in 1983, you wouldn't have felt you'd be in government any time soon. It was different for my generation. It was much easier. They became special advisers. They were given safe seats. I remember when Yvette got the safe seat of Pontefract, thinking, "Wow, she's all set now." It felt like a great career choice.'

Morgan is troubled by how unreflective the Golden Generation seemed to him. 'They had complete self-belief. They believed that they would be the leadership of the Labour Party. They didn't hope it. They totally believed it. I wished they'd been more modest, more questioning, more curious.'

In the early 1960s, JFK's young policymakers played squash to keep fit, a departure from their predecessors under Dwight D. Eisenhower, who preferred golf. The Golden Generation were similarly obsessed with vigour and competition. Their favoured sport was football, which they played with competence and aggression, sometimes with one another, sometimes against one another.

'I remember our team from ITV played Demon Eyes at football,' Morgan said. 'We thought they might be this effete bunch. But they were brilliant. They were fitter, faster, stronger. We were out-thought and out-fought. David Miliband, Jamie Purnell – they were really good footballers. Yes, they were arrogant – but, in a way, they had a right to be.'

In his great book *The Best and the Brightest*, which is about the causes of the Vietnam War and the failures of the young, brilliant and idealistic but flawed policymakers who worked for Kennedy and Johnson, David Halberstam made a distinction between intelligence and wisdom. That is, between 'the abstract quickness and verbal facility which the team exuded, and true wisdom, which is the product of hard-won, often bitter experience. Wisdom for a few of them came after Vietnam.'

The basic question that prompted the book, Halberstam wrote, 'was why men who were said to be the ablest to serve in government in this century had been the architects of what struck me as likely to be the worst tragedy since the Civil War'.

For some of those who once worked with them, Blair and Brown – so able, so determined, so obviously the best and brightest – are culpable not only for policy disasters such as the Iraq War and for allowing the Labour Party to be hollowed out, but also for the failures of the Golden Generation, whom they nurtured and wanted to succeed them. If political parties are machines for capturing power, it was said to me, they allowed the machine to malfunction.

Blair, unlike Brown, never suffered a general election defeat, and, to the last, he will defend his decision to invade Iraq – the single greatest foreign policy catastrophe since Suez – even if he now concedes mistakes were made in the post-invasion planning. For his part, Brown feels profoundly wronged and misunderstood, and still cannot understand how he lost a general election to Cameron and Osborne, of whom he remains scornful.

'Both Gordon and Tony, in their separate ways, must shoulder a huge amount of the blame for what has happened to the Labour Party because it was obvious to me ten years ago that we were hollowing out,' a former MP told me. 'It was absolutely clear . . . but no one was interested. I can't tell you the degree of apathy, indifference, because every single one of them thought it was going to go on for ever.'

And into these hollow spaces flowed the radical left, activists and members who were disgusted by Blair and by the Iraq War. These activists had never stopped believing their opportunity would one day come again. They continued to organise diligently or cluster in the anti-war movement, fringe groups or other parties: the Greens, Respect. They wanted change, they believed that moderate social democracy had failed. Social media offered them new ways to communicate and connect, and they seized their chance when events forced Ed Miliband to revise the rules by which the Labour Party elected its leader. The party is theirs now. Jeremy Corbyn is their leader.

꩜

Ed Miliband and I have not spoken since he lost the 2015 election, but it's clear to me that defeat has changed and humbled David Miliband and Ed Balls: they seem to have acquired not just greater humility, but wisdom. The Golden Generation were intelligent enough, but were they wise enough? Did they really understand the burden and responsibility of elected office, or the struggles and aspirations of the working people they wanted to represent? They wanted to lead and they wanted power, but, unlike Blair and Brown, did they know what to do with it? As it turned out, early success was no preparation for winning and holding on to power.

Gordon Brown once told me how his generation had to fight, and fight again, to win the right to control the party. They had to debate and take on the Bennite left in dreary smoke-filled meeting rooms, in crowded conference halls, in the public prints, and at rallies. The Golden Generation never had to fight. 'They were bright, decent, public-spirited – but they weren't street fighters,' said Eddie Morgan of his former colleagues. 'They were not venal or corrupt but, yes, they lacked fight.'

Another former friend who knew the gilded group well said: 'Political parties in the end are machines for capturing power and there is a sort of life cycle, and you've got to be absolutely vigilant about renewing it. Blair and Brown thought they could renew the machine with very clever people, but with one or two exceptions they were – what is the word I'm searching for? – they were servants, they weren't masters, they didn't really have a vision of where they wanted to go. In the end, the Golden Generation were culpable for their own fall.'

(2016)

THE RESTLESS
PHILOSOPHER

ONE SUMMER AFTERNOON in 1997, on assignment for the *Times*, I visited Bryan Magee at his flat in Kensington, west London. I read philosophy at university in the late 1980s and my understanding of the subject was transformed through watching Magee's BBC Two series *The Great Philosophers* (1987) and then reading the subsequent book adapted from it. He is unsurpassed in the post-war period in Britain as a populariser of philosophy, and I learned more from the fifteen episodes of that series as well as the book than from any lecture or seminar I attended. It achieved, as the philosopher and biographer Ray Monk has written, the near-impossible feat of presenting to a mass audience the recondite issues of philosophy without the loss either of accessibility or intellectual integrity.

The format was extraordinarily simple. Magee sat alongside an eminent philosopher ('two boffins on a sofa' was how the *Guardian*'s witty TV critic Nancy Banks-Smith described the set-up in a favourable review) and together they interrogated the work of one of the greats: Plato, Aristotle, Descartes, Hume, Kant, Wittgenstein, and so on. Magee asked the questions and clarified or summarised the replies. The series was revelatory – at least to me. So, this is how to read and talk about philosophy!

Magee and I chatted for a couple of hours that afternoon as bright sunshine streamed through the high windows of his sitting room. What I liked about his approach was his willingness to demystify philosophical problems by demonstrating that they were not theoretical but existential – about the nature of reality, encountered in the course of living. Yet as I prepared to leave that afternoon, Magee, who through choice lived alone having once been briefly married, said something that I've never forgotten. 'I get the impression,' he said, 'that you feel I am lonely and unfulfilled.'

There was some truth in this: he did seem unfulfilled, and not because he lived alone. There was something restless in his manner: an irritable reaching after fact and reason, as Keats wrote in a different context. He'd never committed himself fully to one discipline, preferring instead to occupy many different public roles as a broadcaster, politician, teacher, author and poet. And he told me – he was sixty-seven at the time – that he believed himself still to be capable of 'doing great things'. He used a German word to describe how he felt about his own potential, *Machtgefühl*. *Macht* = power, *Gefühl* = feeling or sense. So, in broad translation, *Machtgefühl*: a feeling of or having a sense of power. I have also seen the word translated as 'feeling of superiority' (even though I haven't seen *macht* translated as 'superiority').

As an impressionable younger man, I was pretty impressed by what Magee had achieved already. What more could he do or have done? Why even now such restlessness and vaulting ambition?

In his book, *Confessions of a Philosopher* (1997), which is a history of Western philosophy told through his own intellectual journey, Magee offers what could be a partial answer to these questions when he describes how in his late thirties, despite having a passionate attachment to life, he was driven to the edge of mental illness, even suicide, by metaphysical terror. He learned to control his terror, which, though he did not say so, recalled Blaise Pascal's fear of 'immensity of spaces which I know not and which know not me', through reading the writings of others, notably Arthur Schopenhauer. 'I think the feeling of meaninglessness is worst of all, worse than the fear of death itself,' Magee said. 'The feeling that nothing matters, that there's no point to anything. Certainly, I have experiences, in the forms of extreme existential terror, states of mind that bordered on the intolerable.'

Magee, who is eighty-eight, now lives in one room in a nursing hospital in Oxford. It was there that I went to see him. He'd re-entered my thoughts a couple of years earlier when he wrote a letter for publication in the *New Statesman*. Not long after that, he published a short, haunting book called *Ultimate Questions*, which would serve, he told me in another letter, as his final statement on philosophy while also being, he hoped, an original contribution to the subject. Then, in February, John Cleese tweeted: 'One of my heroes, the philosopher Bryan Magee, has just written a new book. It's called *Ultimate Questions* and I strongly recommend it.'

It was poignant encountering Magee in his hospital room after all this time. He cannot walk and sat with a blanket across his legs in an armchair directly opposite a television – he was watching the BBC news when I arrived, the sound turned up loud. He was wearing a pink open-necked business shirt and on a table before him were a telephone connected to a landline, a copy of that morning's *Times*, a hardback of *Ultimate Questions* and several books of PG Wodehouse stories. Magee is still lucid and his voice is as warm and mellifluous as it ever was. He wears thick-framed glasses that magnify his eyes like marbles, just as they did back when he was performing as one of the boffins on the sofa.

Philosophy has been fundamental to his life for as long as he can remember. Even as a young boy he was absorbed by ultimate questions. The world and its mysteries perplexed and tormented him, from the nature of time (does it have a beginning?) to the riddle of why we sleep. He has described lying awake as a child for hours at night, longing to experience the moment at which he fell asleep, in 'the same sort of way as people try to catch the light in a refrigerator going out' as its door closes. 'An ever-present curiosity became for most of the time my strongest-felt emotion, sometimes the mode I lived in,' he wrote.

Even now, alone in his one room, late in life, he remains wonder-struck. 'What the hell is it all about?' he asked. 'What are we doing here? What's going on? I feel the weight of these huge questions. And I know I can't get the answers to them, and I find that oppressive.' In *Ultimate Questions*, Magee writes of being 'driven to the view that total reality consists of some aspects that we are capable of apprehending and others that we are not'.

Philosophy is by its nature improvable: it is perpetually being revised as each generation makes its discoveries and re-evaluates the best of what has been thought and written. In this sense, with the exception of the permanent truths of mathematics and logic, human knowledge cannot be definitive. As Karl Popper argued, to demand certainty is to demand something you can never have. At best, all we can have is conjectural and provisional knowledge permanently open to improvement. For Magee, 'There aren't explanations for everything; indeed, there are no explanations for anything, and we should be far more agnostic in our way of living.'

Martin Amis, formerly an atheist, said something similar in a 2006 interview with Bill Moyers. Being an agnostic, he said, was 'the only respectable position, simply because our ignorance of the universe is so vast ... We're about eight Einsteins away from getting any kind of handle on the universe. Why is the universe so incredibly complicated? That makes me delay my vote on the existence of some intelligence.'

Magee was brought up in a working-class family in Hoxton, east London. Home was a men's clothing shop, owned by his grandfather and worked in by his father, who was an anti-communist socialist, highly cultured, and ambitious for his son. Magee adored him but disliked his mother. 'She was a loveless person who never loved anybody,' he told me. 'She had no affection for her children, and she told us so – she told me and my sister.'

He grew up in the street, surrounded by groups of other children. 'My mother would give me a meal in the morning and then she'd shut me out onto the street, and say, "I don't want to see you again until it gets dark." All the time she was telling us that she didn't love us, didn't want us and that we were in the way.'

Magee was a clever boy and, at the age of eleven and encouraged by his father, he won a scholarship to Christ's Hospital in West Sussex, a traditional public school founded in 1552 which, because of its generous system of bursaries, attracted boys from all social classes (today it is a co-educational day and boarding school). There, he was educated 'out of the class system'. 'The way I spoke changed – I learned to speak like everyone around me, but not consciously. It just happened. I knew too that after I'd gone to Christ's Hospital I could do anything I wanted to do. I could be a doctor, anything.'

During his national service, he served in the army and Intelligence Corps. Magee then went up to Oxford, where he became president of the union, was a committed socialist, and 'took it for granted that sooner or later I'd be a member of parliament'. After a year of graduate research in the United States, he worked in television as a 'backroom boy, scriptwriter and editor' and later as an on-screen reporter and presenter because he knew that he would not earn enough from writing to support the sophisticated lifestyle he desired. 'I wanted to travel, to go to the theatre, to restaurants, to have a much more metropolitan life.'

During this period, he had many relationships – he describes sex as an 'other-worldly' experience and likens its effects to that of great music, 'the deepest we can penetrate into a world other than this world, the world beyond appearances' – but never came close to remarrying. (He has one daughter from his brief marriage, who lives in Sweden and has three children of her own.)

'What I wanted was complete freedom,' he told me. 'It's always been a dominating feeling with me. I wanted to get up in the morning and think, 'I'll go to Paris for the weekend.' You can't do that if you're living with someone.'

In February 1974, he was elected Labour MP for Leyton in east London. He wanted and expected to achieve high office but he was distrusted by Harold Wilson and was never promoted. He believes Wilson would not forgive him for a television interview conducted by Magee in which he had exposed the contradictions in the Labour leader's position on the abolition of grammar schools.

'After the programme he got up and shook hands with the other people in the studio, the floor manager, the cameramen and so on, he shook hands with everybody else, and he glared at me, and he walked out. He was positively anti-me when I was an MP. I'm virtually sure that was the reason.'

Magee left politics 'enormously disillusioned' having defected to the SDP; he lost his seat at the 1983 general election. 'I had completely adjusted psychologically to losing,' he said. 'If I hadn't lost, I might have stood down anyway.'

𝕏

Through all this, Magee kept coming back to philosophy. He presented radio and television series on the subject and wrote books on Karl Popper and later on Schopenhauer. He also published a book of poetry while at Oxford but regrets having done so, and a novel in which he explored his existential terror, *Facing Death* (1977). Despite all this activity, he was frustrated by his own limitations as he identified them – limitations of intellect and of creative imagination. And he had utopian yearnings: it was not a perfect society he sought but perfect knowledge, or understanding.

'There's nothing I wanted to do that I haven't done,' he said. 'But I'm frustrated that I wasn't able to do it better. What's been wrong with me in life is that I haven't had that extra ability or belief in myself, I don't know what it is, that [would have] made me go one step further.'

Later in our conversation, he said: 'What disappoints me about my achievement is that I expected, when I was very young and more optimistic about myself and my future, to do better. I expected to write better things than I have, but I've done as well as I can. I'm not as able as I would like to be but there it is.'

He has met exceptional individuals. 'I got to know Bertrand Russell in the last years of his life. I knew Karl Popper quite well, and they were a whole class above me in intelligence. It wasn't that I was jealous, it was that I was trying to grapple with these problems with inadequate weaponry.'

Magee believes he lacked originality and, until *Ultimate Questions*, struggled to make an original contribution to philosophy. 'Popper had this originality, Russell had it, and Einstein had it in spades. Einstein created a way of seeing things which transformed the way we see the world and the way we even understand such fundamental things as time and space. And I fundamentally understand that I could never do that, never. I wish I was in that class – not because I want to be a clever chap but because I want to do things that are at a much better level than I've done them.'

Not lonely, then, but still restless and unfulfilled.

But what of the original contribution he claims to have made in *Ultimate Questions*?

'Well, it is to say that we don't know anything.'

You mean the permanent unknowability of total reality?

'Yes, the unknowability of everything that matters.'

Of which more later.

Magee follows the news and politics closely and considers the vote for Brexit to have been a 'historic mistake'. More than that, it has dislocated him, as it has many others. 'What this has made me understand is that I've lost my understanding of what's going on. We must live with the consequences. But we will have serious problems long into the future, and the most serious problem is what you call "the elite being out of touch" and being wrong about one huge thing after another. Society has changed, or is changing in ways we haven't properly grasped.'

As a young man following the example of his beloved father, Magee was on the Bevanite left, but now calls himself a centrist. 'I'm not a conservative and I don't think I could ever be. But the old categorisations of socialism, or social democracy, and conservative have been left behind by events. The parties themselves are now out of touch with the realities of social change. Both our main parties are fundamentally responses to situations that no longer exist or have become very weak. They are responses to a society that isn't there.'

The final paragraph of *Ultimate Questions*, in which Magee speculates on how he might feel at the point of death, is especially haunting. 'I can only hope that,' he writes, 'when it is my turn, my curiosity will overcome my fear – though I may then be in the position of a man whose candle goes out and plunges him into pitch darkness at the very instant when he thought he was about to find what he was looking for.'

Magee does not know what he is looking for because what he seeks – answers to the ultimate questions – is unavailable. He does not attempt to find consolation in religion, in abstract systems or in general philosophies that provide explanations for everything, but nor is he an atheist. He's an agnostic troubled continuously by the unknowability, indeed the incomprehensibility, of total reality; of what lies beyond the world of appearances and can never be breached. 'I do genuinely believe the possibility that death might be total extinction, but it's only a possibility; something else might be the case, and I generally believe that too.'

What for him is 'terminally inexplicable' is existence itself. 'What I feel about this is a double sense of wonder that the inexplicable is actual,' he writes in *Ultimate Questions*.

After I turned the tape recorder off, Magee started to ask me questions – about where I grew up, where I went to school. He said he'd hoped my questions might have led him to some kind of revelation or renewed self-understanding. They had not. So, we talked instead about Harlow new town in Essex, where I was born, its origins and purpose. 'This is interesting,' he said. 'Now I'm learning something!'

He seemed reluctant for our conversation to end, so I stayed on to have a cup of tea and some lemon drizzle cake brought to us by a male nurse. Eventually I could see that he was tiring and I left him there, alone, holding a metaphorical candle as darkness fell.

Bryan Magee may now live in one room in Oxford and be unable to walk, but this remarkable man's intellect is unbounded and his mind roams restlessly free. And just as he did as a child in Hoxton all those years ago, he cannot stop grappling with the human predicament. He is pursuing answers to questions he knows can never be answered, and yet will go on pursuing them for as long as he can, until the flickering flame of life is extinguished.

(2018)

PART 2
POLITICS AND POWER

GORDON BROWN'S
LAST STAND

E ARLY ON AN overcast spring morning at King's Cross
Station in London, Gordon Brown was hurried like a fugitive by Special Branch officers into an economy class carriage of
a train whose final destination was Edinburgh. But this journey
was no homecoming for him: we were entering the final week of
the 2010 general election campaign, with the Labour Party trailing
unhappily in third place in most polls.

Brown must have felt as if he was making his last, long, official
journey as Prime Minister, and yet if he believed that these were
indeed the final days of his premiership, he was not saying. He
declined all opportunity to discuss what might happen in the
event of a hung parliament or of a small overall Conservative
majority, merely asserting, again and again, that he was 'fighting for a Labour majority', and warning about the dangers that
Conservative austerity economics posed to the recovery from the
financial crisis.

There was a hauntedness about Gordon Brown: he had the
forlorn air of a man who believed himself to be profoundly misunderstood. 'I cannot get my message through the press,' he said to

me on several occasions as I sat opposite him at a cramped table as the train headed north. He also said that he believed he had 'grown during this campaign', that he was 'learning all the time', 'still had much to offer', and 'could make a difference'. Above all else, he was convinced that the Tories, if elected, would endanger the recovery. So urgently and persistently did he return to this subject that it began to feel as if his words had a kind of strange clairvoyance: he knew what would happen in the near future and it terrified him.

'I mourn for Gordon,' said Irwin Stelzer, the economist and confidant of Rupert Murdoch who has visited Brown in Downing Street to discuss economics and philosophy. 'I never like to see an election in which personality dominates. This is this man's life. Cameron has another life. You can forget Nick Clegg. But for Gordon to finish in a humiliating third place, that would be a tragedy. I draw comparisons with John McCain, who is engaged in a primary fight in Arizona with some Republican nutcase. There's tragedy there to see John in that fight.

'Gordon and I disagree about economics. He believes in a coincidence of economy and government, that they are the same thing. He believes that he can use the GDP better in the people's interests than they can in their own. He has deep egalitarian instincts, a deep moralism. He can't understand why people would choose to buy flat-screened televisions over necessities and books. There's a grandeur in that, but also a misunderstanding of economics.'

Stelzer continued, 'You could say that he's presided over thirteen years of disaster. He's overspent, overtaxed and over-regulated. His appetite for the expansion of the public sector knows no limits. Yet, when the crisis happened, when the chickens came home to roost, he knew what to do. The Tories did not. Cameron did not. Gordon made the right judgements. When the next crisis happens, and it's coming when Greece defaults, Gordon would know what to do. To handle a crisis, I'd pick Gordon over Cameron any day.'

Up close and in person, Brown looked somehow already monumental, like a figure carved into the granite face of Mount Rushmore. There was a rock-like immovability to him. His big-brained head bulged and loomed. He had endured many hurts and more than enough abuse to break any politician. Because of the financial crash, the worst since the Great Depression of the 1930s, and the crisis of executive legitimacy at Westminster created by the MPs' expenses scandal, his premiership had been one long, extended exercise in crisis management. He often struggled, especially in the art of communication, unable to command the unity of his cabinet – there were three attempted coups against him – and incapable of connecting successfully with the wider electorate. He equivocated and dithered, raged and apologised. Yet when it mattered most, his response to the economic crisis was decisive: the recapitalisation of the banks to prevent systemic collapse and then hyper-Keynesian fiscal and monetary stimulus to prevent mass unemployment and recession becoming depression.

This response to the crisis, he agreed when I put it to him, would be his legacy. 'In retrospect,' he said, 'everything over the last two years has been dominated by the world recession. I have no regrets now about other decisions I might or might not have taken before then [we had been talking about the election that never was in 2007]. It was important that I dealt with the world recession, that I took the right decisions.

'It's a fundamental difference of ideology between us and the Conservatives. It's about the view you have of the economy and how you want it to develop. I can't support a view that says you walk away, you leave people on their own, you leave them isolated in a recession. We will be proved to be right on this. If this was an inflation-led, 'interest rate high' recession we'd had to deal with, you couldn't do what we are doing now, because essentially you would have to deal with inflation by maintaining interest rates high. This crisis is more like the 1930s.'

Brown was accompanied on our journey north by a small, loyal entourage that included his long-time fixer Sue Nye (the 'Sue' who brought Gillian Duffy to meet him so disastrously a few weeks earlier) and press officer Iain Bundred, as well as Gordon's wife, Sarah, the anxiety and strain showing in her pale blue eyes, and Peter Mandelson, wearing an immaculate, purple-striped, open-necked shirt and some expertly applied foundation on his face. No doubt Mandelson was present on what was little more than a hit-and-run raid on Newcastle and Sunderland to prevent Gordon slipping up again, as he did when he called Mrs Duffy bigoted after an encounter with her in Rochdale. Mandelson seemed to be enjoying himself and behaved, at all times, like a fond yet mildly exasperated younger brother, assigned for the day with the task of supervising his more wayward and unworldly elder sibling. At one point, after a visit to the National Glass Centre in Sunderland, where Brown had given a speech during which he was heckled (in fact, it was less a speech than the usual robotic, rat-a-tat-tat warning against the Tories; at such moments Brown has all the spontaneity of an automated voice message), Mandelson attempted to encourage Gordon and Sarah to walk out of the centre, arm in arm, up a small hill and directly towards the massed ranks of waiting cameramen and photographers. 'Go on, this will make a nice opportunity for you,' Mandelson said, urging the hesitant couple forward. Yet no sooner had they set off than Brown veered offline, like a race horse jumping left as it approaches a fence. Mandelson let out an expression of camp frustration behind him: 'Oh, my Gaaad!'

❧

'Gordon was never ideally suited to be prime minister,' Irwin Stelzer said. 'At the Treasury, he had time to analyse the facts and the data and to apply his enormous IQ and historical knowledge to a problem. You can't do that as prime minister. Back then, he would have been perfect as the head of the World Bank or the IMF. Now, he's too tarnished.'

The Conservative MP David Davis told me he thought Brown had been 'deskilled' by his many years at the Treasury. 'Being a chancellor under decent conditions is a positively underemployed job, both in parliamentary terms – no debates or statements, no PMQs – and in public terms – you spend half your year in purdah and can say no to most things. It hurt him.'

Later, when I mentioned Irwin Stelzer to Brown, he looked intensely sad. 'Irwin,' he said, his voice scarcely audible, 'Irwin.' He shook his head. Stelzer had been opposed to the *Sun's* decision, taken by James Murdoch, to come out aggressively against Labour on the morning after Brown's party conference speech in October 2009. 'Labour's lost it' was the headline. Since then the *Sun* has run what friends of Brown call an 'inexcusably vicious' campaign against him.

Did the Prime Minister regret courting the Murdoch family?

'They've got to consider the way they enter politics,' he said. 'Such a highly politicised campaign by the *Sun* against [me] is not within the public interest. That's why it's so important to get my message across directly. I'm not naturally someone who wants to spend my time talking about the faults of the opposition. But I feel I have to, because I can't get through the papers.'

❧

As polling day approached, the sense of unease within the Labour ranks felt all-pervasive. The mood was more than simply jittery: it was becoming defeatist. I received innumerable pitches from writers, members of or affiliated to the Labour Party, who all broadly wanted to say much the same: Labour cannot win this election. Worse than that, the party as a coherent, election-winning force was in mortal danger. There were mutterings of an imminent split, as happened in 1981; of a long, slow drift into irrelevance, as happened to the Liberals after 1918; of the party being supplanted altogether by the Liberal Democrats as the main party of the progressive centre left - the Lib Dems had been endorsed by both the *Guardian* and *Observer*.

Much of this was absurdly alarmist. Labour was not existentially imperilled. In the 1980s it was routine for Thatcherite commentators such as Brian Walden to write that Labour could not win again. But the party found new, pragmatic leaders prepared to adapt and, slowly, it regained confidence and began to renew and remake itself. It remained the one truly national party: capable of winning in England and Scotland and of appealing to a coalition of the working class, aspirational Middle Englanders and the liberal and republican intellectual elite.

But the party had become a victim of fatigue and its own multiple failings of leadership, from the catastrophe of the Iraq War to its failure to build enough houses. It had been unlucky, too: it just happened to be the incumbent party at a time of deep cultural, political and economic crisis. There is widespread agreement among our political, academic and journalistic elites that our political system is broken, that our late-Victorian and Edwardian institutions are ill-suited to the complexities of the twenty-first century, that we are grappling with the consequences of both market and state failure. After the MPs' expenses scandal, the near-complete collapse of the banking system and the subsequent

Great Recession, we are at the end of something profound. We are at the end not just of the entire post-Thatcherite/Blairite neoliberal consensus, but our whole way of doing politics in a media and entertainment culture that is in conflict with deliberation and thoughtfulness.

For many in Labour, the central problem was that the party could not renew while Brown remained leader. 'The problem is the same today as it was a year ago: the leadership of Gordon,' one former member of the cabinet told me. 'Without him, we'd have a very good chance of winning this election. With him, it's a question of damage limitation, though we are doing better the further north you go.'

Another former cabinet minister said: 'My fear has long been that all the work we did rebuilding the party, stretching back to Neil Kinnock, will be wasted if Gordon leads us to a generational defeat. I always knew we couldn't win with Gordon. Can a big defeat be averted?'

While we were in the north-east, I travelled in one of the dark-windowed cars in the Prime Minister's motorcade but also on the media bus. There was little excitement among the journalists on the bus. The mood was apathetic. Nor was the bus full: there were uncollected lunches in brown paper bags scattered across the empty seats and many newspapers had not bothered to send reporters or photographers. Everyone I spoke to believed that power was slipping away from Brown.

Brown had started quoting Eric Liddell, the fervent Scottish Presbyterian who won an Olympic sprint gold medal while refusing to compete on the Sabbath. 'The first half of the race requires outer strength, the second half inner strength,' said Liddell, and this became Brown's mantra as he talked of his ability to absorb shocks and blows and then, the very next day, get up and start all over again. 'It's hard, you take blows, but it's unfair to say that my life is just politics. If I thought I couldn't make a difference, I'd stop. I haven't reached that point.'

I began the day thinking that, because of his late conversion to electoral reform and reversals and compromises on other issues, Brown was Labour's Ivan Ilyich, the character in the story by Tolstoy who, as he lay dying, asked: 'What if my whole life has been wrong?' But later, on the train back to London, as I sat chatting with him and Mandelson, I realised he hadn't changed at all. He remained what he always was – defiantly New Labour. And like his great hero of the Scottish Enlightenment, Adam Smith, Brown was absorbed by the connections between ethics and economics, attempting to construct a moral philosophy of markets.

'Your liberalism is that you are pro-competition and pro-market, pro-business and pro-enterprise,' Brown told me. 'But we know also that markets have got to work in the public interest. Markets are in the public interest but they cannot be automatically equated with the public interest, so when markets falter or fail there is a duty on the part of the government to intervene. That was always a cardinal point about New Labour. Private-public partnerships was the markets working with the enabling power of government. When we came to power we had to end the neglect of our public services, so you had to have a public investment in your services. Then open up diversity of supply. Provide people with choice but also voice. Fairness is what I believe in. And equal opportunity. I believe in equal opportunity for all and fair outcomes. Equality of outcome is not possible but fairness of outcome is something we should aspire to.'

Peter Mandelson interjected. 'So this now is a joint interview?' Brown joked.

'The first ever,' Mandelson retorted.

I asked Mandelson if he regretted saying that he was intensely relaxed about the super-rich becoming even richer. 'I said that because I was trying to show that you could be pro-enterprise and pro-competition, that people could come to Britain and be entrepreneurial. People doubted that before Labour won the election in 1997. They were sceptical of us. I'm still relaxed about people getting rich. But what I've learned from the crisis is that wealth must be accompanied by responsibility. And you must pay your taxes.'

Brown cut in. 'People wanted to create an artificial dividing line, saying that you were either for the state or market. Markets are an essential element of any economy but they've got to work in the public interest. So if the banks stop working in the public interest you have to intervene to make sure they do. If you don't have enough competition in the economy and have monopolies dominating you have to take action to create competition.'

There was an air of leave-taking in all of this: here they were, Mandelson and Brown, reflecting on the early months of the first New Labour government, as if in implicit admission that the project was at last coming to an end. 'If anything, we weren't confident enough,' Mandelson said of the weeks following the landslide victory in May 1997. 'There was a feeling that we had a lot to live down from our past and a lot to prove. We became more confident.'

Brown agreed. 'The public service reforms, they were in the second term, weren't they?'

On the issue of proportional representation and the failed 1998 discussions to reform the voting system between Labour and the Liberal Democrats, Mandelson said: 'What happened about electoral reform with Paddy Ashdown and the Liberals was that they kept raising the bar. They wouldn't settle for AV [the Alternative Vote]. They wanted a fully proportional system. In our view, you couldn't sell that to the party just as you couldn't sell it to the public. They'd just elected a majority stable government with a very popular programme that we were just implementing. You couldn't go to them and say you were changing the voting system. Gordon was not a bar to this.'

As for the MPs' expenses crisis, Brown said that it had broken a bond of trust between the electorate and politicians. 'With a more proportional system and right of recall, people would feel that, under AV, an MP would have more than fifty per cent of their support. This is not a deathbed conversion. The political crisis has made me rethink my position because you can't leave things as they are – the status quo is not acceptable.'

At this point, one of the Prime Minister's aides brought drinks to the table – whisky for Mandelson and a beer for Brown. Before I left, Mandelson said something curious that sounded, in retrospect, like an attempt to claim a kind of victory even in defeat. 'The point about the Conservatives is that they believe they cannot win an election by running against New Labour,' he said. 'They are for the political landscape that we have created.

'The whole point of Cameron's Conservatives is to market his party in a way that leads people to believe they've put their past behind them, that they're a continuum of New Labour. They are not, as it happens. But the fact that they feel they can only win power by marketing themselves in that way says a lot about the strength of New Labour.'

There was an ease between Brown and Mandelson, the ease of two men who have known each other for a long time, have lived and worked together in close proximity, have loved and loathed and been reunited. If this was the end of the New Labour affair, it was somehow fitting to find them together, still on deck and side by side, as the ship went down, the band playing blue cocktail music to greet the arrival of Cameron's Conservatives.

In 1909, Charles Masterman published his remarkable book *The Condition of England*. A Liberal MP and friend of Winston Churchill, he was writing from within the establishment but, influenced by his experiences working among the urban poor of London and despairing of deepening inequality between the classes, Masterman recognised that England was suspended between the old ways of the Victorian world and something quite new and frightening. He wrote of how 'the man who is living amid that long-drawn decline is wandering between two worlds, one dead, the other powerless to be born. It is an age in passing. What is coming to replace it? No one knows. What does it all come to? Again, no one knows.'

My feeling throughout the 2010 campaign, reinforced by my visit to Newcastle, was that no one was telling the truth about the extent to which Britain would be changed by the necessary fiscal retrenchment undertaken in response to the Great Recession, which would be imposed on all of us by whichever party won. The cuts in public spending would be punitive; there could be social unrest. Yet this election campaign had been an elaborate dance of evasion, conducted in the theatre of the absurd that is contemporary British politics, where no one dare speak the truth for fear of being hysterically denounced.

So, it was for us, as it was for Charles Masterman, an age in passing. What was coming to replace it? No one knew. All we knew was that these were the last days of the premiership of Gordon Brown. He would lose power. What was coming to replace New Labour? No one knew.

(2010)

POSTSCRIPT

Gordon Brown lost the 2010 general election but not quite as badly as many of his colleagues feared: the result was a hung parliament. However, Labour's share of the vote fell to twenty-nine per cent, its lowest since 1983 (compared to thirty-six point one per cent for the Tories and twenty-three per cent for the Lib Dems). Labour remained strong in Scotland and in London and other English cities. As a consequence, the Conservatives entered into coalition government with Nick Clegg's Liberal Democrats and introduced the Fixed-Term Parliaments Act, under which a general election must be held every five years. We were entering the age of austerity, the consequences of which are still being felt today.

Brown had long been contemptuous of the Liberal Democrats, whom he always called the Liberals. He believes his disdain for them was vindicated by their embrace of austerity, for which he would say they have been deservedly punished by the electorate.

Brown has remained active in public life, intervening to campaign against Scottish independence in 2014 and against Brexit in 2016. When I had lunch with him at his private office in the City of London a few months before the European referendum, he still could not understand how he lost to David Cameron and George Osborne. And he still had the air of a man who believes himself to be profoundly misunderstood.

Brown's political ambition was to remake Thatcherite Britain as a social democratic country at ease with itself. But Scottish nationalism, Brexit and, within Labour, Corbynism have all defied his hopes. Many contend that he will be remembered for preventing an economic recession from becoming a depression. But he will also be remembered for falling fatally short when he finally acquired the office he craved.

THIS CHARMING MAN:
DAVID CAMERON

I was right years ago – more years, I am happy to say, than either of us shows – when I warned you. I took you out to dinner to warn you of charm. I warned you expressly and in great detail of the Flyte family. Charm is the great English blight. It does not exist outside these damp islands.

Anthony Blanche speaking to Charles Ryder,
from Evelyn Waugh's *Brideshead Revisited*

WRITTEN DURING THE middle years of the Second World War and published in 1945, *Brideshead Revisited* is a graceful, ruminative novel about class and the fatal allure of charm. The narrator, Charles Ryder, is an intelligent but uncertain middle-class adolescent who goes up to Oxford in the early 1920s and there he is befriended by a careless and beautiful aristocrat named Lord Sebastian Flyte. Drawn into his intimate circle of high-born and decadent friends, Ryder is changed utterly. Sebastian is from a landed, Anglo-Catholic family and Ryder is enchanted and beguiled by them – by the grandeur of their ancestral mansion, their wealth and social ease, their natural superiority.

He falls in love first with Sebastian, who is destroyed by alcoholism, and then later with his sister Julia, who is tormented by the demands of her faith.

Brideshead Revisited was lavishly adapted for television as an eleven-part drama serialisation and first screened on ITV in 1981, and then repeated in 1983, the year of Margaret Thatcher's landslide election victory that entrenched the new Conservative market hegemony. It was enormously popular and influenced the wider culture of the time, the way some young people dressed, styled their hair and spoke. It coincided with the cult of the 'New Romantic' in pop and encouraged fashion-conscious young men to grow their fringes long, wear fine white shirts, flannels and cricket sweaters. Several friends of mine, who were contemporaries of David Cameron at Oxford, liked to dress in what we called the 'retro-*Brideshead*' style and Cameron back then was a recognisably neo-*Brideshead* archetype, right down to his floppy fringe, cricket sweaters and membership of the Bullingdon Club (a membership he shared with the fictional Flyte).

Cameron was one of those students at Oxford people knew of and spoke about, even if they didn't actually know him. Journalists such as Toby Young and James Delingpole, who knew Cameron a little back then, write enviously even today of the effect of his youthful hauteur and insouciance. Unlike Boris Johnson and Michael Gove, Cameron stayed clear of student politics and of the Oxford Union. He liked to dress up in white tie and tails, played tennis and always said thank you at the end of a tutorial. He had such good manners and such charm, and together these have carried him a very long way, to the top of British politics as prime minister of the first coalition government since the Second World War. At the start of their shotgun marriage, Cameron and Nick Clegg had promised so much, nothing less than a new transparency and a 'new politics'. This was to be a historic realignment;

not as progressives had long wished for on the centre-left, but on the centre-right: classical liberalism in harmony with modernised Cameroon Conservatism, with David Laws heralded as the new model national Liberal politician. In an essay published in the *New Statesman* in May 2010, Vernon Bogdanor, who taught Cameron at Oxford, wrote:

> The decision by the Lib Dems to form a coalition with the Conservatives brings to an end the project of realignment on the left, begun by Jo Grimond in the 1950s, and continued by David Steel in the 1970s and by Paddy Ashdown, with support from Tony Blair, in the 1990s . . . It seems the Labour Party and the left do not yet realise what a catastrophe has hit them. It is comparable to 1983, though then the left could at least hope that Labour and the SDP-Liberal Alliance might come together.

By 2012, the promised centre-right realignment had not happened. Cameron found himself unable to evolve a coherent political strategy, or to tell a convincing story to the British people about the kind of country he wanted Britain to be when in recession and threatened with break-up, or to demonstrate a basic competence in government as he flip-flopped and U-turned and retreated as policies were introduced, only to be revised or abandoned altogether or simply botched, as with Andrew Lansley's Health and Social Care Bill.

ONE-NATION PRAGMATISM

If David Cameron is not a conviction politician, what and who is he? What are his core beliefs? What motivates him beyond the obvious attractions of power and high office? Why is he in politics at all rather than in merchant banking or corporate PR? What kind of Conservative is he? We have many questions about him but very few answers.

Francis Elliott's and James Hanning's excellent Cameron biography was first published in 2007, revised for the paperback edition of 2009 and has since been fully updated to take account of the early years of the coalition. It is subtitled 'Practically a Conservative', which suggests that even the authors are unsure of Cameron's true motivations or purpose; are unsure of what kind of prime minister he was, or would have been if only he'd won the 2010 election, against an unpopular and exhausted Labour government, and was free of those pesky Lib Dems, who acted as brakes on his more radical desires.

Cameron's back story is well known. He grew up in the Berkshire village of Peasemore, the younger son of an Old Etonian stockbroker, Ian, who was born disabled. Home was the Old Rectory (Cameron's brother, Alex, who is a barrister, still lives there with his family), which has a large garden, with a swimming pool and tennis court. 'Home was decidedly old-fashioned if not notably bookish,' the authors write.

The family was 'very county', we are usefully told. Cameron was sent at a young age to board at Heatherdown prep school and then, inevitably, when he was thirteen, to Eton. At prep school he is described as having an 'easy affability', as well as being 'the most terrible snob at the age of seven'. The gradations of the English class system are fundamental to Cameron's biography and the way he is perceived and perceives the world. He is described here as having 'married up' – his wife, Samantha, is of a landed aristocratic Sheffield family – and at one point as being 'well bred', which makes him sound like a racehorse, but then the aristocracy is obsessively interested in bloodlines and lineage, as well as being so adept at keeping so much of the land of these islands in the family interest and out of the greedy hands of the state.

'Among the eighty or so sets of parents of David's contemporaries,' the authors write of Heatherdown, with the relish of F. Scott Fitzgerald describing the guests at one of Gatsby's parties, 'there were eight honourables, four sirs, two captains, two doctors, two majors, two princesses, two marchionesses, one viscount, one brigadier, one commodore, one earl, one lord, and one queen (the Queen).'

And they were all in it together.

Much later, in an aside that could have been more profitably explored, Elliott and Hanning suggest that those who know Cameron best say that he suffers from 'slight and extremely well-concealed intellectual and social insecurities'. In another aside, they write that, against the settled view, far from being a 'secret admirer of the upper class, Cameron nurses a strong dislike bordering on contempt for the aristocracy', which has its origins in his schooling, when he was surrounded by the landed and titled.

This is fascinating and we have seen moments when Cameron has not seemed quite so at ease in his own skin – such as when being goaded by Ed Balls at Prime Minister's Questions or when in the company of Barack Obama, who is so much his intellectual superior and so indifferent to British interests.

Cameron was not outstanding at Eton, the school founded by Henry VI in 1440 as an institute to educate seventy poor scholars but which has since become the grandest and most famous boys' boarding school in the world. His O-level results were average and his intellectual self-confidence began to develop only in the sixth form. James Wood, now a literary critic and Harvard professor, remembers Cameron as being 'confident, entitled, gracious, secure . . . exactly the kind of "natural Etonian" I was not'. He remarks on Cameron's 'charm and decency [at Eton] – almost a kind of sweetness, actually', though he says Cameron showed little interest in politics. (Rory Stewart, the writer-traveller, Conservative MP and another Etonian, once told me that he thought Cameron and Boris Johnson were the 'wrong kind of Etonians', which leads one to assume that there must be a right kind, of whom Stewart is presumably one.)

Eton: a word of just four letters but with a multiplicity of associations. Eton: a word synonymous with upper class and aristocratic ease and entitlement. Eton: a word that inspires as much anger as it does respect. Etonian: a word that can be used as a statement of fact, as a signifier of status and privileges from birth and as a pejorative adjective, depending on who is using it and in which context. 'Eton Rifles': an angry protest song by the new-wave band The Jam, inspired by the singer-songwriter Paul Weller's memory of boyhood visits to Slough and Eton and the festering sense of class resentment he nurtured. Eton mess: a sweet and sickly pudding, but also a metaphor for unrest in the Cameron government and for the larger failure of intergenerational social mobility in Britain in 2013. Eton style: pupils' amusing spoof of the South Korean pop hit and YouTube sensation 'Gangnam Style' by Psy, but also a sense of the boarding school as one of the ultimate luxury British 'brands', and especially desirable to international plutocrats. Old Etonian: David Cameron is of course one such, and the nineteenth British prime minister to have attended the school.

Ferdinand Mount, a cousin of Cameron's mother, Mary, and a writer and journalist (and, inevitably, an Etonian), recalls the young Cameron 'abounding in self-confidence' when as a student he visited Mount while he was working for Margaret Thatcher in Downing Street. At Brasenose College, Oxford, where Cameron read philosophy, politics and economics, his contributions in classes are remembered by a former economics tutor as being 'thought out and charmingly delivered'. The parents of one of Cameron's early girlfriends were 'impressed . . . with his charm'.

At the Conservative Research Department (CRD) at Smith Square, Westminster, which he joined straight from Oxford in 1988, and where he met and became friends with Steve Hilton and Rachel Whetstone, Cameron is commended by one secretary for his 'superb manners'. His peers there say he was invariably 'charming and fun'. Rupert Murdoch, after speaking to Cameron at length in 2006, said: 'Look, he's charming, he's very bright, and he behaves as if he doesn't believe in anything other than trying to construct what he believes will be the right public image.'

Again and again, Cameron's charm is noticed and remarked upon – his charm and self-assurance and verbal fluency. Cameron has always made friends easily and impressed those he needed to impress, just when he needed to impress them most. He never really chokes and is often at his best at moments of heightened stress or tension, such as when he delivered from memory the brilliant would-be leader's speech to the Conservative party conference in 2005, or reacted with authority and good sense to English urban riots after having been traduced for returning late from a summer family holiday in Tuscany.

Cameron was from early on considered to be the coming man at the CRD, where he was promoted rapidly, and then as a young adviser working for Norman Lamont at the Treasury and Michael Howard at the Home Office, as well as briefing John Major for Prime Minister's Questions. Around this time, Alice Thomson wrote an article in the *Times* that I remember reading when I worked there, in which she identified the leading political talents of her generation and described 'David Cameron, twenty-seven, [as the] current class leader'. He was the one whom other clever, ambitious, young, right-wing politicos wished to be associated with and around whom the likes of Hilton, Whetstone, Michael Gove, Edward Llewellyn and Ed Vaizey gathered. The charming leader of the brat pack.

For those who were not close to Cameron, or who were closed out by him and his friends and allies, or who watched him from afar, he could appear aloof and 'arrogant', as no doubt he often was. Yet like Tony Blair, he seems to have had the gift of emotional or practical intelligence, so lacking in Gordon Brown; of knowing how to manipulate, persuade and win over; how to read the logic of a situation and react accordingly; how to bend others to his will. He charmed as he manipulated and advanced.

The authors describe Cameron's rapid rise through the Conservative Party and the intricacies of his extended friendships in the so-called Notting Hill set with reverence, which at times pushes the book closer towards hagiography than the sceptical, independent biography that it ultimately turns out to be in the updated edition. The final chapters concern Cameron's prime ministership and here the tone begins to harden against him.

In an early chapter, Vernon Bogdanor is quoted as describing his former pupil as a non-ideological 'classic Tory pragmatist'. 'My view is unchanged,' Bogdanor told me. 'He's an instinctive conservative. The nearest comparison is with [Harold] Macmillan or even [Stanley] Baldwin. He feels he has been fortunate, he has come from a fortunate background, and feels he has a responsibility to look after those less fortunate than himself. You might call it *noblesse oblige*.'

The book's largest failure is that the authors, for all the diligence of their research and the many interviews they have conducted, fail to convey a sense of Cameron's inner life. This is perhaps less their failure than that of Cameron himself and here a comparison with Obama is instructive. Obama is a politician but he's also a writer. To get a sense of his inner life and motivations, we can read his memoir *Dreams From My Father*, a literary recasting of his often painful struggles to accept his mixed racial inheritance and identity as a black American, and then read it against what others have discovered and written about him. What Obama leaves out from his story can be as revealing as what he chooses to include. And for an exposition of his political ideas, we can read *The Audacity of Hope*.

Before becoming prime minister, Cameron had published nothing of significance, not even philosophical essays in the tradition of Lord Salisbury. When he is at home, he would have us believe that he would rather watch DVDs or play tennis or snooker than read deeply and widely. Unlike Margaret Thatcher, who used to have tutorials on history and economics after becoming Conservative leader, Cameron gives an impression of knowing as much as he wants to know. But perhaps it is only an impression, because for someone of his background it can be 'bad form' to be seen to be trying too hard. Again, where one seeks clarification there is only mystery and mystification.

In his book about the early years of Obama, *Barack Obama: the Story*, David Maraniss quotes from letters written to an early girlfriend, full of flights of poetic fancy and the extravagance of youthful idealism, and has access to the diaries she kept in which she recorded her thoughts about her lover and their relationship. From these one has a greater sense of the intensity of the young Obama's introspection as he struggled to make sense of his complicated family story and learned who he could and could not trust. 'The only way my life makes sense is if, regardless of culture, race, religion, tribe, there is this commonality, these essential human truths . . . that are universal,' Obama told Maraniss.

By contrast, in an attempt to get a fuller and deeper sense of his ideas, Elliot and Hanning are reduced to excavating thin-spun columns Cameron used to write for the *Guardian* website and his local paper as a new MP in Witney, Oxfordshire. (Unlike Maraniss, they have no on-the-record interview with Cameron to draw on, though no doubt they have spoken to him.) As for his speeches, these are the work of many hands and have no original voice or signature style. When Sebastian Flyte speaks, says Anthony Blanche in *Brideshead Revisited*, 'It is like a little sphere of soapsuds drifting off the end of an old clay pipe, anywhere, full of rainbow light for a second and then – phut! – vanished, with nothing left at all, nothing.' Something similar could be said of most of Cameron's speeches and articles.

Nowhere in the book do the authors quote from Cameron's letters or from youthful journals or diaries written by or about him. The drama of his inner life remains unrevealed, the man himself essentially unknown, perhaps unknowable. Could it be that Cameron is no more than what he appears to be – a clever, confident, fluent, self-contented, upper-middle-class fellow who changes his mind a lot and who became Conservative leader when he did because the party was desperate to find someone presentable who was not the pro-European Ken Clarke, after three successive heavy election defeats? Or is there a complexity and depth to the man that in no circumstances would he ever allow to be revealed? More questions, few answers.

As for his politics, his views seem to be a pick'n'mix of old-style shire Toryism, soft Thatcherism and Notting Hill social liberalism. He is non-ideological and pragmatic, and was sincere in his desire to modernise the Conservative Party and lead it away from unenlightened reaction, but the danger of political pragmatism is that it can lead to incoherence and a lack of direction. If the political world is conceptualised as a conversation, as the sceptical philosopher Michael Oakeshott suggested, Cameron seemed to be listening to too many conflicting voices and opinions, being tugged one way by the right and another by the modernisers and Lib Dems; his voice becoming less and less distinctive as he sought to accommodate and compromise.

HEART OF CLASS

In a letter to a girlfriend, written when he was twenty-two, Obama spoke of being 'caught without a class, a structure, or tradition to support me': 'In a sense the choice to take a different path is made for me.' In the great pioneering American tradition, he would become his own invention. Cameron is very much the obverse: he is caught, even trapped, within a class and tradition and has always had the structure of the high establishment to support him. 'He [Cameron] worked his way up from the inside, floor by floor,' says his friend and fellow Tory Nicholas Boles, comparing Cameron with Blair, the public schoolboy son of a Tory father, who was not part of the Labour tradition but who reached the top of the party by climbing the building from the outside.

Cameron has none of the originality of Margaret Thatcher, who was not constrained by class and tradition and had a story to tell the electorate of where she'd come from and how she intended to remake the nation through strife and market reforms. 'For me the heart of politics is not political theory, it is people and how they want to live their lives,' she wrote in the introductory paragraph to the 1979 manifesto. Enough people believed in Thatcher and her story to carry her along as she set about unravelling the post-war Keynesian consensus. Above all, she was interested in and driven by ideas.

'I have brothers, sisters, nieces, nephews, uncles and cousins, of every race and every hue, scattered across the continents, and for as long as I live, I will never forget that in no other country on earth is my story even possible,' Obama once said, with characteristic bombast. One feels, similarly, that only in England would the story of David Cameron be possible. But in the new political era of great economic and political turbulence and instability, his story may not have the happy ending he and his party would have wished.

(2012)

POSTSCRIPT

I was told a revealing story about David Cameron. One day after a cabinet meeting – this was before he delivered what is known as his 'Bloomberg speech' in January 2013 in which he pledged to hold an in/out referendum on the United Kingdom's membership of the European Union if the Conservatives won the 2015 general election, the then prime minister was pulled to one side by Ken Clarke, the veteran Europhile. 'What are you doing?' Clarke said. 'It's far too risky to hold a referendum on the Europe question.' Cameron looked at Clarke calmly and said: 'Don't worry, Ken, I always win.'

In the event, he lost. When the end came, it was merciless: David Cameron was hurried out of Downing Street in 2016 after the European referendum a humiliated and defeated man, brought down by his own insouciance and gambler's instinct. His is an epic failure, comparable to what befell Anthony Eden after the Suez crisis (Eden won a comfortable majority at the general election of 1955 but was gone less than two years later) or Neville Chamberlain, who is for ever stained by his association with appeasement. Cameron is the prime minister who 'lost Europe' as a result of an attempt to settle an internal party dispute, and perhaps, ultimately, the United Kingdom as well.

As Michael Portillo, a former Conservative minister who

supported Brexit, wrote, 'David Cameron's decision to promise a referendum on British membership of the EU will be remembered as the greatest blunder ever made by a British prime minister. There was nothing inevitable about it. It was a calculation made when he led a coalition and had little hope of gaining a majority at the election that loomed in 2015 . . . But in any case, if he seriously thought that leaving the EU would be calamitous for Britain, there is no defence for taking that national risk in an attempt to manage his party or to improve its chances of election.'

THE INSURGENT:
ED MILIBAND

'Economics are the method; the object is to change the soul.'
MARGARET THATCHER

ED MILIBAND IS feeling replenished having just returned
with his wife, Justine, and their two young children from a
holiday in Greece, his first extended break for three years. He
left his mobile phone behind in London, read no British newspapers and watched no television news while he was away, in
what amounted to a full withdrawal from the demands of the
Westminster merry-go-round. 'It was such a relief and a libera-
tion not having a phone,' he says. If someone needed to contact
him, they were told to ring Justine – 'which of course they were
reluctant to do'.

Marc Stears, the Oxford academic who is an old university
friend of Miliband's, had told me that the Labour leader was
feeling 'quietly confident' and in a 'deep and reflective space'.
'It's good to see him like that,' he said. 'What strikes me
is how calm he is. He knows the party is now settled behind
him. He has this gift of being able to see the midterm and long

term and this helps him through the rough times. I think he feels that people are listening more now and he's in a different place.'

'I've been doing a lot of thinking, Jason,' Miliband says by way of confirmation as he leads me around the side of his imposing house in north London and into the narrow garden. It is one of those rare, luminous September mornings, all the more beautiful because the days are shortening. The garden is overgrown, the grass damp underfoot in the early-morning sunshine. Tom Baldwin, a twitchy and suspicious media aide, pulls up chairs and brings us instant coffee. Miliband is wearing a casual, pale grey-blue shirt and a dusting of powder on his face (for the benefit of our photographer, one presumes).

He looks as well as I've seen him for some time, and there's a drifting, dreamy quality to his conversation. He is animated by ideas and grand abstractions. Policy detail can wait for another day.

As he enters the new autumn political season, the Labour leader is restless to explain where he feels the party has reached under his stewardship and to warn against complacency. On the morning we meet he is refining and editing a speech on the economy – drafts are scattered across a table – to be delivered later in the week. But he begins by telling me what he has been reading on his new Kindle, the ease of use and convenience of which have delighted him. 'I read *The Fear Index*, you know, by Robert Harris, *Skios* by Michael Frayn, which is about Greece. And then I read a couple of more serious books – *The New Few* by Ferdinand Mount, *How Much Is Enough?* by Robert and Edward Skidelsky and also the [Michael] Sandel – *What Money Can't Buy: The Moral Limits of Markets*.'

The last three titles share a family resemblance: deliberative and quasi-philosophical, they seek to question the morality of the market-driven, winner-takes-all model of capitalism that has led to entrenched inequality in Britain and the United States, environmental degradation and a deeper existential malaise.

'We drifted from having a market economy to being a market society,' Sandel writes in *What Money Can't Buy*, which can be read as an indictment of the economic and political consensus of the past thirty years.

'The way I put it is that there are two tasks I feel that I have, two tasks in particular,' Miliband says. 'One is to fill out the policy agenda of an economy that works for working people; how we want to reform our economy – and that's everything from banking to skills to short-termism to a whole range of things – how do we change this economy? I'm interested in saying, "What kind of country can we be?" I think that's what people don't get from [David] Cameron. The government's not just shambolic, and it's not just unfair, and it's not just standing up for the wrong people. It's also – what is the bigger vision for where Britain goes?'

Miliband mentions the London Olympic Games and the euphoria that many of us felt during those heady days of August, when it seemed at times as if the whole country was gripped by a kind of ecstatic sociality, as if we couldn't quite believe that everything was going as well as it was. There was joy and there was relief – as well as a renewed understanding of what kind of country Britain is and has the potential to be. 'That's why the Olympics was such a big moment for my generation,' he says. 'There's a guy – the commercial director for one of the sports teams – who I just happened to meet when I went to an event, and he said to me, "For the first time, I had a sense of Britain's future which made sense to me." That was after Danny Boyle's opening ceremony. And I don't think it was just Danny Boyle, I think it's the sense we had of a country coming together, something really important for a nation.'

How do politicians capture that sense of possibility and make of it something of lasting value? How do you make the restructuring of capitalism a collaborative, patriotic, nation-building project?

'I think that's exactly the right way to put it,' Miliband says, tilting forward in his chair. 'I think the Olympics is a very important moment for me – it was very important for the country most of all, but important for me because I think, for the first time in my life, I got a sense of what my dad [the Marxist academic Ralph Miliband] used to talk to me about, about the wartime spirit, his time in the navy. You can't have a permanent Olympic Games, but I think there's something about "what kind of country do we feel like"? Do we feel a sense of obligation to each other? Do people feel the benefits and burdens of life are fairly distributed? Those things are partly economic but they go deeper than that.'

He pauses and seems perplexed, as if his thoughts are not quite yet becoming the words he wants. 'What are the institutions that we have in common – the NHS, the BBC? Very interesting that the Olympics was only what it was – or one of the reasons the Olympics was what it was – because we had a free-to-air broadcaster which was able to promote the national conversation.'

Miliband outlines three immediate self-imposed challenges. 'One, you've got to have a country where everyone feels that they have a stake. You can't have a country that feels a sense of shared project when there are people left out . . . young people who have got no work, got no chance of work, you know. So that's the first thing.

'Secondly, people have got to feel that this country moves together, this country shares the benefits and burdens fairly. When you get CEOs paying themselves a thousand, two thousand times what their lowest-paid employee [gets], that's not a country that's together. And what is so interesting is that the right is saying that as well.'

You mean the more thoughtful, cerebral right . . . 'Yes, the more thoughtful right. Now, Cameron is cut off from that political project. It might have been Cameron in 2006, 2007, but it's just not Cameron now.'

But Cameron speaks of the iniquities of 'crony capitalism'. He has his own reformist position on the financial crisis and its aftermath.

'I know, but he doesn't believe it, does he?'

Ferdinand Mount thinks he believes it.

Tom Baldwin interjects: 'They are cousins [Mount and Cameron].'

Miliband: 'Well, anyway, look, if Cameron really believes it, you don't cut taxes for millionaires and then raise taxes for everybody else and say a country is coming together. So that's the second thing. And thirdly, I think it's our areas of common life. The NHS, our local school, the local high street, the BBC – all of these are things you nurture, and I don't think you have to be a Conservative to believe this. That's where Blue Labour had an important grain of truth in it. Which is this: there are things we seek to conserve and things we seek to change. And that's my project.'

⁂

Ed Miliband speaks broadly but without precision; he is garrulous but not always articulate. He knows what he thinks but not always how to say what he means, hence his fondness for vague generalities and gnomic utterances. Part of the problem is that he is trying to find a convincing language of economic and political reform. The economic ideas with which he is grappling are necessarily complex; he seeks nothing less, Marc Stears told me, than 'to create a new paradigm'.

Miliband has an instinct for change and understands

fundamentally what ought to be done. Ought implies can. He knows also that there can be no returning to the old Labour ways, even if they were styled as New Labour ways: tax and spend, with the centralised state as the engine of (re)distribution and control. Yet the danger for his model of 'responsible capitalism' is that it could go the same way as the Tories' utopian 'big society' – an opportunity squandered for not being properly thought through, or explained, or widely understood.

In *The New Few*, a disquisition on the rise of a transnational rapacious oligarchy, Ferdinand Mount quotes from a speech Miliband gave in June 2011, in which he mentioned the corrosive effects of inequality and of how a culture of corporate irresponsibility had damaged us all.

I asked Mount what he thought of Miliband as a leader and prospective prime minister. He replied, in an email, saying that he had not been following his recent speeches. 'I do not have much of an opinion to offer re E. Miliband, having not got much further than still thinking of him as the man who shafted his brother. As for my book being taken up by the left, most of my fan mail, such as it is, comes from former directors of FTSE-100 companies, saying that, alas, yes, that's pretty much how it is these days. The truth is, or ought to be, that a campaign to restore transparency and accountability to business ought to be an all-party thing. After all, it was D. Cameron, I think, who coined the best phrase for it, "crony capitalism". More importantly perhaps, much of the reform is going to have to be self-generating (e.g., the shareholder spring), rather than led by government of whatever party, although govt must play an energetic supporting role.'

Miliband's forthcoming conference speech will develop the defining theme of his leadership – which is, how does a party of the centre left achieve social justice when the old statist tax-

and-transfer model of redistribution is no longer affordable?

He believes that last year's conference speech in Liverpool – in which he contrasted 'responsible' with 'predatory' capitalism, but then struggled to explain afterwards what he meant – was misunderstood because 'it was ahead of its time'. Some of those closest to him believe that, even though it had a powerful central message that continues to resonate, the speech was poorly written, paced and delivered, and tonally wrong. 'Too many people were involved in the speech,' an insider told me. 'This year, Ed is working on the speech and talking to Marc [Stears] to avoid those mistakes.'

I ask Stears about his role in Miliband's intellectual and political development. 'I act as a kind of sounding board,' he says. 'It's all about understanding. Last year's speech came out without much preparation. And now he feels some mild form of vindication. First, he had to outline what kind of capitalism he wants to see . . . the core pieces of policy detail come later.

'He's establishing a new paradigm – something different from where the coalition is and where New Labour was. But he has to explain the project first.'

Although he doesn't use these words, Miliband has ambition to create a counter-hegemonic project, something comparable in scale and ambition to that of the Hayekian new right at the end of the 1970s. Margaret Thatcher once said: 'The Old Testament prophets did not say, "Brothers, I want a consensus." They said, "This is my faith. This is what I passionately believe. If you believe it, too, then come with me."'

Milibandism, like Thatcherism, aspires to be something profoundly disruptive, something consensus-breaking. But is his project properly understood? Does he have a coherent set of ideas? What are its main texts and who are its outriders and public intellectuals? 'This is what we believe,' Thatcher used to say, brandishing a copy of Friedrich Hayek's *The Constitution of Liberty*.

Would Miliband have the confidence to use the first-person plural in the same way? Does Milibandism as an ideology amount to much beyond an instinct for fairness, some solid rhetorical positioning and a desire to reform capitalism?

In a recent essay for the *New Statesman*, Neil O'Brien, the director of Policy Exchange and one of the most interesting of the younger thinkers on the right, suggested that Miliband was torn between 'pragmatism and radicalism' and this accounted for his overall lack of clarity and coherence.

But that's not how Miliband sees it. First of all, he accepts that fiscal conservatism is and will be the order of the day and that Labour will have no spare money to spend if it wins the general election in 2015. In January, Ed Balls, the shadow chancellor, with whom Miliband has an uneasy relationship, said: 'My starting point is, I'm afraid, we are going to have to keep all these [Tory] cuts.' In a speech a few days later, Miliband reiterated the position.

This angered Labour's union paymasters and many commentators on the left who believe it is Labour's mission to mitigate the worst excesses of capitalism and to protect the poorest and most vulnerable. Len McCluskey, head of the Unite union, wrote: 'Ed Balls's sudden embrace of austerity and the public-sector pay squeeze represents a victory for discredited Blairism at the expense of the party's core supporters. It also challenges the whole course Ed Miliband has set for the party, and perhaps his leadership itself.'

Little has been heard on this subject from either Balls or Miliband since then. 'But our position hasn't changed!' Miliband protested. 'Look, we absolutely hold to everything we said at the beginning of the year, and what Ed and I said was that the next Labour government is going to take over in very different circumstances and is going to have to have a very different prospectus than the last. And if we came along and said, "Look, we can just carry on like the last Labour government did" – I mean it's politically crackers to do that, because we wouldn't win the election and we wouldn't deserve to win the election.'

What if there were another push back from the unions?

'Look, we are setting out in a different direction. We've learned that tax and benefit policy is important as an instrument of fairness but it's not sufficient, and it's going to be much less open to the next Labour government . . . which is why the rules of the economy are incredibly important.'

So is fiscal conservatism the new Labour orthodoxy? 'Hang on,' he says, 'I don't like the [phrase] "fiscal conservatism", because people sort of think, "Well, what does that mean?" Let me put it in my own terms: what I say is the next Labour government will be far more constrained in terms of what it is able to spend. And therefore the new agenda about how we change our economy is necessary . . . it's accepting an absolute reality, which is a much more constrained fiscal environment.'

If Labour would be seeking to redistribute less in government, one aim would be to 'predistribute' more through the spread of the living wage and through keeping more people in work so that they would become less of a burden on the welfare state; through improved training and skills, having an industrial policy and encouraging responsibility from top to bottom in society. 'The redistribution of the last Labour government relied on revenue which the next Labour government will not enjoy,' Miliband planned to say in a speech on 6 September. 'The option of simply increasing tax credits in the way we did before will not be open to us.'

A long-standing Liberal aspiration has been to switch the tax burden from earned to unearned income, from wages to wealth. In an age when capital is so mobile and the very rich so adept at avoiding taxation, when the international plutocracy live happily in London oblivious to the struggles of the poor around them, surely it is Labour that should be thinking more ambitiously about taxing wealth and static assets – those things that cannot move, such as land and mansions and mobile-phone masts?

Miliband's disappointing reply is to say that he will not 'freewheel on tax policy'.

❧

'The leadership of hopeless opposition is a gloomy affair,' wrote Disraeli, 'and there is little distinction when your course is not associated with the possibility of future power.' Miliband knows that the public feels little love for the coalition government or for its senior ministers and has begun to doubt its basic competence, but nor is there much fondness for any politician. Miliband would have been encouraged by how the crowd booed George Osborne during a Paralympic medal presentation ceremony on the evening of 3 September. For him, at present, opposition feels neither hopeless nor gloomy. He is enthralled by the prospect of future power and what might be achieved with it.

'The truth about modern politics is that the only way in which you can feel long in the future that you've done the right thing is by doing what you believe,' he says. 'What have I learned most in the job? Follow my instincts.'

Because it can be brutal, can't it?

'Yeah, but I think what you learn most of all is, er – is it Zen? I'm not sure Zen is quite right, but I'm a pretty stoical guy. You know it's not a walk in the park . . . but I'm sanguine. I know that conventional wisdom can swing one way, it can swing the other. I think I've just got to keep doing what I think is right and setting out my agenda. I think it's the right agenda for the country. We're going to expand it and broaden it in the months ahead.'

Boldness and an unbreakable self-belief have carried Miliband a long way and those who once ridiculed him have been forced to pause and reflect and even to start listening to what he says. Disaffected social-liberal supporters of the Lib Dems have begun realigning behind Labour. He has held his party together when many expected it to fragment, even if the coalition of forces in and around Labour remains fragile – witness how the unions and the left mobilised against Balls and Miliband.

As a manager of people, he is pragmatic and flexible. He has good practical, or emotional, intelligence, so important in a politician. And his thinking is becoming increasingly heterodox. He is forming surprising alliances and he remains intellectually open, as he demonstrated by asking the Blue Labour thinker Jon Cruddas to lead the party's policy review.

Miliband understands the depth of our crisis and accepts the Gramscian analysis that we are suspended uneasily between the old order that is dying and the new one that is struggling to be born. What flows into the interregnum? 'It's deep what's happened with the Tories,' he says. 'Honestly, it's deep. There's the incompetence, there's the plan having failed and there's also who they stand up for. I could see it in Cameron's eyes when I was challenging him after the Budget [after the announcement of the cut in the top rate of income tax]. He was suddenly thinking to himself: "Why did I do this?"'

He does not want Milibandism to be defined as a state-based project: 'People are out of love with an uncontrolled market but they're certainly not in love with a remote state.' He speaks about mutualism, localism, devolution and the decentralisation of power. He wants to invest in the green economy because 'actually the future of the economy is green'.

Miliband has self-belief and a direction of travel but his ideas are inchoate. He has an instinct for reform but not a plan. Policy is in the process of being recalibrated. Everything is in flux, as it must be in the midterm of a fixed five-year parliament and after such a profound election defeat. In person he has the enthusiasm of a young progressive headmaster, high on the thin air of his own ambition, excited by the books he's read, preparing for the start of the new term. But is he convincing?

Once red, Ed is now wrapping himself in the blue robes of fiscal conservatism (sorry, responsibility). He is pulling the leading Blue Labour thinkers into a tight embrace: Cruddas, Stears, Jonathan Rutherford. Of the old-band members, only Maurice Glasman, whom he ennobled, is absent from his inner circle.

But can Ed be both blue and red? Can he, as Neil O'Brien asks, be both pragmatist and radical? The paradox is this: Miliband believes he can reform capitalism in an age of austerity, not through redistribution but through predistribution and procurement, not through the tried and tested state-based method of tax and transfer but through . . . what, exactly? That remains the Big Unanswerable.

'I think this is a centre-left moment,' he tells me optimistically. 'Because of issues of fiscal responsibility, which is why we must be strong on that. But for me it's a centre-left moment because people think there's something unfair and unjust about our society. You've got to bring the vested interest to heel; you've got to change the way the economy works. That's our opportunity.'

Like Margaret Thatcher, Ed Miliband has told us what his 'faith' is and what he passionately believes. Economics are the method: the object is to change the culture, even the soul of the nation. But can he reform capitalism in one country while globalisation prevails? And will enough of the people believe in and come with him?

(2012)

POSTSCRIPT

Many of the failings of Ed Miliband's leadership were evident in this interview – notably the confusion over whether Labour should accept the Conservatives' austerity programme or break radically from it. On 5 November 2014, unconvinced by the Miliband leadership and certain that he was leading Labour to defeat, I wrote a column about his struggles that became something of a media sensation. The response to it intensified the crisis in the party (Ed Miliband had been the *New Statesman*'s preferred candidate in the 2010 leadership contest and we were perceived to be turning against him), and in the days following the publication of the column there were reports of plots against the leader. A week later, Miliband was forced to 'relaunch' his leadership after rumours of a botched coup against him. He did so by giving a speech in which he quoted Nietzsche's dictum that 'what does not kill you, makes you stronger', and, with the BBC's political editor, visiting Harlow in Essex, my home town. Among other criticisms, I had written that he did not understand the aspirations of Essex Man and Woman. After the publication of the column, Miliband never spoke to me again. The *New Statesman* was refused permission to interview or travel with him during the 2015 general election campaign.

RUNNING OUT OF
TIME: ED MILIBAND

Eearly one morning in September 2012 I visited Ed
Miliband at home in north London. He had just returned
from holiday in Greece and this was to be his first interview of the
new political season, his big re-entry. He remembers the interview
as the one in which he was photographed 'sitting in the bushes'. I
remember it as the occasion on which he showcased his new Big
Idea – 'predistribution', a concept adapted from the Yale political
scientist Jacob Hacker.

Having commendably held his party together when many had
predicted it would split into warring factions, Miliband had grand
plans. His mission was to change the rules of capitalism and to
direct markets for the common good. Inequality was the scourge
of our age, he told me. People felt the system was rigged against
them. But the financial crisis and the Great Recession had created
a social-democratic moment.

'For me it's a centre-left moment because people think there's
something unfair and unjust about our society. You've got to
bring the vested interest to heel; you've got to change the way
the economy works. That's our opportunity.' Not once did he

mention the rise of UKIP or even countenance the possibility that a right-wing populist insurgency would erupt into the space that progressive politics hoped to occupy.

Miliband has a deterministic, quasi-Marxist analysis of our present ills. The UKIP insurgency, Scottish nationalism, the hollowing out of political parties, Islamist radicalisation, the loathing and distrust of elites: all are manifestations of a failed economic model.

He is a politician of unusual self-confidence. Considering his appalling approval ratings and the lack of enthusiasm many of his MPs have for him, he has exceptional resilience. It's as if he is driven by a sense of manifest destiny, always dangerous in a politician. But what if he is wrong? What if the majority of people do not share his world-view? What if they want something more prosaic: economic competence, prosperity for themselves and their children, social justice and for their government to protect them against the havoc being wreaked by globalisation? Miliband would argue that this is what he is offering through 'responsible capitalism'. Yet there exists a gulf between the radicalism of his rhetoric and the low-toned incrementalism of his policies.

From the beginning, Labour was always an uneasy coalition of the organised working class and the Fabian or Hampstead intellectual. Later it also became the party of public-sector workers, social liberals and dispossessed minorities. Miliband is very much an old-style Hampstead socialist. He doesn't really understand the lower middle class or material aspiration. He doesn't understand Essex Man or Woman. Politics for him must seem at times like an extended PPE seminar: elevated talk about political economy and the good society.

At present, he and Labour seem trapped. His MPs sense it and the polls reflect it. UKIP is attracting support in the party's old working-class northern English heartlands and winning converts in key Home Counties swing seats that Labour would once have hoped to win. In Scotland the SNP has become the natural party of government.

In a recent interview, Alex Salmond was scathing about Miliband, describing him as 'more unelectable' than Michael Foot. He had none of 'Foot's wonderful qualities or intelligence. He's more unelectable than Neil Kinnock was; and Kinnock had considerable powers of oratory, and didn't lack political courage.' One would expect Salmond to be dismissive of a Labour leader but it is worrying for the party that even allies now speak similarly of him and his failings.

Miliband is losing the support of the left (to the SNP, to the Greens) without having formed a broader coalition of a kind that defined the early Blair-Brown years. Most damaging, I think, is that he seldom seems optimistic about the country he wishes to lead. Miliband speaks too often of struggle and failure, of people as victims – and it's true that life is difficult for many. But a nation also wants to feel good about itself and to know in which direction it is moving. Reflecting many years afterwards on Labour's landslide victory in 1945, Clement Attlee said: 'We were looking towards the future. The Tories were looking towards the past.'

Labour wins well when its leader seems most in tune with the times and can speak for and to the people about who they are and what they want to be in the near future: Attlee in 1945, Wilson in 1966, Blair in 1997.

Miliband does not have a compelling personal story to tell the electorate, as Thatcher did about her remarkable journey from the grocer's shop in Grantham and the values that sustained her along the way or Alan Johnson does about his rise from an impoverished childhood in west London. I went to Oxford to study PPE, worked for Gordon Brown, became a cabinet minister and then leader of the party does not quite do it. None of this would matter were Miliband in manner and approach not so much the product of this narrow background.

He understands and has analysed astutely capitalism's destructive potential but not perhaps its resilience and ability to absorb shocks. As Lenin said, there are no 'absolutely hopeless situations' for capitalism, as we are again discovering. There are deep problems for Labour and for all social-democratic parties that transcend any one leader. But as we enter an unstable era of multi-party politics, the fragmentation of the British state and intensifying Euroscepticism, Miliband's chief problem is not policy but tone. He needs to find a distinctive voice to articulate people's feelings about the present moment. And he might have to accept before long – or the electorate will force him to – that Europe's social-democratic moment, if it ever existed, is fading into the past.

(November 2014)

POSTSCRIPT

In the event, Miliband led Labour to a terrible defeat in the 2015 general election; the party lost twenty-six seats and, even after prolonged austerity, the Conservatives won a majority. Miliband believed until the exit poll that he would become prime minister (when he saw the projections he exclaimed with incredulity that they must be wrong). He never contemplated a Conservative majority. Indeed, he thought such an outcome was impossible in a 'progressive' age. His defeat and immediate resignation were a personal humiliation and a family tragedy.

He challenged his elder brother David for the leadership of the Labour Party in 2010, destroying their relationship, because he was convinced it was his destiny to become prime minister and to lead Britain in a new direction. Far too late, he made a desperate attempt to reframe Labour as the party of fiscal rectitude by including a so-called budget responsibility lock (which guaranteed that every policy in Labour's manifesto was fully funded without requiring any additional borrowing) – a matter of months after forgetting to mention the deficit in his party conference speech. Meanwhile, he was complacent about events unfolding in Scotland, where Labour would be routed in 2015.

Throughout his leadership and encouraged by his loyal aides, Miliband styled himself as an 'insurgent', challenging a nefarious establishment: big business, the multinational banks, the press barons, the energy companies. Some of his positioning was bold and, indeed, courageous. But it never seemed to dawn on him that he, too, was an emblematically establishment figure. And his long-anticipated social-democratic turn never happened. He was far from alone in misreading the political moment: social democrats across Europe believed that the financial crisis would enable their revival.

As it turned out, nothing that Miliband did or said during the protracted election campaign – no boast about his toughness nor late-night tryst with Russell Brand – would change the people's fundamental view that he was simply not up to the job of being prime minister. In the words of the political philosopher John Gray, it was as if Miliband had been 'trying to lead a country that did not exist'. His legacy, however, was to shift Labour to the left and to change the rules by which the party elects its leader, opening the way for the takeover by the Corbynites.

THE SCOTTISH QUESTION:
ALEX SALMOND

ALEX SALMOND IS in the mood to celebrate when we meet for an informal Sunday lunch at a Westminster hotel. Never lacking in confidence, he seems even more satisfied than he was when I last interviewed him at Bute House in Edinburgh in 2013 and physically heavier than he was when he resigned as first minister last autumn after the Scottish people rejected independence ('I'm about to go back on my diet,' he says). He is buoyed by the publication of his first book, *The Dream Shall Never Die*, an acerbic account of the last one hundred days of the referendum campaign, a copy of which he produces and signs for me ('For Scotland and progressive politics,' he writes). He is naturally delighted by the SNP surge and the consequent collapse in support for Labour in Scotland, and by the prospect of his imminent return to the Commons in May as the MP for Gordon in Aberdeenshire, the long-time seat of the Liberal Democrat Malcolm Bruce.

'Big Alex' is unconcerned by the Conservatives' demonisation of him in a series of propaganda posters and, most recently, in an animated cartoon in which Ed Miliband is portrayed compliantly dancing to Salmond the piper's tune. 'You should never put your opponent - any opponent - on one of your posters,' Salmond replies when I ask about them. 'What government puts the leader of the opposition outside Downing Street? As leader of the opposition you should be unbelievably pleased. It's the concession of the election.

'What Miliband should have done, rather than run from the Tories, is to have pointed at Cameron during Prime Minister's Questions and simply said, 'You've just conceded the election.'

As we settle down at a table, Salmond orders a bottle of pink champagne - 'to toast my book' - and it enhances our fish, chips and mushy peas and helps to quicken our conversation. As with Nigel Farage and Boris Johnson, the former first minister is a politician of skill and cunning, at ease in his own skin and fully absorbed by the game of politics. 'If you don't enjoy the game you shouldn't be a politician,' he says. 'But if you don't have a purpose you most certainly shouldn't be a politician.'

Salmond remains largely a mystery even to those who work closely with him. 'No one knows him well,' says David Torrance, his unauthorised biographer. 'He doesn't really have friends. Halfway through his time at university he became absolutely possessed by politics and has been ever since. If he has a hinterland, it comes across as a bit contrived or phoney. He claims to be interested in football, horse racing and gambling - but there's not a lot of evidence that he is. It's all about politics for him.'

'Of course Alex has friends,' Alan Taylor, the influential columnist and editor of the *Scottish Review of Books*, told me. 'It's just that he's not very clubbable.'

More than ever Salmond is convinced that his destiny is not only to inspire his ancient nation to independence - 'It's not a question of if, but when,' he says of a second referendum - but also to play a significant role in the next UK government. The latest polling forecasts that the SNP could win between thirty-five and fifty of the fifty-nine Scottish Westminster seats (in 2010 it won six to Labour's forty-one). For his part, Salmond will offer no precise figure but predicts simply that 'we will win a barrel-load'.

The mood among the electorate in Scotland reminds him of the final weeks of campaigning in the 2011 Scottish election, when, having been trailing in the polls, the SNP won a landslide in a proportional voting system that was designed to prevent such an outcome, setting us on the road to where we are today, with the British people so divided and the United Kingdom fracturing. 'That night,' Salmond says of 2011, 'I was just watching things fall one by one. It's happening again.'

The decline of Labour in Scotland is deep and has been a long time in the making, the result of institutional complacency, failures of leadership and profound structural changes – deindustrialisation, the decline of the trade unions and of cross-border class solidarity, globalisation, the London effect, and so on – and also the Iraq War. Yet it has been accelerated by the 2014 referendum campaign and the perception among many Scots that, as Salmond puts it, 'Labour was hand-in-hand, hand-in-glove, shoulder-to-shoulder with the Conservative Party.' It didn't help that, with the exception of Gordon Brown and romantic unionists such as the historians Tom Holland and Simon Schama, few in and around the Better Together camp were able to elaborate a persuasive moral and cultural account of why the United Kingdom should be cherished. The No campaign was transactional and utilitarian – Alistair Darling addressed Scots like a financial director warning of a downturn in profits – and now, in an astounding reversal of fortune, those who lost have the swagger and exuberance of winners.

Reflecting on the final, frenetic days of the referendum campaign, Salmond says: 'I've no doubt that Gordon Brown saved the day for No. I had assumed there would be a last-minute offer, because [the Labour strategist] Douglas Alexander had discovered Quebec [he is referring to the Quebec sovereignty referendums of 1980 and 1995]: everything was game-played on Quebec, even down to "Non, merci". It's not subtle. But I also assumed that the people making the offer – Cameron, Clegg, Miliband – had no credibility. Which was why Brown had a role. To convince one in twenty: that's all the "Vow" needed to do.'

The three main party leaders' 'vow', published on the front page of the *Daily Record* two days before the vote and offering Scotland what Salmond believes was 'home rule, devo-to-the-max or near-federalism', was made in great haste, with little consideration for its implementation or how it would affect England, Wales and Northern Ireland. And now, the British state is grappling with the consequences of what exactly was meant by 'home rule' for Scotland and confronting the prospect of a second independence referendum.

❧

Born into a lower-middle-class family in Linlithgow, West Lothian, the son of civil servants, Alex Salmond became politicised at St Andrews University in the 1970s, where he studied economics and history. The great Scottish universities, especially Edinburgh and St Andrews, have long been attractive to upper- and upper-middle-class, public school-educated students from England whose sense of entitlement irritates Scots.

The 1970s were a period when, to use a phrase of the young Gordon Brown, Scots' nationalist ambitions were 'oil-fired'. 'We suggest,' Brown wrote in 1975, 'that the rise of modern Scottish nationalism is less an assertion of Scotland's permanence as a nation than a response to Scotland's uneven development – in particular to the gap between people's experiences as part of an increasingly demoralised Great Britain and their (oil-fired) expectations at a Scottish level.'

The historian Tom Nairn, who is a nationalist, has long described Britain as a pseudo-state, without democratic or moral legitimacy. According to the historian Linda Colley, the forces that 'forged' the British nation after the Act of Union between England and Scotland in 1707 were Protestantism, wars with Catholic Europe, especially with France, and imperialism. These were what united the disparate peoples of these islands.

In his 2012 Hugo Young Lecture delivered in London, Salmond spoke about how the 'social union' between England and Scotland would deepen after the break-up of Britain. It was a good speech because it also raised the English question. Englishness has been a less assertive national identity than Scottishness, perhaps because it is much more confident: for many English people their identity is coterminous with Britishness, in spite of all its complicated associations with post-imperial decline and present anxiety about the European project.

One of the paradoxes of Scottish independence is that its supporters long to break free from political and economic union with England but are equally eager to share or surrender sovereignty to the European Union.

❧

The SNP leadership expects that, in spite of the Conservative Party's enduring unpopularity but because of its strength in the populous south and south-east of England, the Tories will end up winning the 2015 election, perhaps as the largest party in a hung parliament. The SNP, in turn, will form the most powerful bloc of nationalists at Westminster since the emergence of Charles Stewart Parnell's Irish Parliamentary Party, which indulged in wrecking measures and filibustering during the struggles over Irish home rule. (Under the later leadership of John Redmond, the IPP eventually formed a coalition with Herbert Asquith's Liberals in 1910, a government that passed the Parliament Act of 1911 that belatedly curtailed the House of Lords' power of veto, by which the aristocracy had resisted progressive reforms and defended its class and landed interests.)

There had been discussion among Conservatives about whether Cameron should be prepared to negotiate with the SNP. The editor of the ConservativeHome website, Paul Goodman, suggested that Cameron could utilise 'his First Mover Advantage as the serving prime minister . . . by coming to an arrangement with as many of the minor parties as he can, under which they agree not to bring down his minority government. This, in turn, would mean striving to come to one with Alex Salmond.'

But this is a non-starter. Salmond tells me that the SNP would not negotiate with the Tories, nor would it seek any compromise with them: instead, the SNP would act to bring down a Cameron minority government by voting against a Queen's Speech. 'The Tories would have to go straight effectively for a vote of confidence, usually the Queen's Speech, although it could be otherwise, of course, and we'd be voting against,' he says. 'So, if Labour joins us in that pledge, then that's Cameron locked out. And then under the [Fixed-Term] Parliaments Act that the Westminster parliament's passed but nobody seems to have read, you'd then have a two-week period to form another government – and of course you want to form another government because this might be people's only chance to form another government.'

Would he expect Ed Miliband still to be Labour leader at this point?

'I have no idea,' he says. 'But somebody will be. I mean, one of Labour's big fibs – there are a number – but one of them has been that the party with the most seats forms the government. No, the party that can command a majority in the House of Commons forms the government as Ramsay MacDonald did [in 1924] . . . so it's the party that has the majority. And the Parliament Act reinforced that, because it limits the ability of the incumbent to dictate an early election, and puts more power in the hands of parliament and indeed in the hands of your party.'

Some of those closest to Salmond believe that, offered an opportunity – any opportunity – to become prime minister, Miliband would be prepared to enter into full coalition with the SNP, even though he has said that he would not. 'If I were him, I wouldn't have ruled it out. I wouldn't give an inch to the Tory press or to the Tory party . . . Nicola [Sturgeon, the SNP leader and First Minister] has always said that she thought full coalition was unlikely. But she didn't rule it out: she said it was highly unlikely. So all they've done thus far, all Miliband's done thus far, is rule out something which has already been defined by Nicola as highly unlikely.'

Unlikely but not impossible? 'I think,' Salmond says, leaning in as if taking me into his confidence, 'probable would be vote-by-vote [support for Labour], and possible would be confidence and supply. This arrangement is . . . a narrow range of policies, and a narrow range of supported votes, obviously: that's confidence and supply. And then in turn, of course, there has to be an agreed number of policies . . . not like the full coalition, where you take responsibility for every dot and comma, but a narrow range of policies, in return for which you make it possible for the government to function – over a period of time. Vote by vote is what I faced as leader of a minority government in Scotland [from 2007–2011].'

In the event of any deal, or pact, the Labour Party would be expected to soften its stance on austerity and to move closer to the position of the SNP, which styles itself as an anti-austerity party and which, rather than cut public spending as the Tories and Labour would do, has pledged to increase it on departmental budgets by half a per cent a year in real terms. Salmond says the SNP would make amendments to any proposed Labour budget to introduce 'progressive tax measures'.

Like Labour, the SNP opposes a referendum on UK membership of the European Union, and Salmond has no interest in seeking to renegotiate British membership. He is unashamedly in favour of immigration and, indeed, wants more of it. 'Does Scotland need more people? Yes.'

⚜

Let's return to the early morning of Friday 19 September, 2014. Alex Salmond knows that the Yes campaign has lost and that he will be announcing his intention to resign as first minister and SNP leader later that day. And yet, even in defeat, with those around him exhausted and despondent, he suddenly sees a way back for the independence movement. He is watching on television as David Cameron, who shortly before had been speaking to Salmond on the phone, steps on to the pavement outside 10 Downing Street and makes a mistake. A big mistake. Instead of being magnanimous in victory, the Prime Minister seeks cynically to address the English Question – the matter of Scottish MPs voting on English laws – in an attempt to appease his restive backbenchers and Nigel Farage, who, as it happens, is the first politician interviewed by the BBC at the end of Cameron's short address to the nation.

'I was asked this morning by a correspondent,' Salmond says. 'He says, "But if Cameron were to offer you everything you wanted, you would want to do a deal with him, would you not?" I said no. He was obviously upset. The reason for me is, why on earth would you trust somebody who comes up to Scotland, makes promises, and then saunters out and says, "Sorry, I forgot to mention about this English vote thing in tandem [with more devolution to Scotland]." I mean, that's as bad as you get. Bad politics has created a fantastic opening for us to take matters forward.'

And now, the former first minister and soon-to-be MP for Gordon is preparing for the general election and his return to Westminster - he represented Banff and Buchan in parliament from 1987 to 2010 - because, as he says more than once, 'I think the stars might be in alignment.'

❦

The referendum campaign energised and changed Scotland and the effect of this national awakening has been to create one of the most politically sophisticated electorates - perhaps the most - in Europe. Visit Scotland and you have a sense of a nation moving inexorably away from England. There's restlessness for change, for alternatives, for new possibilities, for the creation of a fairer, more equitable society, and this desire has only grown stronger since the Scottish referendum, powered by social media. The Scots are relishing what the writer Gerry Hassan calls 'an independence of the mind'.

'Absolutely head-on,' Salmond says. 'That's dead right. The Scotland of 2015 is not the Scotland of 2014, never mind the

Scotland of twenty years ago . . . We had a bad – by and large, a bad twentieth century. If you do things by the century, we had a bad twentieth century. There were reasons for it, of course . . . Yet last year I was looking forward to the Commonwealth Games, the Ryder Cup, the referendum, and Cameron said he was going to, as he put it, celebrate the First World War. Now, Scotland is a martial nation, fiercely proud of what it fought for, but we don't "celebrate" the Great War. It's not to be celebrated. The point is, Cameron thought that pride would come from the Great War, with regards a bloody, devastating carnage. And the relevance to your point is this, Jason – that in Scotland, in many communities, it wasn't a decimation; it was a three times decimation of men of fighting age. And I think the impact was very substantial. Scottish heavy industry should have transformed into light industry and it didn't happen, and one of the reasons – one of the reasons; not the only one, but one of the reasons – it didn't happen was that the people that would have done it were nae there.'

But now there are opportunities. 'If the stars align,' he says again, 'we could have the delivery of what Scotland was promised last September – devo to the max, home rule.'

If the Vow was honoured, would that be enough for the SNP? Would federalism, or neo-federalism, satisfy you?

'No. The SNP is a party of independence. But, of course, the people the question should be asked of are the Scottish people. The great secret weapon of the SNP is that it is a cause, an objective and an ideal. And when you've got an objective and an ideal the rest of the stuff is not nearly as important. I'm having another tilt at Westminster because I think the stars might be in alignment. I wouldn't come to Westminster to make up the numbers.'

(2015)

POSTSCRIPT

Published a few months before the 2015 general election, this profile was seized on by the Tories. The notion of Alex Salmond and the SNP conspiring with Labour and other parties 'to lock' the Conservatives out of power or scheming to bring down a minority Cameron government was not well received and no doubt damaged both Labour and the Lib Dems in the final poll. The SNP won fifty-six of the fifty-nine Scottish Westminster seats in 2015; Alex Salmond returned to Westminster in triumph, as he knew he would. But he lost his seat in the snap election of 2017 which, following the Brexit vote, saw a Tory revival in Scotland under the leadership of Ruth Davidson. A third of SNP supporters were estimated to have voted for Brexit.

Salmond's insistence (if not hope) that the 2014 referendum was a 'once in a generation' event may yet prove correct. The nationalist insurgency has receded; the SNP, wearied by office and outflanked from the left by Labour, no longer enjoys the extraordinary potency it briefly possessed. But it remains the natural party of government in Scotland and a second independence referendum cannot be ruled out.

THE ASCENT OF
THE SUBMARINE:
GEORGE OSBORNE

IN 2005, AS the newly appointed shadow chancellor, George Osborne explored possibilities for introducing a flat rate of income tax, citing Estonia as a model and inspiration. Back then, at the age of thirty-four, he seemed to be a conventionally Eurosceptic, low-tax, small-state right-winger. Even if he self-identified as a moderniser and social liberal – as a metropolitan he was relaxed about many of the issues that unsettled social conservatives: from race and immigration, to gay rights and the equalities agenda – his free-market economics were bone-dry. In his early years as Chancellor, a role he assumed in 2010, Osborne seemed to be conforming to stereotype as he compared Britain's economic woes to what was happening in Greece and, against Keynesian orthodoxy, introduced deep spending cuts to both the current account and the capital budget. 'Slasher Osborne', he was called by David Blanchflower, a former member of the Bank of England's Monetary Policy Committee.

At the 2012 Paralympics in London, Osborne was booed by the crowd during a medal presentation ceremony. It hurt him deeply. This was the same year as the 'omnishambles' Budget, the carelessness of which undermined his reputation for strategic brilliance. In 2013, a ComRes poll for the *Sunday Mirror* and the *Independent* adjudged him the politician people would least like to share Christmas with, or run the country. Unfairly or otherwise, Osborne had become Britain's most reviled politician, caricatured as a caddish Tory baronet wilfully inflicting hardship on the poor.

'It was perfectly understandable,' Osborne said, reflecting on that period when we met in Newton Aycliffe, in the north-east of England. He and David Cameron had just addressed the regional media while sitting in the show carriage of one of the new-model trains that will be built at Hitachi's factory. 'You're in an incredibly difficult economic situation, you set out a difficult plan, and to begin with, all people can see is the difficulty of the plan, they can't see the results. Now, of course, there's much more evidence of the results.

'You have just watched a Conservative chancellor and a Conservative prime minister be interviewed by the local press of the north-east of England. These are not the kind of questions we would have had three or four years ago.'

The reporters' questions were brief and respectful – mostly about jobs and business matters in the region – and each was answered courteously. The Prime Minister, who was deeply tanned, and his friend and ally, the Chancellor, had an easy rapport. Once so awkward in public, Osborne was relaxed and self-assured, further evidence of the startling transformation in his fortunes. The whole show was a bit like watching two first-rate tennis players knocking the ball across the net to each other in the warm-up before a big match: there was no strain.

For all the artificiality of the setting, I found it fascinating to observe Cameron and Osborne together, so comfortable in each other's company, and so unlike Blair and Brown, especially in the terminal phase of their relationship, their mutual trust corroded by years of feuds and resentment. Cameron operated as if he were the chairman, delegating questions of detail to his younger chief executive. The Chancellor, ever alert to an opportunity, could not resist making an anti-Labour gibe ('We are supporting industry in the north-east and not putting all our bets on the City of London as under the last Labour government') as he extolled the virtues of the 'Northern Powerhouse' and reaffirmed his commitment to reviving British manufacturing, which has fallen to ten per cent of GDP (part of the blame for which lies with the deindustrialisation policies of the Thatcher government). Earlier, before assembled dignitaries and senior Japanese executives from Hitachi, Osborne had introduced the Prime Minister affectionately as 'my boss'.

Later, as we sat at a table drinking tea, Osborne attempted to explain why he and Cameron had worked together so successfully for so long. 'First of all, we are very good friends,' he said, keeping his shrewd eyes averted. 'We're personal friends, we're very similar in our outlook. And we've been determined to make this relationship work. You're very much shaped by the political world in which you become an MP: just like Blair and Brown were shaped by Margaret Thatcher's Britain, so we were shaped by what happened to the Conservative Party as we became MPs, and by the Tony Blair premiership, the rows between Blair and Brown – the lessons you learn about what happens if you don't work together.'

Osborne recalled being asked by Michael Howard in 2005 whether he wanted to stand to be leader of the Conservative Party. He was already shadow chancellor, having risen rapidly since entering Conservative Central Office as a young Oxford graduate and impressing with his strategic intelligence, talent for the game and single-mindedness. 'I thought about it briefly,' he told me. 'I just didn't think that it was right for me at that point and, speaking to my friend David, he had a very clear idea of what he wanted to do with the job. And so, far from running myself, I ran his campaign.'

Cameron and Osborne, who knew each other from Central Office but not that well, became close only after they were both elected to parliament in 2001. 'People always think we're friends from years and years ago, but we actually became friends when we became new MPs. And I remember . . . we became MPs just as September 11 happened, and that was the big defining event of that parliament. In the big debates that happened that autumn about anti-terror legislation, I noticed that the other new MP who turned up to listen was David.'

In all the years since, Osborne said he had 'never looked at David and thought, "That should be me." I think Gordon Brown thought that every time. He wanted to depose Blair, he wanted to replace him . . . I don't have that sort of sense of injustice – which I thought was ridiculous in Brown, but anyway – I don't have that at all.'

It was obvious that Osborne was Cameron's preferred choice as successor and that, when we met, he was being presented as prime minister-in-waiting. Having relished his reputation as a Machiavel and arch-manipulator – he had been discussed as if he were some kind of Tory Bond villain, pulling the strings of government from his subterranean lair in Whitehall – Osborne had changed. He was slimmer, fitter and more confident in public. But the change in him was more than cosmetic; it was as if philosophically he had become a different kind of Tory.

Had he made a conscious effort to amend his personal style and politics?

'I think the way our country is run is broken. The model has failed and my views have changed on this. I grew up in the middle of London [but] I've been a north-west MP for fourteen years and it has changed my perspective. I realise of course that not everything in the country happens inside the Circle Line and that's been a very important development for me as an adult. I've also changed my view about the capability of central government to get everything right. I have much more confidence in strong local government, both to make successes and also to get things wrong but then be held to account.'

He joked about discovering his inner Michael Heseltine, and he was interested in, to adapt a phrase of the *New York Times* columnist David Brooks, 'building relationships across differences'. Consider the Northern Powerhouse project. Richard Leese, the Labour leader of Manchester City Council, told me that he considered Osborne to be 'a very political animal'. And yet, he added, 'here's a right-wing Chancellor supporting a northern Labour authority. He's been prepared to do what we need to do to benefit the northern authorities and he's been prepared to do it at a pace that Whitehall is not used to.'

⁂

Danny Alexander, the Liberal Democrat and a former chief secretary to the Treasury under Osborne, told me that the Chancellor was deeply learned in British and American history. I'd heard a story of how Osborne wrote a handwritten letter to the novelist Neel Mukherjee, saying how much he enjoyed *The Lives of Others*, the saga of a Bengali family in Calcutta which went on to be shortlisted for the Man Booker Prize. Like Boris Johnson, Osborne has a hinterland, but unlike Johnson, the exhibitionist and showman, he is reluctant to reveal it. 'Why? I think it's because he's really quite shy,' Alexander said.

I asked Osborne about the nature of his conservatism. It seemed to me that the Chancellor was far more flexible than his image as a cold-eyed austerian suggested and that his conservatism is less about ideology and a fixed body of ideas than it is a disposition, a sentiment, a way of reacting to the world. After all, he is a free marketeer who wants to intervene in markets to force employers to pay a national minimum wage higher than anything proposed by Labour.

'I think there are two powerful strands in conservatism and they both need to be brought together,' Osborne said. 'One is the economic rationalism of Nigel Lawson: you've got to make the sums add up. There is a strong incentive to create simpler and flatter taxes, a modern state that is not overburdened by complexity; and without that, nothing else is affordable and nothing else works. But you also mustn't then lose sight of the very powerful role for government in regenerating areas that have been left behind.

'So that was the Michael Heseltine. You've got to have Nigel Lawson telling you, "You can't have ninety-eight per cent rates of tax," and you've also got to have Michael Heseltine's vision to say, "You know what? I'm going to go in to the Albert Docks in Liverpool, or Canary Wharf, or the Isle of Dogs in London, and there's a big positive role for government." I'm a Conservative who understands, perhaps more than I did ten or fifteen years ago, the positive role for government in making things happen, and using the enormous resources that the state spends, in very particular interventions that help areas, or indeed industries.'

❧

In 2011 Osborne was ridiculed for saying in his Budget speech that he wanted 'a Britain carried aloft by the march of the makers', but he had not been deterred from the belief in the need for a revival in British manufacturing, which lagged behind the service sector. During the 2015 election campaign, he was seldom seen at photo shoots without a hard hat and high-visibility jacket. Contrast this with Ed Miliband, who spoke continuously about the need to build houses but rarely if ever visited a building site; instead, he stood mostly at a lectern, like some economics professor delivering his latest treatise on inequality.

'What I'm trying to do in politics is to take the things I believe in and the ideas I have and put them into practical effect, and that involves political decisions,' Osborne told me. 'The political game as you described it would not be worth playing if it was just a game. There has to be an endpoint.'

⚘

Those who had worked closely with Osborne, including civil servants, said he was more likeable and open than his public image would suggest. 'George is warm and amusing,' Danny Alexander said. 'He is very loyal and people are loyal to him in return. I'd say his knowledge of history is unrivalled – in meetings, he often liked to pull out some analogy from British history from one hundred and fifty years ago. [Osborne studied history at Oxford, not economics – which some critics of his policies use against him.] But there's a big difference between the private and public person and that's been one of the difficulties for him. In the early years – when he was known as "the Submarine" – he avoided attention. It was not him but me who went out to explain our policies. That not fronting up became a problem for him.'

Alexander said that Osborne's reputation as a 'tricky political tactician' was justified. 'But he also has a world-view. You shouldn't doubt that he is sincere in his conviction of trying to do the right thing by the British economy.'

Surely the same could be said of all chancellors?

'Well, you must realise that in the Treasury you have ideas and you drive policies forward, but you rely on other departments for their implementation. I'd say the implementation of some of the coalition's policies, especially on welfare – I never approved of the bedroom tax – was too rough around the edges, and that's what caught people's attention.'

During our several conversations, Osborne referred often to Tony Blair, either directly or more cryptically by appropriating buzz-phrases of the man some Tories call 'the Master'.

'I think now there's a big responsibility for the Conservative Party to hold to the centre, to represent working people, to continue these reforms that previously have had cross-party support. And you know what? I can say it's the Conservative Party that is looking forward, not back.'

'Forward, not back' was, of course, a favourite phrase of Blair's, the slogan under which Labour contested the 2005 general election. Osborne also referred to the 'forces of conservatism' – that is, those opposed to his reforms – another appropriation from Blair.

Following the 2015 election, David Cameron sought to recast the Tories as a party of One Nation, even as the multinational United Kingdom was undermined by its discontinuities and contradictions. This might have been wishful thinking or mere rhetorical positioning. It might also have been recognition of limitations and that the Tories had a slender majority and grudging mandate. 'An intelligent reading of the election is that the Tories did not win an endorsement for their ideas; it was more that the electorate could not accept the alternative [of a Labour/SNP alliance],' Danny Alexander said. 'I think George understands that, which is why he is trying to hold the centre ground and not be pulled to the right by backbenchers.'

Meanwhile, the Tories' desire to run a Budget surplus, welfare reforms and cuts to tax credits had created many victims. In an essay published in the *New Statesman*, Amartya Sen, the Nobel Prize-winning economist, criticised the government's austerity policy, saying it was unnecessary as the ratio of public debt to GDP was much smaller than in the two decades after the Second World War, when it caused little alarm. Moreover, Sen argued, austerity had not worked: 'price-adjusted GDP per capita in Britain today is still lower than what it was before the crisis in 2008' and the recovery had been slower in Britain than in the US and Japan. Robert Skidelsky, the cross-bench peer and biographer of J. M. Keynes, also wrote faulting Osborne's economic logic. 'Historians will debate his motives but I believe that this intensely political Chancellor saw in a manufactured crisis of confidence a once-in-a-lifetime opportunity to cut the size of the state.'

Osborne listened as I attempted to explain why the Tories remained so unpopular with so many and why Professor Sen and others were so critical of him. His austerity policies and benefits sanctions regime affected the poorest and the disabled: did he think about that?

'What I think is the victims are people who are victims of when an economy fails. When you get these decisions wrong about your national economy, it is not the richest in the country who suffer. It is the very poorest: they are the people who lose their jobs, they are the people who have their opportunities snatched from them. This government has to deal with a huge Budget deficit. So, you know, the victims of economic failure are the poorest. And in the end who are the beneficiaries of creating jobs, growing the economy? Again, it's not the person who's always been employed in the hedge fund. It's the person who was previously out of work and now has a chance in life, like these young apprentices I've just been meeting in Nissan.'

Osborne was not only denounced by Keynesians and the left. Many on the free-market right urged him to be bolder and to cut deeper and faster. Why not revive some of the more libertarian, Randian ideas of his younger days? Why not cut income tax and roll back the state even more quiickly?

'I don't think the Conservative Party's response to the Labour Party's lurching to the left should be a lurching to the right,' he replied. 'I think it's a huge opportunity and responsibility for us to hold the centre of British politics. Now, the centre doesn't mean you can't change the centre, you can't shape the centre . . .' – he paused and looked directly at me – 'the whole argument about the country living within its means: these are shaping the new centre of British politics.

'We should not be heading off into the wilderness at the same time as our opponents are. We should be staying very firmly rooted in the centre, but that's not a static thing. I always think [of] a sort of motto I have: which is, in politics, in opposition, the pressure is always to move to the centre; when you're in government you can move the centre. I would take education reform as a kind of classic example of that.'

As to his own future prospects and speculation about who might eventually succeed David Cameron, Osborne was evasive. 'I guess my approach has always been to try and focus on the task at hand and not to be thinking about the next job. Of course, there will be a point when the Conservative Party runs a leadership contest. I'm absolutely determined not to allow that to overshadow what I'm trying to do now. I'm just mentally able to say, "I'm not addressing that now. I'm not thinking about that now." If I started going on about the next job, I think it wouldn't make me a very good Chancellor.'

To translate: he wanted to be prime minister. The Submarine was submerged no more.

With that, he rose, shook my hand and left the room. I watched as, soon afterwards, he and Cameron were led to a waiting car. They sat side by side in the back seat and were quickly absorbed in conversation – two close friends and colleagues who, in their early years in the Commons, learned so much about politics and power from observing Tony Blair and Gordon Brown, learned both what was best about their relationship, and worst, and then, with patience and fortitude as well as luck, set about winning and holding on to power, just as Blair had. Meanwhile, divided and seeking renewed self-definition, the Labour Party moves further to the left under Corbyn, just as Osborne would have wished. He is in the clear now.

(2015)

POSTSCRIPT

George Osborne was far from being in the clear, as it turned out. His political career, like that of his 'boss', was destroyed by the European referendum. Early on the morning of 24 June 2016, as it became apparent that the country had voted for Brexit, George Osborne, who had cautioned David Cameron against holding a referendum to settle the Europe question, is reported to have said, 'Well, Dave's fucked, I'm fucked, the country's fucked.' After Theresa May became Conservative leader and thus Prime Minister, she sacked Osborne, telling him that he 'should get to know the party better'. Having hoped to be foreign secretary, he returned to the backbenches before, in April 2017, resigning as an MP 'for now'. Then he became editor of the *London Evening Standard* and has used its editorial pages to campaign against Brexit and undermine the May premiership. He is reported to have told colleagues that he will not rest until May is 'chopped up in bags in my freezer'. Osborne is also a highly-paid adviser to BlackRock, the fund management firm. He and other liberal Tories now claim to feel 'politically homeless' (like the Brexiteers and the Bennite left before them). But intermittent – and often tedious – talk of a new centrist party has led nowhere.

OUT OF EXILE:
TONY BLAIR

Tony Blair enters the room at his London offices wearing a navy-blue crew-neck sweater, an open-neck pale blue shirt, informal dark trousers and dark shoes. This relaxed, casual style is strikingly reminiscent of how he was dressed when he appeared alongside George W. Bush during their first fateful meeting at Camp David in February 2001, the beginning of a relationship that set Britain on the road to war in Iraq, the reverberations from which continue to destabilise the Middle East and distort the legacy of Labour's most electorally successful leader.

Protected by his personal security team, Blair travels incessantly, a habitué of the first-class lounge and the luxury international hotel, and on this damp, early Monday morning, he looks puffy-eyed and tired. He sits to my left, in a stiff-backed chair, leans forward, his legs slightly splayed, and asks for some coffee. There is a TV screen mounted on the wall and several small bottles of water in a bucket of ice on a sideboard. The blinds are partially closed, lending our meeting a conspiratorial atmosphere.

Blair, who in conversation is personable and animated, is not quite a fugitive in his own land but, because of the Iraq War and his extensive business operations since leaving office, as well as some of the dubious company he has kept among the global plutocracy, he is widely reviled, a fate that frustrates him but to which he is resigned. 'I gave up a long time ago, worrying as to whether life's treated you unfairly,' he says.

But these are turbulent new times and Blair is planning a fresh start and a renewed engagement with British politics. In September, he announced that he would 'close down Tony Blair Associates and wind up the Firerush and Windrush structures', two companies in the group through which the revenues flow. While he will keep some personal consultancies, Blair said that he will concentrate on his charitable and not-for-profit work. 'The substantial reserves' – estimated to be around £8m – 'that TBA has accumulated will be gifted to the not-for-profit work,' the Office of Tony Blair said in a press statement, which noted that his group of organisations employed two hundred people in twenty countries. Blair was clearing the ground for a comeback. At the age of sixty-three, his political journey was far from finished.

The day before our meeting, the *Sunday Times* reported that Blair was 'positioning himself to play a pivotal role in shaping Britain's Brexit deal'. He was also alleged by unnamed sources to have called Jeremy Corbyn a 'nutter' and Theresa May a 'lightweight'. The report irritated his aides and Blair alluded to it several times during our conversation, as if eager to correct any misunderstanding.

There has been speculation to the effect that he wants to set up a new political party. He says that he does not. Nor does he want a direct role in Brexit negotiations, or to lead the resistance to it. But he wants to participate in public life, engaging with new ideas and policy initiatives. He wants to be heard and to influence the wider debate – because, as he told me, the state of Western politics simultaneously dismays and motivates him. His dismay is motivating his re-engagement. He is determined once again to become an agent of influence in British politics, on issues from Brexit to reviving what he describes as the 'progressive centre or centre left'.

His allies call for a new 'muscular centre'. They are discussing how best to counter the populist surge on both the radical left and radical right. 'You've got to unpack, first of all, what bits of the so-called liberal agenda have failed and what bits haven't,' Blair told me. 'And you've got to learn the right lessons of Brexit, Trump and these popular movements across the Western world. Otherwise you're going to end up in a situation where you seriously think that the populism of the left is going to defeat the populism of the right. It absolutely won't.'

Our new emerging political order, he believes, is defined less by a conflict between left and right than by one between 'open and closed', and this is a theme he has been exploring since 2007.

'Open *v* closed is a really important debate today, because in a curious way the populism of the left and the populism of the right – at a certain point they meet each other. They tend to be isolationist. OK, the left is more anti-business, the right is more anti-immigrant, but they tend to be protectionist and they have an attitude to the process of globalisation that says this is a policy that is given by government and we can stop it and should stop it. Whereas my view about globalisation is that it's a force essentially driven by people, by technological change, by the way the world has opened up. You're not going to reverse that. The question is: how do we make that just and fair? That is the big question of our times. The centre left does not provide an answer to that, and we can and should.'

Blair knows that he is unpopular, especially with the left, and why. But does he feel misunderstood?

'Well, I think there was huge misunderstanding of what we

were about and why we were about it. That's partly one of the reasons I'm changing everything.'

Changing everything: the phrase is resonant and refers not only to Blair's decision to close down most of his commercial and business interests, but also to his renewed political engagement. 'What I'm doing is to spend more time not in the front line of politics, because I have no intention of going back to the front line of politics, to correct another misunderstanding . . . but in trying to create the space for a political debate about where modern Western democracies go and where the progressive forces particularly find their place . . . I'm dismayed by the state of Western politics, but also incredibly motivated by it. I think in Britain today, you've got millions of effectively politically homeless people.'

His voice quickens even as his body language betrays frustration. 'I can't come into front-line politics. There's just too much hostility, and also there are elements of the media who would literally move to destroy mode if I tried to do that . . .'

So, what can he do? Is there someone in whom he can invest his hopes? He says that his first priority is to 'build a platform' that will allow people to debate ideas and formulate solutions, without the abuse or vilification that has become so prevalent in modern politics. 'The best thing I can do is use [my] long experience, not just as prime minister – I've learned a huge amount being out in the world these past nine or ten years . . .'

The platform will be driven by technology. 'One advantage of today's social media is that you can build networks. Movements can begin at scale and build speed quickly. The thing that's really tragic about politics today is that the best ideas about politics aren't in politics. I find the ideas are much more interesting in the technology sector, much more interesting ideas about how you change the world.'

Tony Blair believes that Brexit can be halted. 'It can be stopped if the British people decide that, having seen what it means, the pain-gain cost-benefit analysis doesn't stack up. And that can happen in one of two ways. I'm not saying it will [be stopped], by the way, but it could. I'm just saying: until you see what it means, how do you know?'

Attempting to secure access to the single market will be the defining negotiation. 'Either you get maximum access to the single market – in which case you'll end up accepting a significant number of the rules on immigration, on payment into the budget, on the European Court's jurisdiction. People may then say, 'Well, hang on, why are we leaving then?' Or alternatively, you'll be out of the single market and the economic pain may be very great, because beyond doubt if you do that you'll have years, maybe a decade, of economic restructuring.'

But, I suggest, the Remain side made numberless dire economic forecasts during the long, dispiriting referendum campaign and they were ignored. The public understands well enough the risks of Brexit.

'But this is what I keep saying to people. This is like agreeing to a house swap without having seen the other house . . . You've got to understand, this has been driven essentially ideologically. You've got a very powerful cartel of the media on the right who provided the platform for the Brexiteers who allied themselves with the people in the Tory party who saw a chance to run with this. And, OK, they ended up in circumstances where there was a very brutal but not particularly enlightening campaign. They won that campaign.'

He pauses to reach for his coffee cup.

'I think, in the end, it's going to be about parliament and the country scrutinising the deal. So, for example, the deal that was done with Nissan' – to persuade the Japanese carmaker to expand its production in Sunderland after Brexit – 'I don't know what the terms of that deal are, but we should know. Because that will tell us a lot about what they're prepared to concede in order to keep access to the single market.'

⚜

Blair says that he has never met Donald Trump, although he knows his son-in-law, Jared Kushner, the real estate multimillionaire. Trump's venality, belligerence, isolationist rhetoric and narrow definition of the national interest has alarmed the Anglo-American foreign policy establishment, which considers Trump to be a clear and present danger to the rules-based liberal world order. The urgent challenge facing the West in an age of intensifying nationalism, great power rivalry and demagogic plutocracy will be to hold together the alliance structure that has defined the world for the past seventy years.

Under Trump's presidency, the political scientist Robert Kagan has written, the US is likely to retreat into 'national solipsism'. It could be much worse than that, but Blair's response to Trump's victory is to invoke realpolitik. Neither for nor against Trump – in public, at least – he wants to understand and explain.

'Look, he's been elected president of America and [I agree with] the comments that Barack Obama has made about working with him, trying to make sure that those things that people are worried about don't materialise. That's our obligation now. He's the American president, duly elected through their electoral college system, and that's it. He won because people want to change. Because there are various issues upon which the Republican platform was stronger than the Democrats. And this is part of a general global movement, which is partly a reaction to globalisation and partly economic. But it is also a lot to do with culture and identity, and people's feelings that the world is changing rapidly around them and that the left doesn't get this.'

He believes that Trump's preoccupation with questions of identity and belonging, as well as his appeal to people's anxieties about immigration and Islamist terror, was fundamental to his appeal.

Blair's response to the fragmentation of globalisation is not to reject but to reaffirm his commitment to it and to free market economics and the open society. In other words, he favours not less but more liberalism. 'Against the received wisdom, I think the absolute essence is to revive the centre. Progressive forces, if they're not coming at this from a strong centrist position, are likely to find themselves just enough off-centre on the debates around culture and identity, never mind the economy, where they're going to be defeated by a populism of the right. And if you put a populism of the left against that, which is where some people want to go – it's where the British Labour Party's gone [and] many Democrats argue that, really, if we'd had Bernie Sanders, we'd have done better – if we go down that path, we'll just get beaten bigger.'

⁂

Is this the beginning of Tony Blair's second act in British public life? Will enough people be prepared to listen to him, or is the stain of the Iraq misadventure and subsequent pursuit of personal wealth too pronounced? The property portfolio that he and Cherie Blair own, which includes a main residence in Connaught Square in London and a country home in Buckinghamshire, is worth at least £27m, according to the *Guardian*. Blair's total wealth may be at least twice that, according to media reports, though he said in 2014 that it was less than £20m.

'We are suffering a crisis of global leadership,' says one former

ally and associate of Blair's. 'There's an absence of a strong centrist foreign policy voice. We need someone to make the case
for NATO and for the alliance system. Blair could do that. But
it will be difficult for him, because he's never found a way of
acknowledging the mistakes he made. If he wants to talk about
Brexit and Trump, he needs to do so with humility and not be
so Manichaean about it. He has long spoken of the clash between
Islamism and Western civilisation – now we have a problem with
Western civilisation, don't we?'

In his long interview with the *Atlantic*'s Jeffrey Goldberg in
April 2016, Barack Obama discussed the moral limits of American
power and explained what he called his doctrine of 'tragic realism'.
Like the philosopher-theologian Reinhold Niebuhr, whom he has
read carefully, Obama acknowledges the existence of evil (as the
more religious Blair does) in the world, but also the difficulties
and dangers inherent in confronting it. Obama, who opposed the
Iraq War, understood the risks of attempting to impose, through
violence and conquest, Western values of freedom, democracy and
the rule of law. Obama's foreign policy, unlike Blair's, was defined
by a sense of cautious 'realism'. Great power carries the burden of
responsibility and demands the necessity of restraint – perhaps
far too much restraint, in the case of Obama and the Syrian War.

'We cannot do good without also doing evil,' Niebuhr wrote
in *The Irony of American History*. 'We cannot defend what is
dearest to us without running the risk of destroying what is even
more precious than our life . . .'

In his response to the Chilcot inquiry, Blair accepted responsibility for the failures of post-invasion planning, but defended
the original decision to invade and occupy Iraq. Because his
voice was hoarse and weakening, he was described as resembling
a 'broken man' by some commentators during the press conference at which he replied to Chilcot. Yet, in person, he seems

anything but broken: he is alert, vigorous, surprisingly optimistic about the prospects for globalisation, and determined to fight back against the populism sweeping the West. He believes that the arc of history still bends towards progress and enlightenment.

Talking to him, I was reminded of the speech he gave at the 2001 Labour party conference, shortly after the 9/11 attacks. 'The kaleidoscope has been shaken,' he said, and as a consequence it was time to reorder the world. For Blair, 9/11 was a profound shock but also an opportunity. The catastrophe enabled him to find a public voice commensurate with the moment, a voice that George W. Bush could not find, and he saw an opportunity to influence Bush and, at the same time, internationalise US foreign policy, drawing the world's one essential nation away from hermit security.

Trump's 'America First' isolationism is today an exaggerated caricature of Bush's pre-9/11 positions on foreign policy. In the 2000 presidential debates with Al Gore, Bush said, 'I'm not so sure the role of the United States is to go around the world and say this is the way it's got to be.' How incredible that now seems.

'Every American president I've ever dealt with, and I've dealt with three now, has always come to power with an essentially domestic programme,' Blair told me. 'And all of them have ended up, because this is America's inevitable role in the world, being highly engaged in global affairs. And even in relation to a President Trump and President Putin, let's see what happens. Let's see what happens when they actually have to negotiate.'

Asked about the threat posed by Russia to the West, Blair says: 'It's important in my view that we in the West stand up for our essential values. The language that President Putin understands is strength. He will take advantage of any weakness. This concept of a sort of new authoritarianism, I think, is a real risk in the world as a whole, but again the best way of dealing with that is to respond to those people who want some authority and order. I mean the electorate, even in the West. There was a poll I saw in *Le Monde*, the other week, with an astonishing amount of people worried that democracy didn't actually work. The answer to that is to have a centre ground that is strong and radical. And the centre ground has become flabby and managers of the status quo.'

With his flag planted firmly in the 'progressive centre ground' and with opposition to the Tories so divided, Blair is preparing for his re-entry into public life. It's almost as if he believes he's on an ethical mission, that he has unfinished business. But the ground beneath his feet is crumbling. Liberals are losing everywhere he looks.

What if America under Trump ceases to be the last best hope for the world and becomes something darker and more malevolent? This isn't something that Blair wishes to contemplate. He and millions like him may feel 'politically homeless', but he remains, at heart, a liberal optimist. But is his optimism no more than misguided faith founded upon a misreading of the present?

'In a world of uncertainty, people want strength in their leaders,' Blair says. 'It's our job to make sure that that does not bleed across into authoritarianism. And that's why, when we were in government, we introduced real reforms, not least around the Supreme Court, the European Convention on Human Rights being incorporated into British law . . . We had more devolution, more giving away of government power at the centre. But it was still a strong government, with a very clear sense of where it was going, and it had control of the political agenda. And this is not a lesson of politics that's only relevant to this time but to any time.'

Trump, Brexit, Corbyn – Tony Blair keeps ending up on the losing side, though the years when he was winning sustain him in his convictions and extraordinary self-belief. He cautions against fatalism and he remains defiant. And he never doubts he's on the right side of history.

'Of course, history has a direction,' he says, dismissing my scepticism. 'There is progress, we are making progress, even in our own countries. If you think of the world your son is growing up in and the world my grandfather grew up in, if you think what he's going to have and what my father had, I mean, come on! There's a lot to celebrate. There is absolutely no reason to be pessimistic about the human condition.'

(2016)

THE TIME OF THE REBEL:
JEREMY CORBYN

O NE DAY IN June 2016, as the 'coup' to oust Jeremy Corbyn gathered momentum in the immediate aftermath of the vote for Brexit, Owen Smith visited the Labour leader in his office at Portcullis House, Westminster. A vote of no confidence had been tabled against Corbyn and shadow ministers were, at choreographed intervals, resigning in protest at what was perceived to be his failed leadership. Many blamed him personally for Brexit, believing that he was a 'secret Outer'. (He was not.) Corbyn's allies had long anticipated a move from within the Parliamentary Labour Party (PLP) against the leader – they thought that it might come as early as the day after the local elections in May – and they were determined to defend their man to the last. Would Corbyn be similarly resolute?

Long isolated and irrelevant, the far left had waited more than three decades since the end of the Bennite wars of the early 1980s to be in a position to control the Labour Party. 'This is what it's all about,' John McDonnell, Corbyn's long-time ally and neo-Marxist shadow chancellor, said to me as he publicly urged Corbyn to stand his ground against their gathering enemies in the PLP.

With a hostile media camped outside his house in north London, Corbyn was unsettled. He was anxious about the effect of the relentless scrutiny on his wife, Laura Álvarez, and his neighbours, many of whom he considered friends. 'But they all said, "Stick at it. We're with you," Corbyn told me on a trip to Prague in December 2016 for the annual conference of the Party of European Socialists. 'Friends, family, neighbours – they said, "Don't give up. Don't give in to what's going on." And I didn't.'

A former lobbyist for the biopharmaceutical multinational Pfizer, Owen Smith was elected as the MP for Pontypridd in 2010 and purported to be from the 'soft left'. His high self-regard and considerable ambition compensated for a lack of ministerial experience, and he had an ingenious plan he wanted to put to Corbyn when he visited him in his office. The plan was simple: Corbyn should resign and Owen Smith should become the leader of the Labour Party. Smith told the Labour leader that if he moved aside gracefully, his reward would be to become the president of the party.

'What do you think of that?' Smith said, peering at the Labour leader expectantly. There was silence and then Corbyn spoke, his voice betraying no irritation. 'There's no vacancy for president, Owen,' he said, 'because the position doesn't exist.' He then offered to make Smith a cup of tea.

In the event, Corbyn crushed Smith in the ensuing leadership contest, 'burying the soft left along the way', as one senior Labour figure put it to me.

❧

Labour had been 'captured by the far left for the first time in the party's history', Tony Blair said to me in sorrow. But Corbyn had not coerced his way to the leadership. No one forced the membership and activists to vote for him. Corbyn never disguised who he was, what he represented or what his anti-capitalist and anti-imperialist positions were. He was the leader the members wanted – perhaps the leader the party deserved – and he drew his inspiration and determination to carry on from the hundreds of thousands who had joined Labour to support him. 'The mandate I was given by members on two occasions and the support I get from a lot of people – that's why I do it,' he told me. 'And the pleasure, because I enjoy travelling around, I enjoy the campaigning work and I enjoy representing my constituency.'

Corbyn certainly enjoyed himself in Prague, where he was the star turn, repeatedly being stopped for photographs, selfies, and handshakes, to which he responded with warmth and patience.

I sat on the front row as Corbyn took part in a panel discussion on the 'future of democracy' in Europe in the main conference hall of a drab communist-era building. Leaning forward in a chair, his reading glasses perched on the end of his narrow nose, Corbyn spoke from notes, his voice quickening whenever he wished to be emphatic or to convey urgency. He seemed delighted to be in the company of four left-wing women onstage. 'I like being in the minority as the only man on this panel, just as we will have a majority of women ministers in a Labour government,' he said to loud applause.

'We can't make a politics for straight, white men,' said one of the panellists, a blonde-haired woman from the Karl Renner Institute, the political academy of the Austrian Social Democratic Party. Corbyn nodded vigorously.

The Labour leader – his image projected on a large screen behind him – said that politics had been shaken up across the world and that corporate America had 'bought up industrial America, deindustrialised it and sold it off'. He and his fellow socialists had to be 'agents of change'. Injustice had been 'brought about by free market economics', he said, and: 'We should stand up to unfettered capitalism . . . We cannot be protectors of the status quo.' His speech was a hymn to socialist internationalism. I sat listening alongside Corbyn's charming Mexican wife, Laura. She used her phone to take photographs of her husband as he spoke, which she then shared with me. 'Do you like this one!?'

Corbyn performed creditably on the panel. He is at his most comfortable in these situations, speaking to fellow true believers, scourges of global capitalism and far-right nativism. 'We need a socialist economic strategy across Europe for the redistribution of wealth and power,' he said. When asked from the floor about his role in the EU referendum campaign, Corbyn said that the vote for Brexit was 'a cry from the heart from neglected communities'.

One questioner, a woman from Andalusia, said: 'Jeremy, you are an icon, a rock star, but we European federalists cannot forgive you for your poor performance during the referendum. Why did you let us down?' Corbyn seemed unmoved by the criticism.

'I tried as hard as I could,' he said. 'My message was "remain and reform". But if we rejected the result now, what message would that send to the Labour voters for Brexit?' Then he declared that what was needed above all else was 'the redistribution of wealth across Europe', and everyone applauded again.

Afterwards, Corbyn met a group of Czech journalists in a small, overheated room and took quick-fire questions from them. Moderate social democracy was finished, he said, because it attempted to 'manage the system, rather than transforming it'. He repeated the need for a 'redistribution of wealth and power' and said that the 'management model' did not work as it had created a 'free-for-all market economy that blames minorities for the inequalities'.

Since his victory over Owen Smith in the second leadership contest, Corbyn had begun to feel more confident in his role, even as Labour's ratings had collapsed – one poll put the party seventeen points behind Theresa May's Tories. While we were in Prague, the result of the Richmond by-election came through and Corbyn seemed unconcerned that the Labour candidate had lost his deposit. Why was he so calm? What did he know?

To observe Corbyn in Prague – as he mingled with other European politicians, paused for selfies and did several television interviews – was to observe a politician increasingly at ease with his responsibilities and revelling in the attention. (Laura said: 'If Labour charged a pound for every selfie, it would be very rich.') Corbyn was heavier, especially in the face and around the stomach, than when I interviewed him in July 2015, when he was still the improbable insurgent, the rebel leader in waiting.

'I was the last to be convinced we could win,' he said, reflecting on that heady summer of campaigning. 'I took a lot of convincing. People kept saying, "You're going to win." I said, "No way." And then the pressure I got was from a neighbour who put a great deal of money on me, and he hasn't got a great deal of money. I suspect he borrowed the money to put it on. So every time I saw this guy, I had this feeling of responsibility towards him! He said, "You are going to win, aren't you?" And I said, "Well, I hope you're going to vote." And he said, "No, no, I didn't register." Thanks mate.'

Corbyn admitted that he was completely unprepared for what he would do if he won. He was elected on a Saturday and four days later had to face off against David Cameron in the House of Commons. After that first Prime Minister's Questions, which I watched from the press gallery, Cameron, impressed, told one of his aides that Corbyn's hands 'were not even shaking' as he read his prepared questions in what was his first ever appearance at the despatch box, at the age of sixty-six. 'Did he say that?' Corbyn asked. 'I don't get nervous. I just thought, "Well, we've been through so much." I finally got in there and sat down, ready to go up at the despatch box, and looked around and the place was absolutely packed. You couldn't move. Every single seat was taken. I thought, "Wow." There must have been about two thousand people there in total, I suppose, inside the chamber. The galleries and everything, completely full. I thought, "Wow – two thousand people. And about one thousand nine hundred of them don't want me to do well!"'

Moving on from the Commons, Corbyn went a few days later to the Labour Party conference in Brighton, where he made forty-one speeches in three days, and then the next week to a rally in Manchester that was planned to coincide with the Conservative party conference taking place in the city, after which he and Laura took a brief holiday. 'Laura and I went up to Scotland and we were accused of taking a lengthy holiday. Two days, and one of them was in Fort William on a bicycle. It's not luxury. The small-mind-edness and the way in which many of our media will always believe the worst of you. We were eating a bag of chips. And suddenly this guy sells a story about me eating chips to the *Sunday Times* – I hope he got well paid. So things have changed a lot.'

Seumas Milne, the *Guardian* journalist turned spin doctor and chief strategist, had told me that Corbyn worked relentlessly and was much tougher and more determined than his mild demeanour suggested. 'He's a generous man,' Corbyn said of the friend he addresses in jest as 'Comrade Milne'. 'He does the same [works relentlessly].'

I was told Milne hadn't had a day off since Boxing Day 2015. Corbyn laughed. 'He hasn't. What breaks have we had?' He turned to Laura. 'We had that infamous holiday during the referendum

campaign which amounted to one and a half days. We went to
Exmouth at Easter for one day. We were going to stay for three,
but then I went to Port Talbot [because of the crisis at the steel-
works]. And then we had two days at the beginning of June in
Swanage. Cycling. And we took a journey on a steam train.'

Corbyn's aides believed that he was finally learning to stick
to agreed positions – or 'lines' – in interviews. The running joke
among his entourage was that, after an interview or television appearance, they would check 'not against delivery but to see if a line
was delivered at all'. His appearance was smarter – in Prague, he
wore a dark suit and an open-necked pale blue shirt – and he was
more willing to play the game and to make more of the necessary
compromises of leadership.

He was also more comfortable in shadow cabinet meetings.
Encouraged that he had more allies on the Labour front bench, he
knew that he had silenced most of the PLP, at least for the time
being. There was little speculation about a second attempt to oust
him any time soon.

Labour MPs had ceased using Twitter to condemn and mock
Corbyn's every statement and public performance. As things
stood, Corbyn would lead Labour into the next general election,
which his aides believed could be as early as May or June 2017.
'We are preparing for a May or June election and we are ready,'
I was told. As for his and the party's dire poll ratings, Diane
Abbott, the shadow home secretary, had said that these would
steadily improve.

Labour MPs were clearing the ground for Corbyn to fail, in
his own way, on his own terms. Many of the party's more influ-
ential MPs – Chuka Umunna, Dan Jarvis, Yvette Cooper, Liz
Kendall, Rachel Reeves – would not serve under him. By contrast,
Keir Starmer, whose Commons performances shadowing Brexit
Secretary David Davis were impressive, believed that he could best

serve his party and country by demonstrating his competence in opposition and by seeking to hold the government to account on what was the defining political and economic issue of our times.

'Jeremy will be responsible for the manifesto and the outcome,' one senior Labour MP said to me. 'He has to understand that he's the establishment now. Win or lose he must take responsibility.'

❧

How does it feel to be Jeremy Corbyn? How does it feel to be adored by activists and members but traduced by your MPs, reviled by the 'mainstream media', while presiding over catastrophic poll ratings for the party you lead? How does it feel to have spent three decades on the back benches pursuing various radical and fringe causes unconstrained by the usual career considerations or by the discipline of collective responsibility – only to find yourself in late middle age becoming the accidental leader of a great national political party at a time of profound crisis for the left?

As Martin Jacques, the former editor of *Marxism Today*, put it to me, Corbyn has unlocked something long repressed on the left. His consistency, his uncompromising socialism and his hostility to American power and the liberal world order have inspired many who turned away from Labour after the Iraq War to re-engage with politics. He has awakened, too, the interest of young people who are angry about entrenched intergenerational inequalities of wealth. Why, in the era of the hipster beard, even the facial hair is working for him.

But Corbyn is also an epiphenomenon: his election to the leadership is a symptom rather than the cause of Labour's malaise, as well as more generally of the rejection of mainstream social democracy and what Tony Blair calls 'muscular progressive centrism' by voters throughout Europe.

From the United States to France to Germany, the left is losing. This is an era of authoritarian Big Men: Donald Trump, Vladimir Putin, China's Xi Jinping, Recep Tayyip Erdoğan in Turkey, Egypt's Abdel Fattah el-Sisi, Rodrigo Duterte in the Philippines, Narendra Modi in India.

Corbyn has a simple answer to the question of the struggles of the establishment left. He believes that for too long progressive parties have pursued the wrong policies and have been too-willing servants of 'neoliberalism'. In America, Donald Trump won the presidency because he 'was a well-funded opportunist who doesn't appear to put forward an entirely coherent message other than one of blaming women and minorities', and because he 'somehow managed to present himself as a "saviour" to people who were suffering the trauma of industrial decline'.

Corbyn's analysis is broadly Marxist: a far-reaching economic transformation of the exploitative system of market capitalism will lead to political transformation and the creation of a new society. 'Social-democrat parties haven't offered enough hope and optimism to the left-behind communities, haven't offered hope that their housing issues are going to be dealt with,' Corbyn told me. 'There also has to be a challenge to the power of globalism [by which he means, I think, financial capitalism], because we are told that the only solution to globalism is to retreat from the consensus model of a welfare state and roll back on it. And that's what has been rolled back on in the USA and has left people very angry, and the Democratic Party couldn't offer an alternative to it.'

The paradox of ultra-liberal globalisation and EU federalism is that these have resulted in what Corbyn describes as a 'retreat into local identity agendas' and in the emergence of 'strong separatist movements in Spain and France to a lesser extent'. As for the Scottish National Party, it offers a form of what he calls 'identity nationalism'. Is the SNP a party of nativists? 'To some extent. They are also very broad. And like all national movements, become very contradictory.'

Even after the vote for Brexit, Corbyn supports freedom of movement within the EU and strongly favours immigration. He is a cultural liberal but an economic protectionist. You might say that he is left-liberal on culture and left-liberal on the economy. He favours open borders, at least within Europe, but less open and much more tightly regulated markets. I asked him about the failures more generally of liberalism and of the post-liberal turn, but he didn't quite understand what I meant. He is simply baffled by the reaction of some on the left against what the American writer and academic Mark Lilla has called 'identity liberalism'.

'I don't know why everything always has to be identified as "post-something". I'm not sure we've had "post" lots of things. How about we say this is the time for opportunity for social justice? I know it's a bit of a mouthful. But as an idea, surely it's a bit more optimistic than saying we've come to the end of some kind of era. I'm not sure eras are something people recognise when they're in the midst of it.'

⁂

Corbyn's entourage in Prague comprised his wife, Laura, Seumas Milne, Jennifer Larbie – a former National Union of Teachers organiser appointed to advise Corbyn on foreign affairs – as well as the aides Gavin Sibthorpe and Mark Simpson.

One afternoon, we headed north-west out of Prague and drove for sixty kilometres into northern Bohemia, where we visited Terezín (formerly Theresienstadt), the site of a Nazi-era concentration camp and a Jewish ghetto. Long before that, it had been a Hapsburg military fort and small garrison town. It was intensely cold – the temperature was well below freezing – and frost was already forming on the grass beneath our feet when we arrived. Laura stood by watchfully and removed a red tie from her bag, which Corbyn put on dutifully – 'Because of where we are,' Laura said, 'we must be respectful.'

We were taken on a tour of the camp and into various cell blocks, where more than one hundred and fifty thousand Jews (including fifteen thousand children) were imprisoned in appalling conditions before being transported to death camps: Mauthausen, Auschwitz. We were also shown the claustrophobic cell where the young Bosnian-Serb nationalist Gavrilo Princip spent two years after he assassinated Archduke Franz Ferdinand in Sarajevo in 1914, the shot that was heard around the world. The experience in the camp was harrowing.

As we prepared to leave, a Czech Social Democrat asked Corbyn to deliver on camera an impromptu message to 'the young people of my country'. Corbyn reasserted that he opposed all forms of racism and that we should be especially vigilant because the far right was rising again in Europe. Corbyn knew that Labour had a serious problem with anti-Semitism, which was presumably why he took time out to visit Terezín. Anti-Semitism would not be tolerated in the party, he told me.

'I am very concerned about any reports I receive of any racist activity, or any anti-Semitic activity of any sort,' he said. 'I've asked [for] an investigation to take place, and where it's been reported and where there is any evidence, a suspension may well follow, following the investigation.'

But, I put to him, why didn't he condemn anti-Semitism in and of itself (he always used the wider frame of 'all forms of racism')? 'I have totally condemned anti-Semitism on its own terms,' he said.

I asked what he made of Terezín. 'I've been to other concentration camps and I remember as a young man going to Dachau, near Munich, which was awful, obviously. It was designed to be. We went to Auschwitz about five years ago, maybe more. It was a bitterly cold January day, and that was the right time to see Auschwitz. And today, this camp – very well presented, I thought, beautifully presented, and the guide, well, you were there with me. I thought he was very good. And I thought it was very moving to see it . . . The inhumanity that people can descend into.'

He had not been to the Yad Vashem Holocaust memorial in Jerusalem but said that he 'will be there' the next time he visits Israel.

⁂

By the time we returned to our cars, it was dark. Corbyn's aides were becoming concerned that he hadn't eaten since breakfast. There were sandwiches waiting for him in one of the cars, but these turned out to be ham or tuna – as a vegetarian, he could not eat them. Someone passed him a slice of bread from which the meat had been removed. He took a couple of unenthusiastic bites and then drank some water. I had been warned that Corbyn could become 'a touch robotic' if he was tired and hadn't eaten and, on the journey back to Prague, we chatted but many of his answers were indeed robotic, like an actor delivering tired lines.

I asked him about Russian war crimes in Syria and whether a serious consequence of the disastrous invasion and occupation of Iraq was the reluctance of Western powers to intervene in the Syrian War, even to prevent humanitarian catastrophes such as in eastern Aleppo – which Peter Tatchell likened to the horrors of Guernica when he disrupted a Corbyn speech in London.

'The slaughters are appalling,' Corbyn said to me of the Syrian tragedy. 'Had we gone in, would there have been any difference?

I'm not sure whose side we would have gone in on, and it would have been a three-way civil war [sic].'

I asked if he thought that Putin was a neo-fascist. 'His government is very repressive in many ways. I disagree with a lot of his policies, particularly his human rights policies, but one has to recognise that Russia is a place of enormous self-consciousness as a country. I think there has to be an engagement in Russia that is critical but at the same time hopes to bring about some kind of de-escalation of tensions. These tensions can get very dangerous.'

Why have so many politicians, from Viktor Orbán in Hungary to France's Marine Le Pen and UKIP's Nigel Farage, been attracted to Putin? Even Donald Trump seemed sympathetic.

'I'm not entirely sure. I think that they like it that he's the mirror they put in front of themselves. They see him as a very strong leader, which he is, and that he expresses his determination on behalf of his country.'

I asked again about Russian war crimes in Syria, and he said: 'I would want to see them investigated. The bombing that's gone on is appalling, particularly the bombing of the UN convoy, and as one who has spent a lot of time at UN human rights councils over the years, I would want to see an investigation on that. And so, if war crimes have been committed, then they must be charged.'

Towards the end of our conversation in the car, Corbyn pushed back against Blair's claim that Labour had been captured by the far left. 'I don't know where the definitions of left and far left come from. You'll have to ask Tony Blair. If I call myself a socialist, that's because I am a socialist.'

Then he checked the English football results on his iPad.

⚜

How serious is Jeremy Corbyn? Is he for real? This is what one

Czech journalist asked me after meeting him. Because of their history of occupation and communist oppression, the Czechs have a sophisticated sense of the absurd. The Czech Republic is, after all, the land of Kafka, Jaroslav Hašek and Milan Kundera. There is a tradition in central and eastern European literature of the holy innocent or idiot who may or may be not be feigning his idiocy.

In Hašek's celebrated novel *The Good Soldier Švejk*, about the misadventures of a Czech soldier serving in the Austro-Hungarian army, the hero mimics the absurdities and idiocies of the military bureaucracy in which he finds himself. As an empire crumbles around him, his performance is so convincing that no one can tell if he is merely acting the fool or if he means quite what he says and does.

As Nicholas Lezard has written, 'Švejkian means an enigmatic mixture of idiocy and cunning, deep folly and deep wisdom, an incarnation of human stupidity and yet also with something of the divine about it.'

For his supporters and detractors, it is something like this with Jeremy Corbyn, who can seem guileless in his self-deprecating affability and unworldliness, even innocent, as he repeats his stock phrases, chats about his allotment and preaches the virtues of peace and justice and an end to all war and conflict.

Is Corbyn as guileless as he can seem, or would have us believe? No one would doubt that he is politically sincere. Yet does he sincerely believe that his politics can have wide appeal? Does he believe that enough of the British people are yearning for a full-on socialist transformation of society?

Labour has long been an uneasy coalition of the working class, minority groups, public-sector workers and metropolitan intellectuals – and today that coalition is fracturing as its voters find themselves on different sides of the Brexit divide.

Another difficulty for Corbyn is that he drags his past behind him like a ball and chain. Some people will never forgive him for inviting members of Sinn Fein to Westminster only a few weeks after the IRA attempted to murder Prime Minister Margaret Thatcher and many of her cabinet in a bomb outrage at the Grand Hotel in Brighton. I put it to Corbyn when we were back at his hotel in Prague that he had sided with the IRA over the British state. 'Not true,' he shot back. 'I was always wanting there to be peace in Ireland. I recognised what was happening in Ireland and that there had to be peace and there had to be an end to the war ... I represent a very strongly Irish community – it's more mixed now, but then it was very strongly Irish. And I always firmly believed that the only way you would ever bring about peace in Ireland is by talking to people.'

❧

Jeremy Corbyn is a smarter and more adept media performer than he is given credit for. He's good at deadpanning television interviewers and at deflecting questions about Trident or NATO by making reference to his jam-making. He is at once ideologically inflexible and pragmatic. His economic policies so far are in essence little more than reheated Keynesianism. He has compromised on any number of positions since becoming leader, including on his opposition to NATO (membership is party policy, he told me) and unilateral nuclear disarmament (which isn't party policy). He is a Eurosceptic, yet he campaigned sincerely, though never as passionately as some colleagues would have wished, for Remain. (David Cameron and George Osborne believe they were 'let down' by Labour and Corbyn during the campaign.)

In her biography *Comrade Corbyn*, Rosa Prince suggests that the Labour leader's world-view has been unchanged since he returned from working as a young man for the Voluntary Services Overseas (VSO) scheme in Jamaica. 'I personally have always seen Jeremy as a Peter Pan figure, just not a grown-up,' one unnamed friend told Prince.

His aides see him differently, as a 'quintessential Englishman' of a type that Orwell would have recognised. Every Thursday, Corbyn sends his aide Gavin Sibthorpe out to WHSmith to buy a copy of a railway magazine and the most animated that I saw him in Prague was when he received a text or email from a Labour councillor who was a train driver, offering Corbyn a 'ride in his train cab'. 'Look at this, look at this!' he said to Milne when the message landed on his phone. Dressed in a dark suit and dark polo neck sweater and drinking a double espresso, Milne smiled peaceably.

Corbyn has been caricatured as sectarian and as a humourless Spartist. But in person, he is humorous and often self-mocking. He has a hinterland, speaks Spanish and reads widely – he enthused about the novels of Edward Upward and of Orwell, especially the earlier works of low-key provincial English realism, such as *Keep the Aspidistra Flying* and *Coming Up for Air*. On the way to the Terezín memorial, he chatted to Milne about East German cars and recalled travelling through Czechoslovakia on an MZ 349 motorbike in the 1970s. 'You had to change a fixed amount of money every day but there was nothing to spend it on. Everything was excessively bureaucratic and the officials were bad mannered.' He ended up buying some glass trinkets on the border to spend some money. 'It's not a good idea to carry glass on a motorbike,' he said. 'But I think we got some back.'

Back at the hotel, as Laura poured us some tea, I asked Corbyn about his two years in Jamaica. 'I'm not sure changing politics is a good thing,' he said in reference to the comment of the unnamed friend in Prince's biography. 'Yes, it was a dramatic experience.

Here was me, a country boy from Shropshire, grown up albeit with a radical family, or left family, I suppose; didn't do particularly well in school, and was suddenly bizarrely taken on the VSO to Jamaica. I went there and was suddenly told you had to teach seventy kids geography. Also, I took a lot of kids on camping trips, which I enjoyed, and that got me interested in a lot of other things. I started turning up at a lot of random evening classes at the University of the West Indies when I had an evening off. Anthropology, history, cultural stuff. Anything really. Just turn up and listen for a while. And talk to people, and then I went on a journey around Latin America, where I saw unbelievable repression and poverty.'

One Corbyn ally told me that the Labour leader has something special – what the Andalusian activist in Prague described as 'rock star' charisma. 'Jeremy has something powerful – Boris [Johnson] has it, too. He appeals to people, especially young people. We've got to capture that and use it better, because he offers something hopeful, a different way. It's a kind of populism of the left.'

Is this what Corbyn feels he's offering, too, a populism of the left to confront the new populism of the right?

'You need a community of endeavour,' Corbyn told me, somewhat prosaically. 'A community of endeavour to achieve social justice and social change ... There is a growing feeling that there have to be economies developed that are more sustainable and more rational and that Europe doesn't have to succumb to the globalisation of the trade agreements.'

He seems unconcerned by Labour's poor poll ratings, blaming the MPs' coup against him and a summer of internal conflict.

'We were distracted by the leadership contest when we could

have been attacking the Tories. We'll see how they [the polls] develop as we develop our economic programme. We have got to be optimistic. We have got to offer hope, not blame.'

Why aren't people listening? 'It's extremely noisy, there is a lot of hate out there,' he said. 'But people also think about things more deeply than many give them credit for. And a lot of media tend to speak to a lot of other media and don't recognise that there's a whole parallel system of information going on through social media that never touches the rest of it. Listen, I recently spoke to the CBI [Confederation of British Industry] conference and I said that I represented a very successful enterprise known as the Labour Party. Which, in less than two years, has doubled its membership, paid off all debts and all mortgages and has put a stash of money away for the next campaign that we're involved with. I think we deserve congratulations for that.'

If he deserves congratulation, why are Labour MPs so unhappy?

'Some people are just never satisfied. Look, I hope they all have a wonderful Christmas. We are on the way. We are hopeful. We are confident. And we are committed.'

(2016)

POSTSCRIPT

During one of my conversations with Seumas Milne in Prague, he said something that has stayed with me. What he said was this: the Tories would call a snap general election in the early summer of 2017; Labour would be ready for the election and, because of the party's hundreds of thousands of new paying members, it would have the funds to contest it well; the party would exploit its social media expertise; and Jeremy Corbyn would campaign as a Bernie Sanders or Donald Trump-style anti-establishment populist. He said Corbyn and the party would confound expectations. I remember thinking: 'Good luck with that strategy, sir!'

Yet much of what Milne forecast happened after Theresa May called the snap election that destroyed her authority and resulted in an extraordinary surge of support for the Labour Party, which had begun the campaign adrift by more than twenty per cent in some polls (Corbyn, after a dynamic campaign and popular left-wing manifesto, delivered the biggest increase in Labour's general election vote share since 1945, from thirty per cent in 2015 to forty per cent in 2017).

Like all populists Corbyn positions himself against malign or unaccountable elites and against an *establishment*. His form of politics (perhaps unfairly) has been called 'public-school radicalism' or 'bourgeois left populism'. It's fair to say Corbyn captured the imagination of party members and voters uninspired by technocratic social democracy. Austerity created the political space for a radical critique many deemed irrelevant.

Because of the Corbyn ascendancy, Labour is no longer a party of mainstream social democracy. It has become a radical socialist party in thrall to a movement, Momentum. Those Corbyn-sceptic Labour MPs – the majority – who wish to reclaim their party will have a long wait. A realignment has taken place and the left are in control.

Once dismissed as a perennial protester and irrelevance, Jeremy Corbyn now sincerely aims to become prime minister. Should he succeed, a major European country will be governed from the socialist left for the first time since François Mitterand's 1981 election in France.

THE BREXIT PRIME
MINISTER: THERESA MAY

QUIET RESOLVE: IF you read Theresa May's speeches carefully, you will notice this is the phrase she uses when explaining the motivation for Brexit. With 'quiet resolve', the Prime Minister likes to say, the British people voted to leave the European Union. It's also a phrase that could characterise her earnest, unflashy approach to politics and, more specifically, to the premiership-making-or-breaking task of delivering Brexit. Talk to May - perhaps the most inscrutable politician to reach 10 Downing Street in modern times and the first sitting home secretary to become prime minister since Lord Palmerston in 1855 - and certain words and phrases repeat in her conversation: civic duty, responsibility, playing by the rules, the common good.

In May's speech to the 2002 Conservative party conference - through which she first came to national prominence - she called her party 'nasty' and complained that Tony Blair's Labour government, which had won its second landslide election victory the year before, had borrowed 'some of our rhetoric'. Something similar could be said in reverse of May's discourse since becoming Prime Minister - because, with its echoes of some of the pro-state interventionist positioning of Ed Miliband and Vince Cable, it is strikingly different from what we have come to expect from the Conservatives.

David Cameron came to the leadership eager to soften the image of the Tories. In his early tree-hugging, hoody-embracing, Notting Hill-inflected phase, he announced with considerable banality that there was such a thing as society, as if anyone doubted it, but: 'It's just not the same thing as the state.' For all its soft-focus social liberalism, Cameron's government was 'neoliberal', determined to cut back the state and reduce public spending to thirty-five per cent of GDP. In power, empowered by the Liberal Democrats, he and his chancellor, George Osborne, were doctrinaire austerians, but also liberal globalisers, with an open immigration policy and mercantilist foreign policy. Osborne was also a self-described 'liberal interventionist'.

May is moving the Tories in a different direction. Tory MPs say that, unlike her predecessor, she has a 'people' and she is far more at ease with the average Tory activist than the Cameroons were (one could always imagine them muttering about 'swivel-eyed loons' as they left a village fête). It was emblematic that, when May sacked George Osborne at the start of her premiership, she told him to get to know the party better.

The vote for Brexit has unlocked possibilities for her and created an opportunity, she believes, for a new political economy. It was Brexit that opened the door of 10 Downing Street to her, not least because the alternatives – Boris Johnson, Andrea Leadsom, Michael Gove – were so wayward and divisive. Unlike Johnson, who seems to have no consistent or coherent world-view, May believes in an interventionist, even moral, state. 'The key thing about her is her belief in the efficacy and, so to speak, compensatory function of the state, the important positive functions – you might even say the moral functions of the state,' said the philosopher John Gray.

⚘

When I visited Theresa May one morning in her office in Downing Street, we discussed her trip to Davos, Switzerland, in January 2017. In an address to the World Economic Forum, she told the citizens of the world gathered high in the snowy Alps that 'those on modest-to-low incomes living in relatively rich countries around the West' feel that the forces of globalisation are not working for them, hence the 'quiet resolve' protest vote for Brexit.

I asked what she meant by the phrase, which carries an implicit suggestion of approval. Indeed, I asked her, given the resilience of the British economy, which according to the Bank of England's revised forecasts is expected to grow by two per cent this year, whether she regretted not voting for Brexit, so completely had she embraced it. She smiled and said she never answered 'hypothetical questions like that' but conceded that, much to the irritation of the liberal Remain wing of her party and the forty-eight per cent of Britons who voted for the status quo, a 'clean' Brexit was necessary and irreversible. There would be no turning back.

May referred to a speech she gave in April 2016, at the start of the referendum campaign. 'What I said was, "This is a balanced judgement." The sky will not fall in if we leave the European Union, and it hasn't. And this is where the "resolve" comes in, the sense that a lot of people voted for Brexit because they believed in this, they wanted us to feel that we were a sovereign, independent nation, not dependent on decisions taken elsewhere, and they felt that that might bring some problems, but that we would get over them. And that was, if you like, that – and that we would come through stronger. That's what I'm trying to capture in how we look at this. And the overwhelming view I get from the public, from business, is that, whichever side of the debate people were on before 23 June, the decision's been made, so let's get on with it. This is what I meant by the phrase "Brexit means Brexit".'

My meeting with Theresa May took place a few days after she had returned from meeting Donald Trump in the White House and just as she was preparing to leave for an informal EU summit in Malta. She considered her trip to the US to have been a success, despite Trump's best attempts to undermine it with the timing of his nefarious executive order seeking to ban refugees and citizens of seven Muslim-majority countries from entering America.

To many Britons, May's visit to Trump so soon after his inauguration and the sight of them walking hand in hand were distasteful. She had not met Trump before the visit and had no prior expectations. 'I'd only seen him on television. Somebody asked me this [if he had lived up to expectations] the other day and I said I'm not the sort of person who thinks, 'Well, I'm going to meet X and they're going to be A, B, C, D and E, and how am I going to react?' I just meet them and take them as I find them.'

May is too cautious to condemn the US president but nor will she commend him. Her approach to Trump's White House should surely be the same as her approach to Vladimir Putin's Russia, on which she said she 'wants sanctions to remain': engage but beware.

Since she was mocked on the cover of the *Economist* as 'Theresa Maybe', Britain's 'indecisive premier', May has delivered three significant speeches in 2017 – at Lancaster House in London, in Davos and in Philadelphia – which, read together, offer a coherent exposition of what could be an emerging May Doctrine. The May Doctrine has three pillars: a new realism in foreign policy; the return of the state in domestic affairs; and social and economic reform leading to a renewed commitment to social cohesion and the common good.

In the Lancaster House speech on 17 January 2017, the Prime

Minister confirmed to her audience of diplomats and journalists (I was present) that Britain would leave the European single market and the customs union and take back control of its borders. The speech was praised by Brexiteers, and also in Brussels, where diplomats liked its clarity. However, May has also faced strong criticism over her Brexit strategy, some of it from within her party. In the Commons debate on Article 50, George Osborne suggested that the government had chosen 'not to make the economy the priority'. Instead, he said, 'They have prioritised immigration control.'

I read the former chancellor's remarks to May but she pushed back against them. 'One of the problems with this debate about Brexit is that people look at too many aspects of it in a binary way,' she said. 'They are thinking about this in terms of the power that we've had as a member of the EU.'

What is required is a different approach, she said.

'What we say is: what is the outcome that we want to achieve? And it is possible to achieve an outcome which is both a good result for the economy and is a good result for people who want us to control immigration – to be able to set our own rules on the immigration of people coming from the European Union.'

Charles Grant, the director of the Centre for European Reform, believes that rather than choosing a 'hard' – the Prime Minister prefers 'clean' – Brexit, May should have tilted more towards those who voted Remain. She should have pursued what he calls 'an economically optimal deal, something like Norway but a bit different, where we would more or less have been in the single market with a little bit of restriction on free movement'.

Grant told me that the Prime Minister might have failed, but at least she would have tried. 'She didn't want to invest any political capital in an economically optimal outcome because she might have failed and it would have been embarrassing. So she has gone for a hard Brexit, which she knows is not really good for our economy but the politics come first. But Britain is in a very weak position. As soon as you activate Article 50, the clock is ticking. Therefore diplomacy matters. To get a half-decent deal, you need the goodwill of your partners.'

It is said in Brussels that May is not a natural diplomat. In meetings and phone conversations with European counterparts, she is reported to stick rigidly to her speaking notes. 'She may not realise how weak her hand is,' Grant said.

May does not accept that her negotiating position is weak. Yet, even if she did, she wouldn't say so. 'The reason I don't feel I have a weak hand is because this isn't just about us, it's also about the remaining member states of the European Union. This isn't just about the UK as a supplicant to the EU, it's about arranging a partnership that works for all of us.'

Perhaps May under-appreciates just how embattled the remaining twenty-seven EU member states have felt. Not only has the bloc been destabilised by the eurozone and refugee crises and by the vote for Brexit, anti-immigrant populist and nationalist movements are also sweeping the continent. President Trump, who leads what the conservative American commentator David Brooks describes as not a Republican but an ethnic nationalist administration, unapologetically wants the European project to fail.

In this context, agreeing a mutually beneficial free trade deal with the British might be in the best economic interests of the EU27, but would it be in their political interest? Why should they make it easy for the British, who by leaving the EU are, in the view of the Brussels elites, wilfully weakening the rules-based liberal order?

Many people were offended when, in her 2016 party conference speech, May said: 'If you're a citizen of the world, you're a citizen of nowhere.' Was this an attack on deracinated cosmopolitans, on those whom the writer Pico Iyer calls 'global souls'?

'What I was saying was more about [how] people should have a root in a community, should have a feeling that they are part of a community and that they have responsibilities in a community,' May told me. 'I was talking about the concept that you can be around the whole world and not have those responsibilities anywhere. I wasn't getting at a particular grouping or individual . . . Recently there's been a sense that all that matters is the individual, rather than their responsibilities to other people. I think we need to redress that balance.'

Some of May's closest aides call her 'a new model conservative' because she is neither a Thatcherite nor an old-style One Nation Macmillanite Tory. Her cabinet is more meritocratic than Cameron's (it is the most state-educated since the Attlee government), older and more serious-minded. She does not tolerate fools or frivolity, though she does have a nicely modulated sense of humour. She claims to be a politician of her word and said she would not call an early general election – a notable contrast with the game-playing of Gordon Brown when he became prime minister.

May is not an ideologue but she aspires to be a consensus-breaker, as Margaret Thatcher was before her. In many ways, she is our first post-Thatcherite prime minister, even a post-liberal, but not an anti-liberal: she embraces the liberal reforms of the past two decades, such as equal marriage. To the bewilderment of many on both the left and the right, she is intent on breaking with the orthodoxies of neoliberalism, but from the right.

'To me May is a communitarian,' said Ryan Shorthouse, the director of the right-leaning think tank Bright Blue. 'She has moved left economically and to the right socially. She doesn't like excessive individualism and is making the state central in reforming society. She recognises that globalisation and liberalism have downsides.'

Elected to the House of Commons in 1997, Theresa May, a grammar-school-educated only child who grew up in an Oxfordshire vicarage, is not considered clubbable in the way that Cameron and Osborne were, with their extended network of like-minded, well-born friends in politics and the media: the so-called chumocracy. 'May won the leadership race by not being close to anyone or any faction,' Shorthouse said. 'She isn't part of any tribe. Cameron had his think tanks, like Policy Exchange, and his journalists, and others who were ideologically loyal to him. But May is an independent figure. There are no Mayites. She's hard to pin down. As home secretary, she took on the police but also wants to cut down on immigration. She gives a bit to every wing of the party. It makes her vulnerable if the heat is on.'

Because of her relative isolation, May's closest aides, notably Nick Timothy and Fiona Murray, are extraordinarily loyal to and protective of her, and their loyalty – one of them told me that they would 'run through a brick wall for her' – is fundamental to understanding her style.

If May succeeds in creating a new political economy combining greater social mobility with enhanced social justice, she will condemn Jeremy Corbyn's party to electoral defeat, because, as she told me several times, she intends directly to appeal to disillusioned Labour voters. The Tories won Copeland on 23 February 2017, which was the first time the governing party had a gained a seat in a by-election since 1982.

'I hope there are Labour voters out there who will now look at us afresh and say, "Labour hasn't responded to our concerns, it hasn't recognised what matters to us, but the Conservatives have seen that and are responding to it." I want our greater prosperity not to be confined to particular groups of people or a single part of the country.'

Listening to May, who delights in reminding Labour that the Tories have had two women prime ministers, speak about the need to create a society 'that works for everyone, not just the few', is to understand that her threat to turn Britain into an offshore tax haven if the EU seeks to 'punish' her government for opting for a hard Brexit is no more than a transparent negotiating gambit. Although many on the right yearn for such an outcome, she does not.

THE COMMON GOOD

So far, the rhetorical positioning has been matched by policy initiatives that are modest and incremental at best. May seemed irritated to hear this. 'I don't know which particular policies you're thinking about, but they're not modest or incremental,' she said. 'Look at the industrial strategy. There have always been industrial policies, but this is an industrial strategy that says, "This is about a whole government approach, about looking across the whole country to ensure that we're making the best of the expertise and the advantages that different parts of the country have, but ensuring that we are seeing that growth spread."'

May believes not that government is the problem, as Ronald Reagan once declared, but that it is and should be a force for the common good. In her 2016 conference speech in Birmingham, she denounced the templates of both the socialist left and the libertarian right. I asked what it was about the libertarian right that she disliked. 'I suppose it's the concept that it's only the individual who matters, that there is no common good, if you like. To me, conservatives have always believed in the common good.'

John Bew, the author of *Citizen Clem*, an acclaimed biography of Clement Attlee, believes that May is closer to offering 'some kind of Attleeite new deal for Britain' than any Labour leader for a generation. (May is an admirer of Clement Attlee and referenced him in her 2016 conference speech, but doesn't think in such terms.) 'Her cool-headed realism now as Brexit hysteria dies down,' Bew told me, 'chimes with the mood of Britain, which is why she is doing so well in the polls. Some of it has landed accidentally in her lap . . . But she appeals to a fair-minded, moderate majority. Her vision does not require great virtue from the private citizen like the "big society" – she wants to let people get on with their lives but for the powerful to play by the rules, too. All this is very British in spirit. But is this new credo fit for purpose in this changing world?'

Too often, during the last Conservative government, it seemed as if the poorest were carrying the greatest burden of austerity, as well as being penalised and harassed for minor benefit infringements, while the wealthiest operated by different rules. Yet for May, if the common good means anything, it means business recognising its sense of responsibility to wider society.

'There has been a breakdown in trust,' she said. 'Wages have been stagnant but there are other aspects to it, too. There's been a breakdown in trust in institutions that have always formed the core of our society. There's a sense that business somehow has been playing by a different set of rules, which is unfair. Tax avoidance is one of the issues.'

May's instincts are classically Tory on defence and security issues, but no one close to her doubts her sincerity in wanting improved corporate governance and a fairer deal for the ordinary worker, for those who are 'just about managing'. As it happens, she did not use this phrase once during our conversation, and I've heard it said that she was furious when, early in her premiership, a civil servant referred to this group by the acronym 'Jam' in a written report. May crossed it out and instructed that the acronym should not be used again. Unfortunately for her, it is now in wide circulation.

THE NEW REALISM

Theresa May's Philadelphia speech was the most significant on foreign policy by a British prime minister since Tony Blair's Chicago speech in April 1999, in which, following the NATO intervention in Kosovo, he fervently defended Western values and made the 'moral' case for reordering the world and becoming 'actively involved in other people's conflicts'.

But in Philadelphia, May emphatically broke with the doctrine of liberal interventionism, saying that we should not 'attempt to remake the world in our own image'. The speech was misread by some at first as a statement of classic Tory foreign policy restraint and retreat. It was not. The speech made clear that her foreign policy would not be amoral or ethically neutral. Nor would it be 'idealist' or universalist, as Blair's was. Rather, it would be cautiously 'realist': she reaffirmed Britain's commitment to free trade, to multilateral institutions such as NATO and to the rules-based liberal world order, but conceded the limits of Western liberalism, which, she said, cannot be exported or imposed by military intervention.

May and her advisers understand that liberal values are not absolutes but practices that evolve over a long time and can easily be disrupted, as is happening in Trump's America. These values cannot be merely dropped like bombs on foreign lands, as Blair and Cameron seemed to believe. May is not an advocate of a Pax Americana that is forced on the world by war.

But nor does she rule out military intervention if it should be in the national interest. 'We need to put Britain's interests first but mustn't just assume there's a sort of natural thing for the UK to intervene in order to change places in the way we think they should be changed,' she told me. 'I'm not saying that we don't believe that we would like to see more democratic countries, with a very clear [commitment to the] rule of law, but I think there are different ways of achieving that. I'm not ruling out the possibility of intervention, but we do need to be very clear about when it is in British interests to do that.'

What is the UK's role in the world? It's a question that May believes Brexit has brought into 'sharper focus'.

She believes the UK should stand up for Western values of democracy and the rule of law, for the international rules-based order. 'Internationally, there is a turn towards protectionism and isolationism. That is not what we want to see in the UK. We want to be outward-looking.'

I discussed with her Barack Obama's notion of 'tragic realism': there is evil in the world about which sometimes nothing can be done, not even by the most powerful nation. In an interview with the *New York Times* book critic Michiko Kakutani, Obama cited the celebrated opening to V. S. Naipaul's novel *A Bend in the River*: 'The world is what it is; men who are nothing, who allow themselves to become nothing, have no place in it.'

Obama said that he thought about that line and Naipaul's novel when 'thinking about the hardness of the world sometimes, particularly in foreign policy, and I resist and fight against sometimes that very cynical, more realistic view of the world. And yet, there are times where it feels as if that may be true.'

'I don't think I'd put it in the same way,' Theresa May said of tragic realism. 'But we have to recognise that there are threats out there in the world that we have to deal with.' She then spoke at length about the wickedness of ISIS and of Islamist terrorism more generally.

༺༃༻

Theresa May speaks of 'my method', by which she means her approach to politics, the way she likes to keep her strategic options open for as long as possible. She weighs and balances the evidence and consults with her closest advisers before acting. She considers it wise to make haste slowly and, I was told, allows the 'logic of the situation' to dictate her actions. She chooses the outcome she wants and works backwards from there in an attempt to achieve it.

Her aides say that she is anything but indecisive, but she is deliberative: from the beginning, she understood that the referendum result was a mandate not merely to leave the EU but to reshape the economy and society. And she knew what she wanted from Brexit and that it would require Britain leaving the single market and ending freedom of movement.

May has a nuanced sense of the British national interest and accepts that she can't simply have a narrow, trade-based, mercantilist approach to foreign policy. Values also matter, as her campaign against modern slavery demonstrated. In Philadelphia, she appealed directly to the better instincts of the Republican Party because, although she won't say so, she understands how erratic and unpredictable the Trump White House has become as it turns towards authoritarianism.

One should never underplay the role of luck in politics as in life. May is certainly fortunate in facing such a divided opposition. But the last three Conservative prime ministers before her were, in their different ways, all ultimately brought down by Europe. Is it to be May's destiny to settle the European question, and thus bring peace to her fractious party, or will the combined forces of Trump and Brexit destabilise the European continent and the fragile British state in ways as yet unimagined?

By invoking Article 50, May will lose control of an essential aspect of her foreign policy. She will be at the mercy of events and have to rely on the pragmatic good sense and the kindness of others, by which I mean the spurned EU27. We all live with a sense of the terror of the unforeseen. Theresa May believes in the 'quiet resolve' of her fellow citizens. She is hopeful about our future prosperity. She has a clear sense of where she wants to take the country and how she wishes to transform it. She knows the outcome she wants from Brexit and, after her Lancaster House speech, so should everyone else. Her competence, steeliness and method have taken her a long way, from the vicarage in Oxfordshire all the way to 10 Downing Street. But is she lucky? And given the epic challenge of EU withdrawal, can she ever be more than the Brexit prime minister?

(2017)

POSTSCRIPT

Theresa May's luck held out until 18 April 2017 when, despite having said she would not, she called a snap general election, convinced that she would win the Tories their first commanding majority since 1987 and a resounding mandate for a 'hard' Brexit. The results of the local election on 4 May that same year had merely strengthened her conviction that the polls were correct and that she was on course for a landslide victory. Then the short election campaign began, and we know what happened next: the Tories lost their parliamentary majority and Corbyn's Labour surged.

May's associates are regretful that during what was a disastrous and charmless campaign she did not make one memorable speech: she shrank under scrutiny just when she should have enlarged her vision of the 'new model' Conservatism. She abandoned the communitarian language that had distinguished her early weeks in Downing Street. She had nothing to say to those who voted Remain. And she acquired a new nickname: 'the Maybot', because of her robotic repetition of the phrase 'strong and stable'.

'My biggest regret,' Nick Timothy, May's former chief ideologue, has written, 'is that we did not campaign in accordance with the insight that took Theresa to Downing Street in the first place.' The May Doctrine, such as it was, may turn out to have been nothing more than the Timothy Doctrine: communitarian, pro-state, anti-libertarian, 'realist' in foreign affairs, softly nationalistic. A chance for political and intellectual renewal was squandered.

Tony Blair's aides had a phrase for the 2005 general election: 'the masochism campaign'. After the Iraq invasion, Blair was in retreat and, as he toured the country, he was routinely traduced. Unlike May in 2017, Blair still enjoyed campaigning and was prepared for the worst.

May detests confrontation. She has an unfortunate facial expression, exacerbated under pressure, a look of awkward disdain, of sudden alarm even, as if she is permanently afraid of being embarrassed. She is often at her best when she delivers a long-deliberated speech; at her most uncomfortable when she fears the loss of control in public. She knows her authority is shattered. She knows that many of her cabinet colleagues have been scheming against her. She knows that, when the party believes the time is right, she will be forced out. At international summits, in the company of other world leaders, her face is often fixed in that familiar rictus of unease.

Theresa May has told her friends that she will serve her party for as long as she is required. She will occupy the crease, duck the bouncers and take the blows. She has so far endured as Conservative leader for want of a better alternative. Her Sisyphean fate is to pursue a project – Brexit – which she does not believe in and which, even now, she refuses to say that she would vote for in a second referendum. The story so far of her premiership is an epic of hubris and, indeed, because of the calamitous outcome of the snap general election, humiliation. It is the masochism premiership.

THE ARSONIST:
NIGEL FARAGE

WHAT DOES NIGEL Farage know? What does any successful politician know? What did Tony Blair know that
Ed Miliband did not? What does Jeremy Corbyn know that his
detractors in the Parliamentary Labour Party do not?

In 2009, Michael Ignatieff, a cosmopolitan intellectual and
former Harvard professor, became the unlikely leader of the Liberal
Party of Canada. As he began the slog towards the Canadian
federal election, from which he was initially expected to emerge as
prime minister, Ignatieff was tormented by his inadequacies. High
intelligence, deep, immersive reading and considerable literary and
philosophical sophistication - he was the authorised biographer
of Isaiah Berlin and a former Booker Prize-shortlisted novelist -
were, he discovered, no guarantees for a career in politics or for
winning a national election.

'I've spent my life as a writer, but you have no idea of the
effect of words until you become a politician,' Ignatieff told his
old friend, the *New Yorker* writer Adam Gopnik. 'One word or
participle in the wrong place and you can spend weeks apologising
and explaining.'

It was as if he was already exhausted by the demands of high politics: 'This is by a very long shot harder than being a professor at Harvard, harder than being a freelance writer, harder than anything I've ever done – in terms of its mental demands, its spiritual demands and its emotional demands.'

Ignatieff envied successful politicians, serial winners such as Blair and Bill Clinton. He knew they knew something he did not. But what did they know? What is it that a great politician knows, he kept asking himself. 'The great ones have a skill that is just jaw-dropping, and I'm trying to learn that.'

Ignatieff never discovered the answer to his question or learned the required skills. Unlike Barack Obama, who was also professorial in demeanour, he had no gift for popular communication. Nor was he adept at the game of politics – or perhaps ruthless and fearless enough, though he was more than ambitious enough. He was routed in the 2011 election by the conservative Stephen Harper, even losing his own seat. Soon afterwards he retired from politics and retreated from Canada, humiliated and humbled by defeat, but wiser.

I was reminded of Ignatieff and his pertinent question – what does a successful politician know? – when I visited Nigel Farage at the offices of Leave.EU in Westminster. The previous evening, when I texted a friend to postpone our meeting because I was seeing Farage, he replied: 'Why are you seeing him? I despise him.' This was not an isolated view.

Farage, who now has his own talk radio show on LBC, is widely despised – not least because of his antics during the referendum campaign and his post-Brexit embrace of alt-right movements in America and Europe. He is despised not only by liberals and Remainers: mainstream Conservatives and many prominent Brexiteers, such as the MEP Daniel Hannan, are appalled by him and his closest associates at Leave.EU.

❧

The Leave.EU offices were shabby and had the atmosphere of a poorly resourced magazine or newspaper office the morning after press day – but at least there was an outside terrace, which allowed Farage to slip out for a cigarette on a cold, bright winter morning. The television was on in his office and it burbled away as we talked. A packet of Benson & Hedges was open on the desk, and on the bookshelf nearby was a paperback copy of the Cambridge historian Robert Tombs's *The English and Their History*. One of his aides brought him a coffee from Pret A Manger – 'I can't drink that instant stuff' – then Farage settled down, preferring initially to discuss the Ashes cricket series in Australia: a few overs of gentle conversational looseners before the pace quickened.

I first interviewed Farage in November 2014 at UKIP's London headquarters on the fourth floor of an unremarkable building, in a part of Mayfair that resembled then nothing so much as one great construction site – the clamour and clatter of the machines serving the agents of the global plutocracy plundering the city's property market. Unlike many politicians I'd met, he was curious. He asked questions; he did not merely wish to assert. It was like having a conversation with an opinionated bloke you'd met in the pub – and I guess that was a large part of his act and appeal. 'I'm optimistic,' he told me. 'We need change. There are millions out there who aren't getting an even break. They're being done down.'

During that meeting, Farage described the typical UKIP voter as 'aspirational'. Who votes for UKIP? he asked. 'The people who get up earliest in the morning have the highest propensity to vote UKIP. I'm being absolutely serious about that. A lot of these people are in jobs where they're driving, or working on building sites, or running a small carpentry business, or whatever they're doing; they tend to be people whose political backgrounds from

their parents and grandparents would be red and blue – there'd
be bits of both. A lot of them haven't voted for anybody since the
early to mid-Nineties.'

A former City broker who began work in the metals market
at the age of eighteen, Farage was educated privately at Dulwich
College in London (popular today with Russian oligarchs). As a
young man, he was a Thatcherite but now describes himself as
being neither right nor left but an anti-system radical: he told me
that his hero was John Wilkes, the eighteenth-century parliamentary agitator and pamphleteer, and that he took inspiration from
the nineteenth-century tradition of dissenters and free traders
such as John Bright and Richard Cobden, who helped form the
Anti-Corn Law League. 'We've got to get back control of our
country,' he said to me in 2014. 'We're in deep denial about how
we've given away control of almost everything. When you get back
control of your country you get proper democracy. You get back
proper debate.'

'Get back control': the Brexiteers would adapt this slogan and
use it to devastating effect in the European referendum campaign
in 2016.

***

Unlike my friend, I do not despise Nigel Farage. What does he
know? That's what really interests me. It's not enough to condemn
one's political opponents or antagonists: it's harder, yet more fruit-
ful, to attempt to understand and explain the events and dominant
individuals shaping the history of our era.

Speaking on 14 November 2017 in the House of Commons,
Ken Clarke, the veteran Conservative Europhile, called Farage the
'most successful politician of my generation'. It's hard to disagree,
even though he tried and failed seven times to become an MP.

More than any other politician, Farage created the conditions for Brexit. Through sheer force of will, charisma and a kind of dogged monomania, he transformed what was once a fringe cause into a national movement (the 'people's army'). He galvanised the Eurosceptics in the Conservative Party and harried David Cameron, who in 2006 had carelessly dismissed UKIP supporters as 'fruitcakes, loonies and closet racists, mostly'. It's never wise to insult your potential voters, as Hillary Clinton would discover when she dismissed Donald Trump supporters as a 'basket of deplorables'.

For all of Farage's success at ventriloquising the sentiment of a large section of the population, his behaviour has often been reprehensible: never more so perhaps than when, in the final week of the referendum campaign, he launched the anti-immigrant 'breaking point' poster depicting a column of Muslim Syrian refugees in the Balkans, the wretched of the Earth. Farage deliberately conflated legitimate economic migration with the refugee crisis and illegal immigration: even the former UKIP MP Douglas Carswell called the poster 'morally indefensible'.

Farage was unapologetic. 'Jacob Rees-Mogg says that poster won the referendum, because it dominated the debate for the last few days. The establishment hated it, the posh boys at Vote Leave hated it, but it was the right thing to do. Now, I don't think we'd have won the referendum without Mrs Merkel. But that poster reminded people what Mrs Merkel had done.'

This was a reference to the German Chancellor's decision in September 2015, at the height of the worst refugee crisis in Europe since the end of the Second World War, to open Germany's borders to nearly one and a half million dispossessed people from the Middle East and Africa.

'After the election in 2015, [Farage's close associate] Chris Bruni-Lowe said to me, "If on the Sunday before the referendum we're discussing three million jobs, we've lost." I launched the poster, there was a bit of commentary, I had double-page spreads in five national newspapers. There was the usual criticism of it. It was only when Jo Cox got murdered that they chose to focus on the poster as the big issue.'

The Labour MP was shot and stabbed on 16 June 2016 in Birstall, West Yorkshire, by Thomas Mair, who shouted 'Britain first!' as he attacked her. Farage told me: 'I remember thinking, "Can I live with this?" Not because of what I've done – just the hatred, not my conscience . . . Basically, it's your fault she's dead. I came in here, a bit down. It was rough, and Chris said, "Remember what we said last year: what's the conversation? It's immigration."

'But it was obviously very unfortunate that a young woman got murdered, and all the rest of it . . . I don't think her death ultimately changed the way people voted, but what it did do was kill the momentum. It did kill the momentum. Sorry, that's the wrong word to use. It stopped the momentum. Because we had the "big M" going. Momentum's an odd thing, because when it's going with you, you just feel it. You know it's happening. So, yeah, that was quite a thing.'

That phrase, 'quite a thing': you could call it a euphemism.

⁂

Simon Heffer, a commentator, historian and authorised biographer of Enoch Powell, believes that Farage is one of the most significant politicians of the entire post-war period. 'Enoch was the first British Eurosceptic,' Heffer told me. 'He kept the argument going throughout the 1970s and 1980s when most others had given up. As he faded, Farage took over, at the crucial moment when the Maastricht and subsequent treaties started to raid British sovereignty and democratic accountability. Nigel built up huge momentum over the twenty years before the referendum and, unlike the fantasists of Vote Leave with their £350m a week for the NHS, concentrated on the key intellectual argument for Brexit: the reclamation of sovereignty and the reinstitution of democratic accountability.

'And he galvanised the working class, whose criticisms of the EU and failed aspirations had been ignored by generations of Labour politicians, to support Brexit. He, not Boris Johnson or any of his crew of poseurs, was the key to the Brexiteers' victory.'

I witnessed something of Farage's populist appeal when we went for a drink after that first interview. Farage, wearing his familiar covert coat with velvet collar, his aide Raheem Kassam and I went to a local pub close to UKIP's headquarters in Mayfair. Because Farage and Kassam are smokers, we stood outside, drinking London Pride bitter – what else? We were watched from a short distance away by Farage's security team, two shaven-headed men in black coats whom he greeted with a furtive nod as we'd stepped on to the street. It was cold and bright and the lunchtime crowd swirled around us. People kept approaching to shake Farage's hand – 'Keep it up, Nigel'; 'You're doing a great job, Nigel'; 'Stick it to them, Nige' – and he received them with interest and warmth. I asked if he ever grew weary of the attention. 'Never. It's huge fun,' he said, laughing loudly.

At one point, a man wearing a turban had posed for a selfie with Farage and then three others in suits had joined us, one of whom was from Oldham. He talked about how he'd lost faith in Labour. 'See what I was telling you?' Farage said, turning to me. And then he offered his empty glass to Raheem: 'Let's reload.'

※

Farage winced when I mentioned Simon Heffer's comparison to

Enoch Powell, notorious for his 1968 anti-immigration 'rivers of blood' speech. 'Enoch was, er, a brilliant man,' he said, with unusual hesitancy, 'but somehow the words he used, the analogy he chose, destroyed the debate [on immigration] for a quarter of a century. It made it impossible even to talk about it.'

Farage sensed an opportunity to reopen the debate with the enlargement of the EU in 2004, when ten new countries joined, eight of which had been part of the former communist Eastern Bloc. Of the existing member states in 2004, only the United Kingdom, Sweden and Ireland had not imposed 'transitional controls' restricting the freedom of movement of migrants from the new accession states, a fateful decision as it turned out. The New Labour government forecast that only thirteen thousand migrants would arrive from Poland and other eastern European countries; in the event, more than a million came to live and work in Britain as annual net migration, year after year, rose inexorably.

If – as Isaiah Berlin wrote in a celebrated essay in 1953 – the fox knows many things but the hedgehog knows one big thing, Farage is a hedgehog. The single defining thing that he knows is how to exploit people's unease about immigration. That was his great wager: the revivifying of the immigration debate.

'The European Union and immigration wasn't an issue before 2004,' he said. 'It was the mistake of letting in the former communist countries. Many in UKIP said, "No, no, don't do that, you mustn't do that. They'll call us all the names under the sun." I knew that touching the immigration issue was going to be very difficult. But I think the impact that had on me, the family, I think all of that was bad, yeah. And frankly . . . the only thing that upsets me about it is that, had it been wilfully and overtly a racist message, I might have deserved some of it. But it wasn't. It never was. It never, ever was. It was a logical argument about numbers, society.'

The rise of UKIP destroyed the neo-fascist British National Party, not least because Farage made a direct appeal to its voters. 'The problem was that with the demise of the BNP, the haters on the left had to have someone to hate, and that all transferred to me.'

He did not like the term 'working class' but agreed with Simon Heffer that his rhetoric and plain speaking appealed to those he called 'good, ordinary, decent' people.

'The one thing I had going for me is that I'm able to cross classes. You know I do what I do, I am what I am – people like it or they don't like it, but I'm not confined to the shires or the inner cities. I can do a bit of both. You know how our class system is . . . The sort of middle, upper-middle class never say what they think to anybody, you know, just in case. But the lower down the social scale you go, the more people are very blunt in what they say and how they approach things. So, I use direct language, never trying to come across as being too clever.'

Farage respects Jeremy Corbyn because he is not a conventional career politician. 'Corbyn's a bit different, and maybe that's why he's working with a certain segment . . . Corbyn's popularity among the young is astonishing. But he comes across as very genuine. His technique is so similar to mine in an odd way, and Trump's. He's very similar to Trump, the way he does it!'

What does Corbyn do?

'One, the embrace of social media. He understands it; I understand it. If you look at the social media following of UK politicians, it's just him and me. The rest are so far behind us, it's almost incredible.'

Both Farage and Corbyn have more than a million Twitter followers. I suggested that Ruth Davidson, the Scottish Conservative leader, was excellent on Twitter and understood how to use social media.

'Yes, she is. Her numbers at the moment are very small, but that may change. But she understands it. The rest of them haven't got a clue. I mean Boris Johnson! Boris should be huge on social media and he's not. Corbyn also gets that the big public meeting works. It energises people in the most incredible way.

'And some of the stuff he said in this general election was not entirely dissimilar to some of the stuff that I said in the previous general election. On the fact that you're living in a society where the rich and powerful are richer and more powerful than they've probably ever been . . .

'And he comes across as genuinely caring about those that are having a tough time. And that's his big card. I've got a certain admiration for that. What I don't have an admiration for is the thought of [John] McDonnell running the British economy.'

⚜

Before this interview, the last time I'd seen Farage in person was in November 2016 at the *Spectator* parliamentary awards dinner in London. There, he was presented with a Lifetime Achievement Award by George Osborne. Farage had been drinking and gave a raucous, triumphalist speech during which he mocked the 'pasty-faced' Osborne, whom he loathes, and then told the guests, who included the Prime Minister, Theresa May, that Donald Trump would be 'the next leader of the Western world'. Farage's comments were received with derision. 'Oh, come on,' he said that night. 'What's the matter with you? That's . . . the attitude you all took to Brexit. [You said] it could never happen . . . [But] my achievement was to take an issue that was considered to be completely wrong, perhaps even immoral, and help to turn it into a mainstream view in British politics.'

It was a fair self-assessment and he was correct about Trump winning. Farage, who understands that in the age of social media, outrage cuts through, has had an astounding effect on our politics. He is blamed for coarsening and poisoning the public discourse and inflaming racism and xenophobia, charges that he rejects. Instead, he told me that angry Remainers, such as Alastair Campbell, had created what had become a foul and feculent national conversation.

'I think some of what's happened has been appalling. Alastair Campbell, he's almost lost reason! I mean, the classic example of what's happened since the referendum is the death of the Polish man in Harlow. So, the story is: 'Polish man gets beaten up because of race hate caused by Brexit.' That's the story. It's everywhere: BBC Two's *Newsnight* even ran a report saying, "Nigel Farage has blood on his hands."

'Talk about fake news . . . The collective shock of the liberal establishment, they still can't get to grips with it, and they're trying to find a reason why this illogical thing, as they see it, happened. In this country, they put it down to lies, and in America, it's the Russians!'

Ah, the Russians – let's hope they love their children, too, as Sting once sang.

Carole Cadwalladr, an *Observer* feature writer, has been determinedly investigating the operations of the data mining and analytics firm Cambridge Analytica and its connections to Robert Mercer, an American hedge fund billionaire and libertarian, who is a prominent Trump supporter. Cadwalladr is convinced that Mercer and Farage are at the centre of a network of alt-right white nationalists and libertarian billionaires who are intent not only on destabilising the West but engendering hate and overturning the liberal order.

Cadwalladr has been mocked as paranoid and a conspiracy theorist on social media by Farage associates Arron Banks and Andy

Wigmore of Leave.EU, which also posted a video that abused her on Twitter. The video has since been removed and Wigmore told me that it was meant to have been a joke and he regretted the upset it had caused.

'It seems to me that Wigmore and Banks are using Trumpian rhetoric for effect,' Carole Cadwalladr said. 'It doesn't really ring true. But Farage is ideological. That's the difference. And he's been given a free pass in Britain for too long. It's disturbing. It's made me question our institutions – including the press and media. There's no covert conspiracy with Farage. He's part of this overt, right-wing, pro-Putin bloc. He loves Putin. He supports Hungarian demagogues.'

Farage said that Vladimir Putin was 'a strong leader' but that he would never wish to live in Russia. 'You know, one hundred and twenty journalists have gone missing in the last nine years . . . I wouldn't want Putin as my leader, no, no, no. This is not some unqualified fan club, far from it. But, you know, he's a strong national leader who, when it comes to playing strategic global politics, is a bloomin' sight smarter than No 10.'

※

Before UKIP's post-referendum collapse into irrelevance and Jeremy Corbyn's dramatic rise, Farage successfully reached out to and captured a certain demographic of Labour voters, several million of whom ended up voting for Brexit. One of the most serious mistakes made by Ed Miliband as Labour leader, I think, was to have underestimated UKIP, a party he believed would hurt the Conservatives much more than Labour. By the time of the 2015 general election, however, increasing numbers of voters were abandoning Labour for the so-called people's army.

The Labour-to-UKIP defectors were, on the whole, not

city-dwelling liberals. They mostly lived in towns and were not university graduates. They were anxious about immigration, fearful of change, pessimistic about the future and tired of austerity. Caricatured as those 'left behind' by globalisation, they made themselves heard at the referendum in 2016, an act of rebellion that the Blue Labour thinker Jonathan Rutherford has likened to an Orwellian 'tug from below': a people's revolt.

'Cameron would not have won the election in 2015 had it not been for the UKIP vote,' Farage told me. And if Cameron had not won the election, there would have been no referendum. 'We hurt Labour far more than we hurt the Conservatives. And I remember thinking, "These cretins." The *Daily Mail* didn't understand it! *The Sun* didn't understand! They didn't understand it! We were digging deep into that Labour vote. And that was the gap Miliband created. It was the gap that, Jason, *you* saw earlier than almost anybody, to be frank, and we did well with them. We did very well with them. So, 2015 was an odd moment, because . . . we had four million votes and we'd got nothing for it [UKIP ended up with one MP]. But we had a referendum!'

Call it the revenge of the fruitcakes.

On 14 November 2017, Farage made a speech in the European Parliament during which he denounced George Soros, the octogenarian billionaire financier who funds the Open Society Foundations, which champions civil society and liberal democracy. Soros has been vilified in his home country of Hungary and is the victim of conspiracy theories and anti-Semitism. I put it to Farage that his speech had been interpreted as an anti-Semitic 'dog whistle'. For the first time, he became genuinely angry and his features coarsened.

'Fuck off, for God's sake. Excuse my language – but honestly, isn't that incredible? Is this what we've sunk to? If you attack Soros, you're anti-Semitic? They're desperate aren't they, these people? You know why? They're losing. Because even if Brexit's delayed, even if it's not done properly, public opinion is hardening around the kind of things that I campaigned for, for all those years. They're losing.'

What are they losing?

'Their very nice, comfortable, narrow vision of what the world is and what it should be: that's what they're losing.'

In his book *The Shipwrecked Mind*, the American academic Mark Lilla draws a distinction between the conservative and the reactionary mind. Reactionaries are, in their way, 'just as radical as revolutionaries and just as destructive', he writes. Farage is a radical and a reactionary: his instincts are destructive. He wanted to blow up the British establishment. He wanted to smash an elite consensus. He delights in describing Brexit as an 'earthquake', the aftershocks from which continue to reverberate.

'I've thought for a long time,' he told me, 'that this question about Europe and our relationship with it was one that had the potential to realign British politics. In the last few months, I've been thinking that Brexit might not be the last earthquake. There might just be another one. There may be something seismic still to come. And it could be the Conservative Party that's the most vulnerable to it.'

In 2017, far-right parties suffered notable electoral reversals in France, Austria and the Netherlands but they have not been decisively defeated. We are not witnessing the return of a more liberal, optimistic Europe. Marine Le Pen won thirty-four per cent of the vote in the second round of the French presidential election against Emmanuel Macron, after reverting in the final weeks of the campaign to the politics of her father, an old-style Vichy fascist. To defeat Geert Wilders's anti-Muslim Freedom Party in the Netherlands, the centre-right Dutch prime minister, Mark Rutte, had to adopt some of his rival's positions and borrow much of his xenophobic rhetoric. In the illiberal democracies of eastern Europe – Poland, Hungary – an ugly form of the old right has re-emerged. The Czech Republic has embraced anti-establishment populism after the ruling Social Democrats were crushed by ANO ('Yes'), an insurgent party led by a billionaire oligarch, Andrej Babiš.

Meanwhile, Angela Merkel's centre-right government has been severely weakened in Germany and her standing diminished after the far-right Alternative für Deutschland, energised by the migrant crisis, won nearly thirteen per cent of vote in the federal election in September 2017: it now has representation for the first time and is the official opposition in the Bundestag.

'All that has happened, especially in France, is that the rise of the far right has been paused,' said the philosopher John Gray. 'What's driving all this, I think, is that the emerging European state, or super-state, cannot discharge some of the primary functions of a state. It claims many of the prerogatives and authorities of a state, but it hasn't got the means to deliver on the functions of a state – which do include control of borders.'

As Gray said to me, 'Farage is taking an Oswald Mosley-like gamble. I'm not saying he's a fascist, but he's reinventing himself as an alt-right politician in a culture that, despite everything, has no room for the alt-right. He has made a fundamental strategic error. Let's say he's arrived at a point of non-arrival. There is no alt-right position for him to connect to, because the great achievement of British politics has always been to marginalise the far right. The dark European stain that has re-emerged – and now the American stain – is altogether different.'

❧

At the end of our encounter, Farage accepted that the Brexit negotiations were faltering. He was unsettled by the economic forecasts but accepted no responsibility or blame. 'It's not Brexit that's caused the uncertainty,' he said. 'It's Theresa May. Let's be honest about it: the prospect of a hard-left government with McDonnell as chancellor and Corbyn as leader is scaring business.'

He believed that the Prime Minister had no conviction. 'Brexit is an instruction from the electorate to turn around the ship of state by one hundred and eighty degrees. You cannot do that unless you believe in what you're doing. You have to actually, passionately believe in what you're doing. Ignore all criticism, you just have to do it. It's like an act of going to war . . . And she's managing the different wings of the party as if this is politics as normal.'

The ultimate irony of Brexit is that the UK is now more at the mercy of the EU than it was before the referendum. Farage predicted Labour would offer a second referendum on what would still be the unresolved Europe question in its next manifesto. 'I have a feeling that Labour will fight the 2022 general election, if we go that long – we will not be fully out, we will still be in a transition of some kind – on a ticket of either, "We'll have a referendum to rebalance our relationship" (which would not be fully rejoining, but it could be a single market compromise), or an EEA compromise, or something. That's a very realistic possibility.'

At which point, Nigel Farage might return to front-line politics, perhaps in or at the head of a new party or English nationalist movement. 'My position is this: if they really make a mess of Brexit, and if there's a job that has to be done . . .'

He lowered his voice almost to a whisper and looked straight at me. 'I've got no choice! Actually, I honestly don't really want to. I've done it. I don't want to do it again. You know climbing mountains without crampons is quite tough – you take on the establishment. But, no, if the gap is there, if it needs to be done, if the job needs to be finished, I'll do it.'

(2017)

THE FAILURE OF ELITES:
MICHAEL SANDEL

In the run-up to the European referendum on 23 June 2016, I spoke to the political philosopher Michael Sandel about our age of upheaval. His course 'Justice' is the first Harvard course to be made freely available online and on television and has been viewed by tens of millions of people. He presents the series Public Philosopher *on BBC Radio 4.*

JASON COWLEY: Shall we begin with Brexit? It's very close here at the moment: the Remain side had big leads in the polls but it's narrowed considerably since the conversation moved on to immigration, porous borders and freedom of movement of migrant workers within the EU. What forces are driving the desire for Brexit?

MICHAEL SANDEL: There are really two questions. One is whether Brexit would be good for Europe and the other is the question of whether it would be good for Britain. It seems to me that for Britain to remain in the EU would be a good thing for Europe, but whether it's a good thing for Britain is something that's for British voters to decide.

A big part of the debate has been about economics – jobs and trade and prosperity – but my hunch is that voters will decide less on economics than on culture and questions of identity and belonging.

JC Superficially, the United Kingdom seems becalmed, but we're experiencing eruptions. We had the Scottish referendum in 2014, and we almost saw the break-up of the British state. Now we're having a referendum on whether we should continue to be a member of the European Union. Why are there so many unsettled questions in Britain? Why are the people so restive?

MS The restiveness that you describe reflects a broader disquiet with democracy that we see in most democracies around the world today. There is a widespread frustration with politics, with politicians and with established political parties. This is for a couple of reasons; one of them is that citizens are rightly frustrated with the empty terms of public discourse in most democracies. Politics for the most part fails to address the big questions that matter most and that citizens care about: what makes for a just society, questions about the common good, questions about the role of markets, and about what it means to be a citizen. A second source of the frustration is the sense that people feel less and less in control of the forces that govern their lives. And the project of democratic self-government seems to be slipping from our grasp. This accounts for the rise of anti-establishment political movements and parties throughout Europe and in the US.

JC One of the key slogans of the Brexiteers is to take back control. Why does this resonate? Are you sympathetic at all to that line of argument?

MS It does resonate deeply. I see this not only in Britain, I see it in the US and Europe. A theme running through these various political movements is taking back control, restoring control over the forces that govern our lives and giving people a voice. As to whether I have some sympathy for this sentiment, I do. I don't have sympathy for many of the actual political forms that it takes.

One of the biggest failures of the last generation of mainstream parties has been the failure to take seriously and to speak directly to people's aspiration to feel that they have some meaningful say in shaping the forces that govern their lives. And this is partly a question of democracy: what does democracy actually mean in practice? It's also closely related to a question of culture and identity. Because a sense of disempowerment is partly a sense that the project of self-government has failed. When it's connected to borders, the desire to reassert control over borders, it also shows the close connection between a sense of disempowerment and a sense that people's identities are under siege.

A large constituency of working-class voters feel that not only has the economy left them behind, but so has the culture, that the sources of their dignity, the dignity of labour, have been eroded and mocked by developments with globalisation, the rise of finance, the attention that is lavished by parties across the political spectrum on economic and financial elites, the technocratic emphasis of the established political parties. I think we've seen this tendency unfold over the last generation. Much of the energy animating the Brexit sentiment is born of this failure of elites, this failure of established political parties.

JC One particularly notable trend is the failure of mainstream social-democratic parties across Europe – the Labour Party included. Many people who might once have been inspired by or supported the centre left are now attracted by populist and radical movements of both left and right. Why is social democracy failing?

MS Social democracy is in desperate need of reinvigoration, because it has over the past several decades lost its moral and civic energy and purpose. It's become a largely managerial and technocratic orientation to politics. It's lost its ability to inspire working people, and its vision, its moral and civic vision, has faltered. So for two generations after the Second World War, social democracy did have an animating vision, which was to create and to deepen and to articulate welfare states, and to moderate and provide a counterbalance to the power of unfettered market capitalism.

This was the raison d'être of social democracy, and it was connected to a larger purpose, which was to empower those who were not at the top of the class system, to empower working people and ordinary men and women, and also to nurture a sense of solidarity and an understanding of citizenship that enabled the entire society to say we are all in this together. But over the past, well, three or four decades, this sense of purpose has been lost, and I think it begins with the Ronald Reagan/Margaret Thatcher era.

JC You mean the neoliberal turn at the end of the 1970s – the advent of what you have called 'market triumphalism'?

MS Right. It began there. But even when Reagan and Thatcher passed from the political scene, and were succeeded by the centre-left political leaders – Bill Clinton in the US, Tony Blair in Britain, Gerhard Schröder in Germany – these leaders did not challenge the fundamental assumption underlying the market faith of the Reagan/Thatcher years. They moderated, but consolidated the faith, the assumption that markets are the primary instrument for achieving the public good. And as a result, the centre left managed to regain political office but failed to reimagine the mission and purpose of social democracy, which became empty and obsolete. This remains an unfinished project.

JC Unfinished even after the financial crisis, when this was considered by many on the left – especially here in Britain – to be a potential social-democratic moment?

MS That's right, and I think many of us expected that the financial crisis would mark the end of an era of unqualified embrace of the market faith and the beginning of new debate about what should be the role and reach of markets in a good society. What happened, sadly, is that the financial crisis came and, although we did have some debate about regulatory reform, it was a rather narrowly cast debate. We have not yet had the more fundamental debate about what should be the role of markets in a good society. As a result, social democracy has not only lost the argument, it has failed to articulate a vision of a just society; it's failed to articulate a conception of democracy as self-government. And so, it is understandable that its traditional constituencies in working-class and middle-class communities lost confidence that social-democratic parties could be the vehicle either for a renewed sense of community and mutual responsibility or for collective democratic projects.

JC Is it also because trust has been lost in the state – because of the memory of the economic failures of the mid-to-late 1970s, the unravelling of the post-war consensus, stagflation and so on?

MS That has contributed to a loss of confidence in the state but I think a further source of lost confidence in the state is that, traditionally, the democratic state has as one of its primary purposes to be a vehicle for self-government, to enable citizens to have some meaningful say in how they are governed. Whereas today the state seems more an obstacle to meaningful political participation and self-government than a vehicle for it. Any revival of social democracy would require not only an articulation of a conception of a just society, but also forms of political participation that could renew the democratic promise.

That's as important as articulating a conception of a just society, working out institutions and civic practices that could revitalise the project of democracy as a vehicle for self-government. The existing state fails to do that and I think when people look to the European Union they also feel that it is not a vehicle for democratic self-government. Both the nation state and the European Union are seen to have failed in this regard.

JC Where does this leave us? I guess it leaves us in the UK approaching Brexit?

MS Where it leaves us is with a potent backlash. And it's a backlash that is understandable. I think it's a mistake to view the backlash – and it finds expression in the ways that we've been discussing – simply as people suddenly turning inward and against immigrants as if this were simply a matter of mindless bigotry by people, benighted people, who are ungenerous. It's important for people who make the case for Remain to be able to offer a conception of Europe that could begin to address this unanswered hunger for meaningful self-government, for having a voice.

JC What about the EU as a social market with its own social standards and rules? Is that potentially progressive? It can impose certain transnational legislation on sovereign governments from outside that benefits workers.

MS It's potentially progressive in the policy outcomes but that is not enough. A regulatory state, however effective and desirable its social regulations may be, is insufficient to win people's allegiance unless the regulatory process is connected to a democratic process with which people identify as citizens who have a voice, who have a say.

It's desirable to have the EU promulgate social regulations that moderate market forces and protect workers and protect the environment, protect health and safety. All of that's good but it's insufficient and I don't think it can be supported politically unless it makes people feel they're not being dictated to by faceless bureaucrats from Brussels. Even if those faceless bureaucrats promulgate very good social legislation, people want a voice, people want a say, people want a more robust democratic system. It's a mistake to neglect that.

JC More generally, can free-market globalisation be tamed? And could we be entering an era of more protectionist economics? Consider the rhetoric of Trump.

MS I have no sympathy for Trump's politics but I do think that his success reflects the failure of established parties and the elites in both parties to speak to the sense of disempowerment that we see in much of the middle class. What Trump really appeals to is the sense of much of the working class that not only has the economy left them behind, but the culture no longer respects work and labour.

This is connected to the enormous rewards that in recent decades have been lavished on Wall Street and those who work in the financial industry, the growing financialisation of the American economy, and the decline of manufacturing and of work in the traditional sense. There is also the sense that not only have jobs been lost through various trade agreements and technological developments, but the economic benefits associated with those agreements and those technologies have not gone to the middle class or to the working class but to those at the very top. That's the sense of injustice; but more than that, the fact that the nature of political parties – I'm speaking about those in the US – have become, since the time of the Clinton years, heavily dependent on both sides, Democrats and Republicans, on the financial industry for campaign contributions.

JC One thinks of the Clintons' relationship with Goldman Sachs, for instance – a kind of crony capitalism.

MS Well, there you have an example of how the Democratic Party has become so Wall Street-friendly that it has largely ceased to be an effective counterweight to the power of big money in politics or to the financial industry and its influence in politics. And this is why Bernie Sanders was able to have far more success than anyone imagined. He was originally thought to be a fringe candidate who would maybe get five, ten per cent of the vote. And yet he fought Hillary Clinton almost to a draw in many of the Democratic primaries. No one would have imagined that.

The mainstream of the Democratic Party had so embraced the financial industry that it was unable to provide an effective counterweight when it came to the financial crisis or to the aftermath, the regulatory debate. And oddly enough, Trump from the right and Bernie Sanders from the left have a good deal of overlap. They've both been critical of free-trade agreements that benefit multinational corporations and the financial industry but haven't in practice helped workers.

JC What are the limits to markets? And what is the alternative to market triumphalism, especially when moderate social democracy is in crisis?

MS Social democracy has to become less managerial and technocratic and has to return to its roots in a kind of moral and civic critique of the excesses of capitalism. At the level of public philosophy or ideology it has to work out a conception of a just society, of the common good, of moral and civic education as it relates to democracy and empowerment. That's a big project.

A revitalised social-democratic response to the power of markets would also try to come up with institutions for meaningful self-government – forms of participatory democracy in an age of globalisation, where power seems to flow to transnational institutions and forms of association. It's important also to find ways to promote participatory democracy. This requires political imagination and political courage. It's a long-term project that remains as a challenge, but until we make some progress in that bigger challenge, democratic politics will still be vulnerable to the backlash that we're witnessing, with Brexit in Britain, some of the populist political movements in Europe, and Trump in the United States.

There is an alternative – but the alternative is to go beyond the managerial, technocratic approach to politics that has characterised the established parties and the elites, to reconnect with big questions that people care about.

(2016)

PART 3
LIVES AND LETTERS

EUROPEAN SON: THE
LONG LONELINESS
OF CHARLES HILLS

ONE LATE SUMMER afternoon Charles Hills, an Oxford-educated former editor of the journal PEN, stood in the dock at the Old Bailey in London and pleaded guilty to two counts of soliciting to murder his late mother's former boyfriend. Flávio Rosa, a Portuguese gardener and handyman who is, like Hills, in his early fifties, had befriended Maria José Hills towards the end of her life when she was living in Portugal. In spite of an age difference of almost thirty years, he became the lover of the long-time-divorced elderly woman and, eventually, her live-in partner at the villa she owned on the Algarve. It was there that Hills schemed to have Rosa murdered 'by any method possible'.

Dressed in a jacket, a faded sweatshirt, and dark trousers recently bought for him by a friend, and wearing plastic-framed spectacles, Hills lowered his head as he was sentenced to seven years in prison. It was the end of a disastrous period for him, during which, among many other troubles, he had attempted to kill himself and had also spent several weeks in a secure ward at the Maudsley psychiatric hospital in Camberwell, south London. On his release from the Maudsley, still depressed and confused, he'd asked a neighbour on the Clapham estate where he lived how he could hire a hitman. The neighbour put him in touch with an intermediary who, in turn, introduced him to two contract killers.

Their first meeting took place at night, in a parked car close to Wandsworth Road station. Hills told the men what he wanted, who Rosa was and where the hated man lived. This was his second attempt to engage a hitman; a year earlier, he had given a drifter on his estate £2,500 in cash to murder Rosa. Instead of travelling to Portugal, the drifter had squandered the money on alcohol and then disappeared. Now Hills was prepared to pay as much as £15,000 to have the job done, not by an unreliable amateur, but a professional assassin.

'Charles talked about wanting to have Rosa murdered,' one of his friends told me. 'I tried to talk him out of his obsession. He said he'd been negotiating with hitmen, but I didn't know whether to believe him. He'd had psychotic episodes in the past. He could be unstable.'

Early on the morning of 16 December 2006, Hills was startled from sleep by the sharp crack of splintering wood: the front door of his ramshackle flat was being demolished. The police had arrived to arrest him. As it turned out, the hitmen with whom he had been negotiating were nothing of the kind; they were undercover police officers and had recorded and secretly filmed their meetings with Hills.

Charles Hills is a friend of mine and I received news of his sentence in an email from his closest friend, Mark Casserley. He pleaded guilty after the original charge of conspiracy to murder was reduced to the lesser soliciting to murder. I was told he was resigned to his fate and prepared to accept his punishment. So disordered and disturbed had his life become that I wondered whether prison might not even be the best place for him, a place of discipline and routine where he could perhaps begin to recover a sense of moral purpose.

I first met Hills in 1997 at a party held by the editor of *Prospect* magazine, David Goodhart. Hills was of the party but apart from it, a small, dishevelled figure standing in a corner. Towards the end of the evening, he approached and introduced himself. He had a high, plaintive voice and stuttered slightly. I responded to his courtesy and charm and obvious intelligence, while being a little repelled by his appearance: the shabby suit, the shuffling, awkward manner. He told me that he wrote fiction as well as essays and reviews under the name C. A. R. Hills.

'I think I read something by you recently,' I told him, 'an essay on Pessoa. It was excellent.' Hills seemed delighted, inordinately so, and spent the rest of the evening shadowing me as I moved around the room. It was the beginning of an odd friendship. Later, I asked Goodhart about Hills. 'Oh, he's a bit of a literary saddy,' he said, 'but he writes well.' It would be a few years before I realised just quite how sad being Charles Hills could be.

Hills was born in Archway, north London, on 21 August 1955; the only child of an English father, Arthur Hills, who worked as a company secretary, and a Portuguese mother. He was a young boy when the family moved to Crawley in Sussex. Charles was still at school when his father left his mother for another woman, after which they had little contact. Arthur disapproved of his son, of his homosexuality, eccentricity and literary ambition. When, shortly before his death in 2004, Charles contacted his father seeking reconciliation, he was rejected. Arthur wrote to him to say that he should stay within his 'rotten little life' and not bother him again.

He attended a comprehensive school, where he was an

outstanding pupil, achieving three A-levels at grade A and, unusually for someone from his background and school, winning a place at Hertford College, Oxford, in 1973. 'There were only six A grades in my entire year at school, a huge and mediocre comprehensive, and I got three of them,' Hills told me with evident pride when I went to visit him at Belmarsh jail in south-east London. 'I really was very clever.'

He read geography at Oxford – 'a terrible mistake,' he says now, chuckling, 'the start of my decline'. He felt apart at Hertford, socially ill at ease and sought the company of fellow gay students. His Oxford years passed in a haze of indolence: the urgent rhythms of life, both at university and beyond, seemed to him always to be elsewhere, out of reach. He had no idea what he wanted to do once he graduated, beyond nurturing a vague, romantic attachment to the idea of being a writer and so, without enthusiasm, he did postgraduate research in history at Sussex University and then back at Oxford. And he took more A-levels, in Latin and Greek.

Throughout his twenties, he continued to read as much as he could, worked on his various languages, played the piano and began, slowly, hesitantly, to write: stories and strange, self-revealing essays. 'My great influences were [the painter and novelist] Denton Welch and Somerset Maugham,' he told me. 'I was very influenced by Maugham when he wrote of his three aims for writing: lucidity, simplicity, euphony.'

Hills could not live by his writing alone and supported himself through teaching at various crammers; by working in a second-hand bookshop off London's Charing Cross Road, on a trade journal for the electrical goods industry and, for a period in the early Nineties, as an editor at the BBC Monitoring Service, from where he was sacked in 1994 for telling 'my line manager to fuck off'.

By the time I met him, he was unemployed, impoverished, living on benefits and making what money he could as editor of PEN News and from the scraps of journalism he had published in small magazines. His was an unsettling, shambolic, twilight existence. He inhabited a peculiar literary demimonde, mixing with mostly unpublished or disappointed writers, a world of shabby clothing, intellectual snobbery, drunkenness and, above all, of poverty.

I pitied him, but also believed in his talent and wanted to encourage him. I occasionally bought him lunch but, sitting opposite him at a table, I felt as if I was staring into a mirror which revealed the kind of life that could have been mine had I dropped out in my twenties to pursue the writing life. What sustained him? Why did he keep on trying to find a publisher for his fiction? How did he cope with the rejection, with the continuous hustling for work, for the next poorly-paid review, the next commission? The answer, I guess, is that he, too, believed in his talent. 'I really am an excellent writer,' he told me whenever we met.

He would sometimes send me a postcard commenting on something I'd written, or a print-out of one of his stories or novels. I liked his fiction; there were always passages of interest, he had a distinct sense of place and was adept at juxtaposing tenderness and brutality. Others encouraged him as well, notably literary agent Caroline Dawnay, whose authors include Nick Hornby and Alain de Botton. She wanted Hills to write a memoir, to be called *The Man Who Took A-Levels*, but it was fiction he was determined to publish.

In the late Nineties, I was working as a literary editor and Hills would sometimes turn up at our offices in Victoria, usually on Thursday morning, the early part of which he would have idled away at a WHSmith on Victoria Station's concourse. There, he flicked through the latest editions of the weekly political magazines and cultural reviews he could never afford to buy. When he came to the office, he was invariably looking for books to review and, very occasionally, I commissioned something by him.

Learning from Maugham, Hills has a graceful, limpid style and a fine ear for cadence, for the internal music of a sentence and paragraph, for rise and fall. I especially admired his *Prospect* essays, in which he wrote of his lonely wanderings in and around the rundown estates of Clapham and Peckham, and the encounters he had there. He transformed his south London neighbourhood into a place of shadows and loss, of restless questing and melancholy longing, achieving a distinctive effect, a kind of urban pastoral. It was as if C. A. R. Hills (the name under which he published) were yet another of Fernando Pessoa's heteronyms, living and dying not in Lisbon but on an inner-London council estate. 'See life from a distance,' wrote Pessoa's Ricardo Reis and this was something that Hills understood, as he loitered always on the margins, knocking at the door of the literary club that remained firmly closed to him.

In the early summer of 2000, Maria Hills came to visit her son in London. She had some news that would distract him from his writing and set in progress the events that would lead to his incarceration. She told her son that she had altered her will to give Flávio Rosa a *usufruct* on her house in the Algarve. This would allow him under Portuguese law to live in the house for the rest of his life, even though Hills would ultimately inherit it. 'The house was his mother's principal asset and he was looking forward to owning and then selling it,' says Mark Casserley, his longtime friend. 'I remember he rang me from a cafe to tell me this, on the day he first heard of it, and said he was too angry to speak.'

It was apparent to everyone who met and knew Maria that she was suffering from Alzheimer's. 'She was often confused and forgetful,' says her niece, Maria Streeter, who lives in England.

'She kept asking where she was, where she was going.'

Hills believed that Rosa had manipulated his mother into alter-
ing her will, that he was exploiting an aged and vulnerable woman.
With his mother's condition deteriorating, he moved to Portugal,
staying at a second property owned by her, a flat in Lisbon. For
the next two years, until her death in a nursing home at the age
of seventy-nine in September 2002, he moved between Lisbon and
London, beginning an action in the Portuguese courts to have
Maria's amended will declared invalid and Rosa expelled from the
house. He thought of little but his hatred of Rosa. He resigned
the editorship of *PEN News*, he sold his piano and even ceased to
fret about finding a publisher for his work.

When I met him for lunch one day in 2005, the last lunch I
was to have with him, he was agitated. He told me about Rosa
and how this man had cheated him out of his rightful inheritance.
At the end of the lunch, he said that he would spend the rest of
the year travelling in the Far East and Australia. He did just that
and sent me a couple of postcards from his travels, and one short
story, in which a narrator, not unlike Hills, is brutally buggered by
a male prostitute in a cheap hotel room. There was no tenderness
in that story.

I heard nothing more from him until receiving a telephone
message one evening just after Christmas. It was Charles, but
he sounded distressed, panicked. Someone wanted to kill him,
he said. The man was outside his flat and had a gun. I must call
the police. The message had been left a couple of hours earlier. I
thought about calling back, but then remembering his anxiety and
expressions of irrational hatred when we last met, I decided not
to. I was becoming weary of his melodramas and struggles. But
later that night, I awoke feeling ashamed that I'd not responded
to his pleas for help. What if someone really was trying to kill
him?

I know now that he was suffering from a form of manic paranoia, convinced that his closest friends were MI6 agents and plotting to kill him. His mother and father had been mafiosi and drug smugglers, concealing their true identities from their son. His mother, he believed, was not Portuguese, but a Jewish-Italian from Naples, and his father was a Polish Jew. Discovering that he was really Jewish had brought Hills 'great peace' he told friends. And so it went on: Flávio Rosa was not just his mother's lover; he was also her son, by another man, which made him Charles's half-brother.

One morning, Hills was queuing for a bus when two elderly women pushed up against him. He felt a sharp pain and believed the women had somehow injected him with a lethal poison. 'He went to the public library and sat down to await his death,' Casserley wrote in a private document prepared for Hills's solicitor, Janet Dalton. 'He felt, he said, very liberated. He had often told me, in moments of despair, that he wished he was dead, though . . . nothing happened, of course.'

After recovering from this period of psychosis, Hills became increasingly depressed, mooning away the long, aimless days at home. 'He wasn't taking care of himself,' says his cousin Maria. 'He was feeling so bitter and angry.' He would sometimes leave messages on my answering machine, his high voice fading with the merest echo of a sigh. There would invariably be piano music in the background; he especially admired German lieder, the songs of Franz Schubert, Robert Schumann and Hugo Wolf. I was moved by his plight, but seldom called back – there was no more I could do for him.

Then, early one Sunday morning in August 2006, he got through to my wife at home. He was in the Maudsley hospital, he said, recovering from a failed suicide attempt. He wanted me to come in to see him. During one morning, he had swallowed at least one hundred paracetamol tablets, drunk many glasses of Ribena and then written a short suicide note. It said that none of his friends should feel self-reproach for his death and that he had taken the pills because he believed he would 'never know happiness again'.

After writing the note, he lay on his bed and fell into a deep sleep, from which some time later he was awoken by the sound of the telephone. Scarcely able to rouse himself, he stumbled across the room, vomiting as he went. It was Maria Streeter. She had not spoken to her cousin for several months, but later explained: 'I just knew I had to call him that evening. I think I had a premonition. I knew I had to reach him and picked up the phone on the spur of the moment. He wasn't with it. He didn't know who I was. I knew he'd been depressed. My husband took the phone and asked Charles if he'd taken something. We then called the police and told them to get an ambulance because Charles had taken an overdose.'

'Maria's call saved my life,' Hills recollects. 'I remember, when awoken by it, I felt relieved, relieved to still be here, alive after all.'

On arriving at the Maudsley hospital, I was directed to a secure ward. I sat for five minutes or so in an office with three young female nurses, separated from the patients by a glass screen. You could see the patients, most of whom were black men, moving around as if in a stunned, narcotised trance. I wasn't sure what I was doing there or what I could do for Hills, beyond wishing him well. Then I saw him, a forlorn, slow-moving, overweight, raggedly shaven presence. He smiled through the glass at me and I was taken through to meet him by one of the nurses. She then returned to the office, locking the door behind her.

Several patients gathered around; I surveyed the room to see if there were any male doctors or nurses present. There was no one. I felt isolated and threatened – not by the patients, who were docile enough, and no doubt tranquillised by anti-depressants, but by the extremity of the situation: all these mentally ill men together in the same cramped room and only a few female nurses to control them.

Charles was permitted to leave the hospital for an hour, so after a brief walk in a nearby park, we went to a pub that was adjacent to Denmark Hill station. There, drinking several glasses of white wine, he spoke of having no money and of needing to find a regular paid outlet for his writing. Perhaps that's why he had wanted to see me. Perhaps he thought I could find him something. He said it was difficult to sleep at night at the Maudsley, because of the noise and clamour of those around him, some moaning or shouting out, while others jabbered on solipsistically. Yet he still wanted to stay there for as long as possible because he feared the consequences of being alone at his flat. He didn't once mention Flávio Rosa.

A short while later, I heard that Hills was out of the Maudsley but now in a very different kind of secure unit: he was in prison, awaiting trial on the charge of conspiracy to murder.

I have travelled to Belmarsh in the south-east London suburbs to see Charles Hills. Traffic clogs the narrow roads around the prison; long queues of cars and trucks wait to use the moribund Woolwich Ferry, and near-derelict buildings and abandoned wharves stand alongside new-model estates, where the houses seem so flimsily constructed you feel they could be blown away in a storm. Belmarsh is built on part of the site of the old Woolwich Arsenal and is where Abu Hamza al-Masri, radical jihadist and former preacher at the Finsbury Park Mosque, is incarcerated.

Hills is a category B prisoner, and though his sentence has been reduced on appeal to five years, there's no indication that he will soon be moved to a low-security or open prison as Jeffrey

Archer, another writer and former inmate at Belmarsh, was before him.

As a visitor to Belmarsh, you are subjected to an assault course of indignities: scanned, searched, photographed and fingerprinted, if never quite stripped. Having passed through an airport-style metal detector with my shoes and belt removed, I am asked by a uniformed security guard to open my jeans. He rubs vigorously between my legs, and opens my boxer shorts and peers into them. Meanwhile, two women visitors wearing niqabs are led into a side room by a female security guard, presumably to be searched.

From there, the two women and I are directed through to the visitors' room, the size of a small school gymnasium. It is a few days before Christmas, but there are no decorations. The prisoners, who can receive no gifts, wear distinguishing orange bibs and sit at small tables in hard-backed chairs. But first, I'm searched again and my fingerprints are checked.

I've not seen Hills since that afternoon at the Maudsley, and he looks well. He's much slimmer, his hair is clipped short and his skin has lost much of its sickly pallor. Dressed in an off-white T-shirt, faded sweatshirt and tracksuit bottoms, he wears a rosary. I buy him a cup of coffee and two chocolate bars, which he eats hungrily. Softly, he speaks of his psychological torment: he cannot concentrate even to read in his cell. 'I'm trying to work my way through *War and Peace* but spend most of my time lying on my bed or pacing around,' he says.

The other prisoners are kind to him, considering him to be a harmless oddity. So are the prison officers, who sometimes leave his cell unlocked so that he can wander along the corridor outside. He was writing for *Prospect* again, but this privilege has now been stopped after he identified a fellow prisoner in a recent column.

'I have nothing now,' he says, and laughs, as if at the absurdity of our meeting in such a place. He talks about the writers he most admires – Barbara Pym, Muriel Spark, Jean Rhys, as well as Welch and Maugham – and recalls how when his first story was accepted for publication, by PEN *New Fiction* in 1987, he used the pseudonym David Welsh. 'The story was about being mugged and in it I wrote about being gay. But because I did not want my mother to know, I used a different name.'

He returns repeatedly to his mother; of how much he loved her, of how extraordinarily close he was to her. 'She's the only person I've ever truly loved. I think about her continually and what happened to her in her last mad years.'

As a young man, his ambition was always to travel, but his mother did not want him to leave Europe. He was her European son. Her death, in 2002, freed him to wander and go wherever he wanted: Portuguese-speaking Africa, the Far East, Australia. 'I remember being on Bondi Beach and starting to cry. I'd always wanted to be there, but now that I was, I felt nothing.'

He digresses to say that in Thailand he was 'fucked hard' for the first time since he was an undergraduate at Oxford. 'I was the passive recipient. I've never had much sex myself, because I can scarcely maintain an erection,' he says, chuckling again.

When he's not talking about his mother, or his thwarted sexuality, he touches on his rediscovery of religious belief. 'You are rather cast upon God in here,' he says. And then, self-dramatisingly, his words proffered with an amused flourish: 'I have travelled the world, but now I live in just one small room and I've been delivered into the arms of Jesus.'

Do you believe that?

'I've got to,' he says, this time with pained sincerity. 'Sometimes, I find it hard to believe, but I must.'

We talk about his writing for a while and I mention how much I used to admire his *Prospect* columns. 'And then I was so brutally dropped by Goodhart.' He breaks off. 'I've forgiven him, you know. I've forgiven Flávio. If I don't, the anger will never let me go. It will destroy me.'

He makes no mention of his own culpability, only that he must forgive Rosa. He glances fretfully at the clock mounted high on the bare wall, beneath which two prison officers stand, each wearing plastic gloves. It's almost four in the afternoon – when all visitors must leave. As I stand to go, Hills mutters something in German, lines from a Schubert song, which he translates: 'There where you are not/ There happiness lies.'

Has Charles Hills ever known happiness? Certainly, his writing – his troubling and poignant stories and personal essays – are deeply sad. His narrators are lonely wanderers, lost and bewildered in the world. They long for tenderness and for a transcendence that can never be theirs. And so, the emptiness of their lives is filled with brutality, with random acts of violence: canings, beatings, muggings.

How to account for it, this desire to be beaten and humiliated, a desire that is there in the life as well as represented in the work? Perhaps it can be explained only by this: an absence of enduring love in his life.

As we shake hands, Hills says he has found peace of sorts in prison, through the affirmation of religious belief and because he is well cared for. In Dostoevsky's *Crime and Punishment*, the young protagonist Raskolnikov believes that his superior intelligence elevates him above the common morality of other people, liberating him to live by his own ethical code, in a condition of radical freedom. The test of his superiority is the self-created liberty he has to commit murder, which he does, as an intellectual exercise, only to be immediately enfeebled by guilty conscience and forced, once he has been sent to prison, to submit to the forces of a higher morality, as Hills has done by embracing religion.

Like Raskolnikov, Hills has found a kind of harsh freedom in prison. In the solitude and darkness of his cell, he has begun to see more clearly; to see what was wrong in his old life, destroyed as it was by bitterness and fury, and how everything must be different on his release. 'I was in a pretty bad way on the outside and could have gone under a bus at any moment. Now I must look to a better future.'

He will be encouraged by the knowledge that his civil action in Portugal to have his mother's will annulled has been successful; Rosa has appealed against the verdict and is still living in the villa on the Algarve.

Here at Belmarsh there's movement all around us now, as women lean across to kiss the men they're leaving behind, and children reach out for their fathers' hands. Before I am allowed to leave, my fingerprints are checked once more, just to make sure I am who I say and have decided not to stay on. There's an irritating delay as the scanning machine fails to recognise my prints and I take the opportunity to glance back at Hills who is sitting there in his chair, quite still. He raises his right arm in a formal gesture of farewell. From this distance, it seems to me as if he's smiling.

(2008)

LOST PROMISE: THE SHORT, BRILLIANT LIFE OF MARINA KEEGAN

IN THE AUTUMN of 2011, Marina Keegan, a precocious-ly gifted English major at Yale who was being mentored by Harold Bloom, published an essay in the college newspaper. 'Even Artichokes Have Doubts' (the whimsical title suggests the influence of David Foster Wallace or George Saunders) was about the career choices of elite Ivy League graduates. Keegan, who also wrote and acted in plays, lamented how many of her peers - a quarter at Yale, she calculated - would soon be pursuing high-paying careers on Wall Street or in management consultancy.

This troubled and saddened Keegan, who was an activist in the Occupy movement and served as president of the Yale College Democrats. It told her something important about her generation of millennials and what they wanted, or were coerced into wanting, that she did not like.

The essay reached a readership far beyond her student peers and, after a version of it was republished in the *New York Times*, it inspired, Marina's mother Tracy told me, a wide-ranging discussion about what America's brightest young people should be doing with their lives in the wake of the 2008 financial crisis and the subsequent Great Recession.

Just before she graduated in May 2012, Keegan wrote the cover piece for a special graduation edition of the *Yale Daily News*. 'The Opposite of Loneliness' would be her farewell to a brilliant student career at Yale. It was also a plea to her fellow graduates not to waste time and, as she put it, to 'make something happen to this world'. Keegan wrote often in the first-person plural, as if she were speaking not only for herself but a generation. 'What we have to remember is that we can still do anything,' she wrote in 'The Opposite of Loneliness'. 'We can change our minds. We can start over . . . The notion that it's too late to do anything is comical. It's hilarious. We're graduating from college. We're so young. We can't, we MUST not lose this sense of possibility because in the end, it's all we have.'

The essay was a viral hit and seemed to confirm what everyone who knew Keegan already thought about her: that she was a young person of tremendous promise. One of her creative writing professors, Anne Fadiman, called her a 'self-starting cornucopia'. You sense that Keegan knew she was good, perhaps the best of her cohort. 'Vaguely, quietly, we know we'll be famous,' she wrote in one piece at Yale.

Within a few days of graduating, Marina Keegan, who was preparing to take up a staff job on the *New Yorker* magazine after impressing there as an intern, was killed in a road accident. She and her boyfriend, Michael Gocksch, had been on their way to Marina's father's fifty-fifth birthday party in Cape Cod when the car hit a guardrail and overturned. An inquest revealed that Gocksch had fallen asleep at the wheel. He was unhurt in the crash but Keegan was declared dead at the scene. She was just twenty-two.

When he was told what had happened, Harold Bloom, the literary critic and academic, said the young woman's death was 'beyond human comprehension'. He added: 'It is sixty years since I first came to Yale. I can think of only a few other women and men I have taught whose presence always will be with me.'

Keegan's damaged laptop was recovered from the wrecked car; from its hard drive her mother retrieved her unpublished writings. These, together with short stories and pieces from the *Yale Daily News*, have been collected in a book, *The Opposite of Loneliness*. Edited by Anne Fadiman, it has been a small sensation in the United States, where it has been widely and mostly generously reviewed. Keegan has, indeed, become famous, but not in a way that she or anyone could have imagined or would have wished.

Many of the book's themes – the confusions of romantic love, your first car, college jealousies and rivalries, the strangeness of returning home to your parents after a long period away – are juvenile: Keegan was only twenty-two when she died. Yet there is a surprising preoccupation, too, with death and mutability and this gives the book depth and a kind of macabre retrospective fascination.

Milan Kundera has written about what he calls 'the mathematical paradox in nostalgia: that it is most powerful in early youth, when the volume of the life gone by is quite small'. Keegan seems to have had a keen sense of this paradox: even as she prepared to leave Yale and was excited by her future prospects, she seemed to have been mourning something she understood could never be recaptured, the bright brilliant life of her student experience. 'We don't have a word for the opposite of loneliness,' she wrote in her final piece, 'but if we did, I could say that's what I want in life. What I'm grateful and thankful to have found at Yale, and what I'm scared of losing when we wake up tomorrow and leave this place.'

Tracy Keegan told me when we spoke on an indistinct phone line (she was on a train to New York), that her daughter was extraordinarily driven. 'She grabbed life and ran with it,' she said. 'Compassion, humanism and humour – these are the three strongest ingredients of our family. Marina was driven by her passions but also by a sense of urgency.'

Why such urgency in one so young, I asked. 'Perhaps she had a sense of things to come...' Tracy Keegan's voice faded, and then there was silence.

There is not much footage of Marina Keegan on YouTube, apart from some recordings of poetry recitals she gave at Yale. In one performance, she recites from memory a long poem she wrote called 'Bygones', the last line of which is, 'And I cry because everything is so beautiful and so short.' As she speaks you can see how she is drawing confidence from the audience and the pleasure their enthusiasm gives her.

It's moving to watch this hopeful young woman speaking about everything being 'so beautiful and so short', knowing what happened to her soon afterwards. 'High on their posthumous pedestals, the dead become hard to see,' writes Anne Fadiman in her introduction to *The Opposite of Loneliness*. '[But] Marina wouldn't want to be remembered because she's dead. She would want to be remembered because she's good.'

As an undergraduate I had a macabre fascination with several writers who died much too young, notably Keats, Wilfred Owen and Alain-Fournier, who wrote one enchanting novel, *Le Grand Meaulnes* (1913), before he was killed shortly after enlisting to fight in the First World War. I cherished these writers for what they had written, but also for what they might have written had they lived even just a few more years.

It's something like this with Marina Keegan's first and last book. Her voice is so fresh, her enthusiasm so appealing, her ambition so boundless that you cannot help but wonder what she might have achieved with more life experience and once she was freed from the hothouse environment of an ultra-competitive Ivy League school. 'When we encounter a natural style we are always surprised and delighted,' wrote the seventeenth-century polymath, Blaise Pascal. Keegan had her own surprising and delightful natural style. She persuades by sweetness, not authority. She also had a very American sincerity but was never solemn or worthy. She performed in plays and was active in politics; her friends speak of her wit and warmth. For Fadiman, 'Every aspect of her life was a way of answering that question, "How do you find meaning in your life?"'

I asked Tracy Keegan whether she felt any anxiety about exposing her daughter's juvenilia to the world. 'Marina would have been mortified,' she said, half joking, 'but this is all we had to choose from. What has given me sparks of light in the darkness is the way people from all over the world have responded to [her graduation essay] 'The Opposite of Loneliness'. So many have contacted us to say its message has changed their lives. This encouraged us to push through this whole thing and get more of her words out there in the world.'

Marina Keegan, her mother said, 'was willing to put on paper her fears, hopes, insecurities, foibles, jealousies. She had courage. My daughter had courage in her writing.' And now she has many readers too.

(2014)

ENGLAND DREAMING:
GEORGE ORWELL

GEORGE ORWELL'S LUMINOUS gift was for seeing things, for noticing what others missed or simply found routine or uninteresting; for discovering meaning and wonder in the familiarity of the everyday. Matthew Arnold defined culture as 'the best which has been thought and said in the world'. But for Orwell culture meant something quite different – 'the life most people lead', as John Carey has put it. Orwell seldom distinguished between high and low culture. Nor was he a relativist: all things were not of equal value to him but they were potentially of equal interest. Little escaped or seemed beneath his notice, from boys' comics to the rituals of hop-picking, which was why he was such a good reporter.

There's a scene in *Nineteen Eighty-Four* (1949) in which Winston Smith, the troubled, isolated hero, is being forced to watch propaganda films. He is moved by something he sees in one of the broadcasts: a woman trying to protect a child by wrapping her arm around him as they are attacked from the air. It's a futile gesture. She cannot shield the boy or stop the bullets hitting them both, but she embraces him all the same – before, we are told,

'The helicopter blew them both to pieces.' For Winston, what Orwell calls the 'enveloping, protecting gesture' of the woman's arm symbolises something profoundly human – an expression of selflessness and of unconditional love in a hostile world.

Repeatedly in Orwell's fiction and non-fiction, one encounters moments of clarity such as this, when the reader is startled by something small but significant that the writer has revealed or noticed. One thinks in particular of Orwell's essay 'A Hanging'. Recalling his period as an imperial policeman in Burma, the writer describes looking on as a condemned man steps to avoid a puddle as he is led to the gallows. Why should he care about wet feet when he is about to die? But, Orwell writes: 'When I saw the prisoner step aside to avoid the puddle, I saw the mystery, the unspeakable wrongness, of cutting a life short when it is in full tide. This man was not dying, he was alive just as we are alive.'

One thinks too of the essay 'Shooting an Elephant', in which Orwell recalls the day he shot a rogue elephant and left it to die in agony, not because he wanted to or believed the act was just, but because he feared the derision of the villagers who were watching if he did not.

Seeing Things As They Are, edited by the veteran Orwell scholar Peter Davison, showcases none of the most famous essays but helpfully features lesser-known pieces and book reviews as well as some poems. It's full of interest and curiosities. I was particularly fascinated by 'Awake! Young Men of England', a jingoistic poem about the start of the First World War which Orwell wrote when he was eleven and was published in 1914 in the *Henley and South Oxfordshire Standard*.

Orwell did not have a private income, unlike his old friend and fellow Etonian Cyril Connolly, and his early career was scarred by rejection and hardship. From the mid-1930s until his death in 1950, he wrote compulsively. In the *New Statesman* archive I once discovered a handwritten note in the margins of a back issue in which one of Orwell's book reviews had been published: 'He is keen. Will do more.'

In an appendix, Davison estimates Orwell's earnings from the period 1922–45: when he died, his estate was valued at less than £10,000. Of his books only *Animal Farm* (1945) could be considered a commercial success, after which he complained: 'Everyone keeps coming at me, wanting me to lecture, to write commissioned booklets, to join this and that, etc – you don't know how I pine to be free of it all and have time to think again.'

Orwell lived by what he wrote in small magazines and weekly reviews: the short book or theatre review, the personal column (many of his 'As I Please' columns, in which he anatomised the rituals of English life for the left-wing Labour paper *Tribune* are collected here), the political essay, the eyewitness report, the BBC talk.

Orwell could see things but he could also see ahead, and the limpidity of his prose – he wanted to 'make political writing into an art' – could be explained by his desire to be understood, especially by the general reader.

Published during the Second World War, *The Lion and the Unicorn: Socialism and the English Genius* was Orwell's attempt to discover a new language of progressive patriotism. He denounces revolutionary leftist internationalism and rootless cosmopolitanism, and writes with respect about the patriotism of the ordinary man and woman. 'One cannot see the modern world as it is unless one recognises the overwhelming strength of patriotism, national loyalty. In certain circumstances it can break down, at certain levels of civilisation it does not exist, but as a positive force there is nothing to set beside it. Christianity and international socialism are as weak as straw in comparison with it.'

Orwell was writing in 1941, before the Americans had entered the war, when the British nation was isolated and imperilled. For Orwell, the nation was bound together by an invisible chain. 'At any normal time the ruling class will rob, mismanage, sabotage, lead us into the muck; but let popular opinion really make itself heard, let them get a tug from below that they cannot avoid feeling, and it is difficult for them not to respond.'

'Patriotism and intelligence will have to come together again,' he wrote in *The Lion and the Unicorn*, four years before what he desired became manifest in the landslide victory of Clement Attlee's Labour government. Patriotism and intelligence: the argument will have to be made all over again in our own age of bitter division and upheaval.

Orwell despised jargon. In his famous essay 'Politics and the English Language' he warned against the dangers of the 'inflated style' – against excessive stylistic ornamentation, long words, redundant or strained metaphor, ready-made formulation and use of the passive voice. He wanted to illuminate the times in which he lived – to show as well as tell, to report and discover rather than merely pontificate and condemn.

Both left and right have of course claimed him; the right because of his vigorous anti-totalitarianism, popularised in the late political fables *Animal Farm* and *Nineteen Eighty-Four*, and because he never ceased challenging the pieties of the left or those he contemptuously called the 'orthodoxy-sniffers'. In a 1941 review of Malcolm Muggeridge's *The Thirties*, he writes of the 'shallow self-righteousness of the left-wing intelligentsia'. He rails against those who, as he put it in an essay on Arthur Koestler not included in *Seeing Things*, 'have always wanted to be anti-fascist without being anti-totalitarian'.

Yet, I think, in spite of his pessimism and hatred of the

all-powerful bureaucratic state, Orwell remained of the left and for the left, even if he was also profoundly conservative in his respect for the traditions, codes, institutions and character of English life. As a young man, he was in his own self-description a 'Tory anarchist'; later he called himself a democratic socialist. And he instinctively sided with the outsider and the underdog.

Just as he rebelled against the expectations of his 'lower-upper-middle-class' background – St Cyprian's prep school, Eton, imperial life in Burma – so he refused to submit to the rigidities of doctrinal orthodoxy. No Guru, No Method, No Teacher is the title of a Van Morrison album. It could have been the title of the autobiography Orwell never wrote – except that it would have been too grandiose for his taste.

Some of Orwell's finest writing occurs towards the end of Homage to Catalonia (1938), his account of the betrayals he witnessed during the civil war in Spain when, like many other idealistic socialists, he joined the international resistance to Franco's fascists, only to be wounded in combat. During his months in Spain, Orwell was outraged by what he considered to be the treachery of the Soviet-backed communist government, which was persecuting and killing anarchists and members of the Marxist POUM militia, for whom he fought on the Aragon front.

In 1937 Orwell wrote an indictment of the communist government, which he denounced as a totalitarian, 'anti-revolutionary' force. He called it 'Eye-witness in Barcelona' and sent it to Kingsley Martin, the editor of the New Statesman, from whom he'd received early encouragement. It was rejected (but eventually published in New English Weekly as 'Spilling the Spanish Beans').

As a committed socialist, Martin was concerned that Orwell's report could have 'caused trouble' for the left: a case of you are either on our side or you're not. 'As a sop', says Davison, Orwell was asked to review a book about the civil war, *The Spanish Cockpit* by Franz Borkenau, which Martin also rejected, against the advice of his literary editor, Raymond Mortimer. Orwell was outraged and never forgave Martin, because he had allowed ideological sympathies to influence his editorial independence: Martin's was the 'corrupt face' of censorship.

Homage to Catalonia, which sold fewer than one thousand copies in his lifetime, ends with Orwell's return to England. Disillusioned by his experiences in Spain and with his hatred of revolutionary dictatorship hardening, he finds his home country to be reassuringly, seductively becalmed. The book's wonderful, long final paragraph – one of my favourite in all of Orwell – begins, 'And then England – southern England, probably the sleekest landscape in the world . . .'

The author discovers that 'down here' in Deep England it was still the country he had known in childhood – 'the railway-cuttings smothered in wild flowers, the deep meadows where the great shining horses browse and meditate', 'men in bowler hats and posters telling of cricket matches and Royal weddings', and so he goes on in characteristic style. However, something isn't quite right. The people are 'sleeping the deep, deep sleep of England', yet Orwell knows war is coming and that soon everyone will be 'jerked' awake by 'the roar of bombs', as in time they were.

It's often said the left seeks traitors and the right converts. In 1949, sick with pulmonary tuberculosis and with his judgment becoming increasingly erratic, Orwell compiled a list of 'crypto-communists and fellow travellers' for the International Research Department of the Foreign Office. Some of his acquaintances never forgave this small act of betrayal. On the list were two *New Statesman* editors, Kingsley Martin, whose editorship lasted from 1930–60, and Norman Mackenzie, who worked on the paper for twenty years and used to lunch with Orwell. (Also included was the super-patriot J. B. Priestley, author of *English Journey*.)

In a letter to a friend written on the day of Orwell's funeral, Frederic Warburg – who published *Animal Farm* after it had been repeatedly rejected – described it as one of the 'most melancholy occasions of my life'. Warburg said that 'English literature had suffered an irreparable loss'. He was correct: many have since aspired to write in the Orwellian tradition, most recently and notably Christopher Hitchens, but no English writer has his authority and moral clarity or his mastery of so many different forms: the essay, the parable, the book review, the narrative report. His loss was indeed irreparable.

'The great enemy of clear language is insincerity,' Orwell wrote. As a novelist, perhaps his style was too plain and his realism too simple, even sentimental. As a journalist, when he wasn't reporting, he could be priggish. He was not always right – it was foolish to have drawn up his list of crypto-communists and fellow travellers, for instance – but he was sincere in his commitment to truth-telling, even at the expense of making enemies of former friends, as he did of H. G. Wells.

George Orwell was a radical and a conservative, an English patriot and an English rebel. He disliked imperialism and all forms of tyranny, from the boarding school bully to the Stalinist apparatchik. He was an empiricist, not an ideologue. And he was a moralist who wrote of the world as he found it not as he wished it to be. He celebrated the English character and English civic life as something worth conserving. And he never ceased writing well or loving his country. He was dead at the age of forty-six, yet his influence and example grow more radiant with each passing year.

(2014)

THE LOST BOY:
HANGING ON IN QUIET
DESPERATION IS THE
ENGLISH WAY

O NE AUGUST DAY while on holiday in Cornwall in 1978, Richard Beard, who was eleven, and his younger brother Nicholas, slipped away from their parents for one last swim. They left 'the broad stretch of beach' where the family had set up camp and clambered over rocks until they came to an isolated cove. The boys were boarders at the same Berkshire prep school and they had a fractious and rivalrous relationship, as many brothers do. Together they waded into the sea, but soon the nine-year-old Nicholas (or Nicky, as he was known, the third of four brothers) was in trouble, having been carried out of his depth. Richard was also struggling in the water and was forced to make a decision: should he save himself or try to save his brother? 'I couldn't reach him and I didn't want to go in deeper,' Beard writes in his memoir *The Day That Went Missing*. He is haunted by a final image of his drowning brother, 'his head back, ligaments straining in his neck, his mouth in a tight line to keep out the seawater'.

The Beards went home to Swindon after Nicky's death. There was a funeral, and then they did something astonishing: they returned to the cottage in Cornwall to resume their holiday, *as if nothing had happened*. The family had entered a frozen state of denial: Nicky became the great unmentionable in the family, mourned silently but never spoken about. The dates of his life and death were absent from his gravestone. Richard Beard told me that, after Nicky was buried, his parents never again had a conversation about their dead son.

The Day That Went Missing is a book about a family tragedy that has the momentum of a well-constructed detective novel as, all these years later, the middle-aged author attempts to piece together the shattered fragments of his brother's story, in life and in death. It also has something of the mystery and intrigue of a metaphysical quest, since it is an attempt to capture the essence of someone long dead.

Beard knew what happened that day in Cornwall – he was in the sea with Nicky – but, because of the family's self-imposed silence, he did not know how it happened or quite who was there with them in the extended group on the beach, or why his parents responded as they did. He knew none of this because his parents were in denial and would not discuss it, and also because he had forgotten so much, or chosen to forget.

Beard felt able to approach the subject only after his father died in 2011. He began searching through his father's papers for references to or information about Nicky. He interrogated his mother and two brothers. Beard read Nicky's reports and the letters he'd sent home from prep school, and he studied photographs of his brother, including those taken on the beach in the final hours of his life.

As part of his investigation, Beard returned repeatedly to Cornwall to visit the cottage where the family had stayed on that long-ago holiday and to find the beach where the tragedy happened. One day as he made his way down a cliff path to the actual beach, he began to weep uncontrollably – not only for his lost brother, but also for the waste of all the long decades during which Nicky had been erased from their lives.

Written in pellucid prose and artfully constructed, *The Day That Went Missing* is never sentimental or self-pitying and is all the more moving as a consequence. There is self-reproach, sarcasm, bitterness and anger, and Beard is especially tough on his father, a self-made builder (he described the family as 'arriviste or nouveau riche' when we met) who, in later life, became withdrawn and drank heavily.

Beard later attended Radley, one of the grandest boys' boarding schools in England, but did not feel comfortable there and said he had not spoken to any of his classmates since the day he left. At times, in the book, it's as if he is indicting an entire class of repressed, boarding-school-educated Englishmen – you could say, as Pink Floyd did in 'Time', that 'Hanging on in quiet desperation is the English way'.

It was 'awkward' when Beard first began questioning his mother about her dead son. 'But she was also relieved,' he said. 'More than that, she was happy that someone was taking an interest. He was, after all, a child of hers who had lived to nine years old and who had effectively been deleted during this refusal to talk about him . . . She has read the final book and is very proud of it. She has also said how much time we have wasted by not thinking about Nicky, not allowing him to exist.'

I asked Beard whether he had consciously not used the word 'love' in the book. He seemed surprised. That evening I received an email from him: 'I did the wordsearch, and there are instances of love as a descriptive verb (intensifying 'like') and of 'lovely', so I'm not a total monster. However, I'd say there are only two genuine uses, one on page eighty, regretting the absence of love from the letter-writing home from school, and one at the very end – when I realise I want to run towards the people I love on the beach. Otherwise your hunch is justified, and a little disconcerting.'

He need not be disconcerted – because the book he has written is itself an act of retrieval but also love which honours and memorialises the brother he lost so traumatically. As you read the final paragraph – in which Richard Beard describes placing the manuscript of the book inside a trunk among Nicky's belongings, including his school cap and his blue cricket hat – you're reminded of the final, beautiful lines of Philip Larkin's 'An Arundel Tomb':

> Our almost-instinct almost true:
> What will survive of us is love.

(2017)

AN INNOVATOR IN OLD
AGE: ARSÈNE WENGER

HOW TO ACCOUNT for the essence of a football club? The players and managers come and go, of course, and so do the owners. The fans lose interest or grow old and die. Clubs relocate to new grounds. Arsenal did so in the summer of 2006 when they moved from the intimate jewel of a stadium that was Highbury to embrace the soulless corporate gigantism of the Emirates. Clubs can even relocate to a new town or to a different part of a city, as indeed Arsenal also did when they moved from south of the Thames to north London in 1913 (a land-grab that has never been forgiven by their fiercest rivals, Tottenham). Yet something endures through all the change, something akin to the Aristotelian notion of substance.

Before Arsène Wenger arrived in London in late September 1996, Arsenal were one of England's most traditional clubs: stately, conservative, even staid. Three generations of the Hill-Wood family had occupied the role of chairman. In 1983, an ambitious young London businessman and ardent fan named David Dein invested £290,000 in the club. 'It's dead money,' said Peter Hill-Wood, an Old Etonian who had succeeded his father a year earlier.

In 2007, Dein sold his stake in the club to Red & White Holdings, co-owned by the Uzbek-born billionaire Alisher Usmanov, for £75m. Not so dead after all.

In the pre-Wenger years, unfairly or otherwise, the Gunners were known as 'lucky Arsenal', a pejorative nickname that went back to the 1930s. For better or worse, they were associated with a functional style of play. Under George Graham, manager from 1986 to 1995, they were exponents of a muscular, sometimes brutal-ist, long-ball game and often won important matches 1–0. Through long decades of middling success, Arsenal were respected but never loved, except by their fans, who could be passionless when compared to, say, those of Liverpool or Newcastle, or even the cockneys of West Ham.

Yet Wenger, who was born in October 1949, changed everything at Arsenal. This tall, thin, cerebral, polyglot son of an Alsatian bistro owner, who had an economics degree and was a mediocre player in the French leagues, was English football's first true cosmopolitan.

He was naturally received with suspicion by the British and Irish players he inherited (who called him Le Professeur), the fans (most of whom had never heard of him) and by journalists (who were used to clubbable British managers they could banter with over a drink). Wenger was different. He was reserved and self-con-tained. He refused to give personal interviews, though he was candid and courteous in press conferences, during which he often revealed his sly sense of humour.

He joined from the Japanese J League side, Nagoya Grampus Eight, where he went to coach after seven seasons at Monaco, and was determined to globalise the Gunners. This he did swiftly, recruiting players from all over the world but most notably, in his early years, from France and francophone Africa. I was once told a story of how, not long after joining the club, Wenger instructed his chief scout, Steve Rowley, to watch a particular player. 'You'll need to travel,' Wenger said. 'Up north?' 'No - to Brazil,' came the reply. A new era had begun.

Wenger was an innovator and disrupter long before such concepts became fashionable. A pioneer in using data analysis to monitor and improve performance, he ended the culture of heavy drinking at Arsenal and introduced dietary controls and a strict fitness regime. He was idealistic but also pragmatic. Retaining Graham's all-English back five, as well as the hard-running Ray Parlour in midfield, Wenger over several seasons added French flair to the team - Nicolas Anelka (who was bought for £500,000 and sold at a £22m profit after only two seasons), Thierry Henry, Patrick Vieira, Robert Pirès. It would be a period of glorious transformation - Arsenal won the Premier League and FA Cup 'double' in his first full season and went through the entire 2003–04 league campaign unbeaten, the season of the so-called Invincibles.

The second decade of Wenger's long tenure at Arsenal, during which the club stopped winning titles after moving to the bespoke sixty thousand capacity Emirates Stadium, was much more troubled. Beginning with the arrival of the Russian oligarch Roman Abramovich in 2003, the international plutocracy began to take over the Premier League, and clubs such as Chelsea and Manchester City, much richer than Arsenal, spent their way to the top table of the European game. What were once competitive advantages for Wenger - knowledge of other leagues and markets, a worldwide scouting network, sports science - became routine, replicated even, in the lower leagues.

Wenger has spoken of his fear of death and of his desire to lose himself in work, always work. 'The only possible moment of happiness is the present,' he told *L'Équipe* in a 2016 interview. 'The past gives you regrets. And the future uncertainties. Man understood this very fast and created religion.' At such moments he can sound like the stoic philosopher Marcus Aurelius. In the same interview – perhaps his most fascinating – Wenger described himself as a facilitator who enables 'others to express what they have within them'. He yearns for his teams to play beautifully. 'My never-ending struggle in this business is to release what is beautiful in man.'

Arsène Wenger is in the last year of his contract and fans are divided over whether he should stay on. To manage a super-club such as Arsenal for twenty years is remarkable and, even if he chooses to say farewell at the end of the season, it is most unlikely that any one manager will ever again stay so long or achieve so much at such a club – indeed, at any club. We should savour his cool intelligence and subtle humour while we can. Wenger changed football in England. More than a facilitator, he was a pathfinder: he created space and opportunities for all those foreign coaches who followed him and adopted his methods as the Premier League became the richest and most watched in the world: one of the purest expressions of let-it-rip, winner-takes-all free-market globalisation, a symbol of deracinated cosmopolitanism, the global game's truly global league.

(2017)

POSTSCRIPT

To the frustration of many Arsenal fans, Arsène Wenger signed a new two-year contract in the summer of 2017. He should not have – and, after another difficult period, he announced on 20 April 2018 that he would finally leave Arsenal at the end of the season, his departure hastened by a board of directors who had lost faith in his methods. Late-era Wenger was defined by disappointment and unrest. And the mood at the Emirates Stadium on match day was often sour: fans in open revolt against Wenger, against the club's absentee American majority shareholder Stan Kroenke, against the chief executive Ivan Gazidis, and sometimes even against one another, with clashes between pro- and anti-Wenger factions. As Arsenal's form became ever more erratic, Wenger spoke often of how much he suffered. 'There is no possibility not to suffer,' he said in March 2018. 'You have to suffer.'

The younger Wenger excelled at discovering and nurturing outstanding young players, especially in his early seasons in north London. But that was a long time ago. Under his leadership, Arsenal became predictable in their vulnerability and inflexibility, doomed to keep repeating the same mistakes, especially defensive mistakes. They invariably faltered when confronted by the strongest opponents, the Manchester clubs, say, or one of the European super-clubs such as Bayern Munich or Barcelona.

Wenger's late struggles were a symbol of all that had gone wrong at Arsenal. The vitriol and abuse directed at this proud man was, however, often painful to behold.

How had it come to this? Wenger suffered from wilful blindness. He could not see, or stubbornly refused to see, what others could: that he had become a man out of time who had been surpassed by a new generation of innovators such as Pep Guardiola and Tottenham's Mauricio Pochettino. 'In Arsène we trust'? Not anymore. He had stayed too long. In the words of football writer Simon Kuper, Wenger shows that no one can be a pioneer twice. Sometimes the thing you love most ends up killing you.

NATIONAL NOVELIST:
IAN MCEWAN

THE ATTACKS ON New York and Washington, DC on 11 September 2001, so extreme and audacious, left many of us silenced: the horror of what had happened seemed beyond articulation. These events were 'unimaginable' and 'unspeakable', it was said. But Ian McEwan, writing on 12 September in the *Guardian*, offered a swift and articulate narrative response to this world-historical shock. Three days later, he published another article. He had been thinking about those passengers on the hijacked airliners who, confronted by the certainty of their own deaths, had in their final desperation used their mobile phones to call loved ones. 'A new technology has shown us an ancient, human universal . . . There was really only one thing for her to say, those three words that all the terrible art, the worst pop songs and movies, the most seductive lies, can somehow never cheapen. I love you . . . There is only love, and then oblivion. Love was all they had to set against the hatred of their murderers.'

Perhaps the gravest failure of the hijackers, McEwan wrote, was that of imagination: a failure to imagine how it must have been to be a prisoner on one of the doomed planes. 'Imagining what it is like to be someone other than yourself is at the core of our humanity. It is the essence of compassion, and it is the beginning of morality.'

On Friday 8 July 2005, the morning after the jihadist attacks on London (the so-called 7/7 suicide attacks), McEwan reported from the bomb-shattered streets in and around Bloomsbury, London. He wrote with clarity and imagination and empathy about what had happened and what he thought it meant. What we were witnessing here was nothing less than the emergence of McEwan as the closest thing we have to a national novelist: the bestselling literary author who, because of his continuous, imaginative engagement with the people and events creating the history of our era, aspires to speak to and for the nation at times of shared crisis and stress. How had he come to occupy such an exalted position of public influence?

One June evening in 1988, as the high tide of Thatcherism broke across the country, a group of writers and intellectuals gathered at Harold Pinter and Lady Antonia Fraser's grand house in Campden Hill Square, Holland Park, west London. They were there to discuss how best to respond to the hegemony of the Thatcher government. The response to the creation of this 'informal discussion group' was derisive, notably from the *Sunday Times*: what did these preposterous *bien-pensants* really know about politics and the condition of England?

Among those present that evening was the young McEwan, in the process of reinventing himself as a writer. Since the publication of his debut collection of stories, *First Love, Last Rites* (1975), he had seemed to be more a chronicler of personal obsession than a writer of public engagement: the disturbed, isolated, amoral protagonists of his early fictions pursued their fantasies with vigour: killing, maiming, bullying, masturbating.

So seemingly devoid of redemptive impulses were these early fictions that reading them felt almost like an act of voyeurism. McEwan appeared to have no love for his characters; instead, he dissected them. Here was, as John Updike said of Martin Amis in a different context, 'an atrocity-minded author' – but one with a clinical and fastidious prose style.

The early McEwan was no pornographer: he already wrote too well, his intentions were too serious, and his fictions, despite their splatter effects, were really about the disturbed imagination and about power – the power parents have over children, a brother has over a sister, a man over a woman, and the state has over the individual. Many of these early stories, which he wrote under the guidance of Malcolm Bradbury as the first student of creative writing at the University of East Anglia (UEA), were experiments in form: the interior monologue, the fractured or unreliable confession. Yet those stories, with their insistent linking of sex with death, were mostly chilling. Love was absent from them, as if their very bleakness were an expression of an entire, despairing world-view.

McEwan's cruellest book, the one in which the violence can seem most gratuitous and nasty, is *The Comfort of Strangers* (1981). It's a novella about a young British couple who are on a trip to an autumnal Venice, which McEwan portrays as a city of shadows and fear. It marked a point of transition for him as a writer; he has spoken of having 'written himself into a corner': after this, and a long period of silence, he returned as a different writer. The instinct for cruelty remained but it was mitigated by a much deeper, more sophisticated, even feminine, moral and aesthetic sensibility. From *The Child in Time* (1987) onwards, he was less a postmodernist than an emerging realist, with a nineteenth-century interest in character, agency and storytelling, in what can be called the human predicament. He had a modernist's concern with consciousness, and began to experiment with different ways of representing it. In his long novel *Atonement* (2001), a character called Bryony writes fiction in which she seeks 'to show separate minds, as alive as her own, struggling with the idea that other minds were equally alive'.

McEwan was now writing from inside out: thought determined action, and there was a new descriptive density to his writing (he is a great admirer of Updike). Where once he had compressed, he now expanded and inflated. He was no longer a miniaturist, and yet he was still a writer of intense, self-contained set-pieces. Long before 11 September 2001, he created whole novels out of moments of sudden terror: the disappearance or kidnapping of a child from a supermarket (*The Child in Time*, 1987), a scene of such exquisite panic that it would torment any parent who read it; a balloon crash-landing in a field in Oxfordshire (*Enduring Love*, 1997); or the malicious allegations of a little girl, in an England caught uneasily between two world wars, that condemn an innocent man to imprisonment and perpetual separation from the woman he loves.

McEwan's fiction can be too tidy and schematic, too over-determined. Yet what unifies his work is a preoccupation with the randomness of human endeavour in a post-religious, Darwinian world: his novels invariably turn on one sudden, unaccountable, life-changing event or moment of fatal equivocation.

Born in Aldershot in 1948, the son of a middle-ranking Scottish soldier, McEwan grew up in North Africa and Singapore, where his father was posted. He later attended a state-run military boarding school in Ipswich, Suffolk, where, as he has said, he felt permanently cold, hungry and alone. From there, he went to Sussex University and then, after following the hippie trail in North Africa, he moved to Norwich to work with Bradbury at UEA. 'I arrived in this lovely foreign town [Norwich], took a room and had a meeting every three or four weeks with Malcolm,' McEwan once told me over breakfast in a quiet upstairs room of a pub in Primrose Hill, north London. 'He offered no strictures and showed no shock at the content of my stories. He was remarkably tolerant. It was a great piece of luck; having a reader with no egotistical wish to shape me to some preconceived end meant that I was free to find my own voice.'

Shortly before the American-led invasion of Iraq, McEwan wrote an article for the openDemocracy website in which he expressed his ambivalence about the threatened conflict. Compared to the often strident and bellicose certainties of those arguing either for or against the war, his commentary was restrained and uncertain. 'The hawks,' he wrote, 'have my head, the doves my heart. At a push I count myself – just – in the camp of the latter. And yet my ambivalence remains . . . One can only hope now for the best outcome: that the regime, like all dictatorships, rootless in the affections of its people, will crumble like a rotten tooth; that the federal, democratic Iraq that the Iraqi National Congress committed itself to at its conference can be helped into existence by the UN, and that the US, in the flush of victory, will find in its oilman's heart the energy and optimism to begin to address the Palestinian issue. These are fragile hopes. As things stand, it is easier to conceive of innumerable darker possibilities.'

In January 2005 McEwan published his long-deliberated fictional response to the attacks of 11 September 2001 and the wars that followed: *Saturday*, perhaps the most discussed and debated literary novel of recent times, and exploring innumerable darker possibilities. It is set on a single day – 15 February 2003, when more than two million people marched in London in opposition to war in Iraq – and is told exclusively from the point of view of one man, Henry Perowne, a forty-eight-year-old neurosurgeon. So, the novel, as well as being a political text, is an attempt over a single day to represent what Virginia Woolf called 'the quick of the mind'.

Perowne, like McEwan, lives a comfortable life in central London. He loves his wife and is the father of two well-adjusted young adults, one a published poet (by Faber, no less), the other a promising blues musician. There the similarities end: Perowne, though intelligent, is resolutely unliterary. He cannot understand the impulses of the artistic mind: he is a scientific reductionist. He strips and reduces human behaviour to its biological essentials. 'There is much in human affairs that can be accounted for at the level of the complex molecule,' he suggests.

Yet out on the inner-city streets and beyond in our interconnected, globalised world are true dangers and little control: not everyone is as rational as Perowne, or thinks as he does. He encounters one such person when, on his way to play squash, his car collides with another driven by an aggressive thug called Baxter. There follows a menacing confrontation. Baxter, who Perowne immediately (and perhaps too conveniently) understands has a degenerative brain disorder, believes that he has been humiliated. Later, Baxter returns, violently, to confront Perowne at home, where he is preparing for a family dinner, with brutal and then surprising consequences.

McEwan is a determined binarist: what continues to interest him are stark dichotomies, the clash and interplay of stable oppositions. Repeatedly in his fiction he sets reason against unreason, science against art, the mind against the body, technology against nature. He has spent much of his writing life conjuring up some of the darkest possibilities in contemporary fiction. Yet *Saturday* is his most fearful novel so far, perhaps because it is also his fullest expression of the war-shadowed times in which we live. It is a novel suffused with anxiety – about the conflict in Iraq and its likely consequences – but also with a sense of how increasingly vulnerable we are in our terrorist-threatened cities, where suicide bombers can strike at any time and anywhere . . . and do. To read this novel – indeed, to read most of McEwan's fiction alongside his journalism, as I like to do – is to discover, as Shakespeare wrote of Hamlet, a writer who seeks 'to show . . . the very age and body of the time his form and pressure'. He is our national novelist.

(2005)

POSTSCRIPT

On the evening of Margaret Thatcher's death in April 2013, BBC Two broadcast a special edition of Newsnight. The novelist chosen to participate in a discussion about her life and legacy, via satellite from New York, was Martin Amis. Like Thatcher, his career-defining work was done in the 1980s, and on Newsnight he recycled old jokes and riffed on the names of some of those who served under Thatcher – 'the Keiths, Normans and Cecils'. It was an amusing cameo but no more than that: it was striking that Amis, once such a perceptive cultural critic, had little that was original or notable to contribute. McEwan would have been a better guest.

Barbara Kingsolver has said literature 'doesn't tell you what you think. It asks what you think.' But perhaps it is not a question of either/or. Perhaps a better definition of the engaged political novelist is one who simultaneously asks questions of the society in which they live and tells important truths about it. After the London bombings of July 2005, I described McEwan as being the closest thing we had to a national novelist. The phrase resonated: it is now how he is routinely described when he is profiled in the

New York Times, the *New Yorker*, the *Sunday Times*, the *Financial Times*, and so on.

What I continue to like about McEwan is that he is interested in politics, not as an activist or controversialist, but in the broadest sense. It was no surprise that he should write one of the more thoughtful reflections about Margaret Thatcher after her death. In the 1980s McEwan was one of a group of literary writers in London – others included Salman Rushdie, Angela Carter, Harold Pinter and Hanif Kureishi – who were radicalised by Thatcherism. They loathed and scorned the woman who won three general elections while, I believe, never really attempting to understand what she represented or the consensus-breaking forces she unleashed. As the New Left thinker Stuart Hall explained, 'When I saw Thatcherism, I realised that it wasn't just an economic programme, but that it had profound cultural roots. Thatcher and [Enoch] Powell were both what Hegel called 'historical individuals' – their very politics, their contradictions, instance or concretise in one life or career much wider forces that are in play.'

In Rushdie's *Satanic Verses* (1988), Thatcher is caricatured as 'Mrs Torture'. In McEwan's *The Child in Time* (1987), she is not named, but the novel's repulsive, domineering female prime minister, whose voice is 'pitched somewhere between a tenor's and an alto's', is obviously influenced by her. But now, in late middle age and after her death, McEwan could write more reflectively about Thatcher: 'She forced us to decide what was truly important . . . Her effect was to force a deeper consideration of priorities.' A deeper consideration of priorities: an admirable task for a novelist.

THE LOST MAGIC OF
ENGLAND: PEREGRINE
WORSTHORNE

O NE MORNING OUR subscriptions manager happened
to mention that Peregrine Worsthorne was still a *New
Statesman* subscriber. A former editor of the *Sunday Telegraph* and,
during a long Fleet Street career, a self-styled 'romantic reactionary'
scourge of liberals and liberalism, Worsthorne used to be something
of a pantomime villain for the left, a role he delighted in. He had
close friends among the 'Peterhouse right', the group of High Tory
intellectuals who gathered around Maurice Cowling at the small,
conspiratorial Cambridge college. He was a frequent contributor
to *Encounter* (which turned out to be funded by the CIA) and an
ardent Cold Warrior. His social conservatism and lofty affectations
offended lefty Islingtonian sensibilities. On several occasions, he
was the *Guardian's* reviewer of choice for its annual collection of
journalism, *The Bedside Guardian*, and he invariably delivered the
required scornful appraisal. There is no suggestion, he wrote in 1981,
that the '*Guardian* ever sees itself as part of the problem; itself as
having some responsibility for the evils its writers described so well'.

His prose style was more Walter Pater than George Orwell. It was essential not to take Worsthorne too seriously, because he delighted in mischief-making and wilful provocation – one of his targets for remorseless ridicule was Andrew Neil, when Neil edited the abrasively Thatcherite *Sunday Times*. He ended up suing Worsthorne, who was famous for his silk shirts and Garrick Club lunches, for libel; Neil was awarded damages of £1, the then cover price of the *Sunday Times*.

'I wrote that in the old days, editors of distinguished Sunday papers could be found dining at All Souls, and something must have changed when they're caught with their trousers down in a nightclub,' Worsthorne told me when I visited him at home. 'I had no idea he was going to sue. I was teasing. I occasionally run into him and we smile at each other, so it's all forgotten and forgiven.'

After his retirement in 1989, Worsthorne seemed to mellow, and even mischievously suggested that the *Guardian* had replaced the *Times* as the newspaper of record. In the 1990s he began writing occasionally for the *New Statesman* – the then literary editor, Peter Wilby, commissioned book reviews from him, as I did after I succeeded Wilby. Like most journalists of his generation, Worsthorne was a joy to work with; he wrote to length, delivered his copy on time and was never precious about being edited. (Bill Deedes and Tony Howard were the same.) He might have had the mannerisms of an old-style toff, but he was also a tradesman who understood that journalism was a trade.

Shortly before Christmas, I rang Worsthorne at the home in Buckinghamshire he shares with his second wife, Lucinda Lambton, the architectural writer. I asked how he was. 'I'm like a squeezed lemon: all used up,' he said. Lucy described him as being 'frail but not ill'. I told him that I would visit, so one morning I did. Home is a Grade II-listed old rectory in the village of Hedgerley. It is grand but dishevelled and eccentrically furnished.

A sign on the main gates warns you to 'Beware of the Dog'. But the dog turns out to be blind and moves around the house uneasily, poignantly bumping into objects and walls. At lunch, a small replica mosque in the dining room issues repeated mechanised calls to prayer. 'Why does it keep doing that?' Perry asks. 'Isn't it fun?' Lucy says. She then turns to me: 'Have some more duck pâté.'

As a student, I used to read Worsthorne's columns and essays with pleasure. I did not share his positions and prejudices but I admired the style in which he articulated them. 'The job of journalism is not to be scholarly,' he wrote in 1989. 'The most that can be achieved by an individual newspaper or journalist is the articulation of an intelligent, well-thought-out, coherent set of prejudices – i.e., a moral position.'

His *Sunday Telegraph*, which he edited from 1986 to 1989, was like no other newspaper of the era. The recondite and reactionary comment pages (the focus of his energies) were unapologetically High Tory, contrary to the prevailing Thatcherite orthodoxies, but were mostly well written and historically literate. Bruce Anderson was one of the columnists. 'You never knew what you were going to get when you opened the paper,' he told me. 'Perry was a dandy, a popinjay, and of course he didn't lack self-esteem. He had a nostalgia for Young England. In all the time I wrote for him, however, I never took his approval for granted. I always felt a tightening of the stomach muscles when I showed him something.'

⁂

Worsthorne is ninety-two now and, though his memory is failing, he remains an engaging conversationalist. Moving slowly, in short, shuffling steps, he has a long beard and retains a certain dandyish glamour. His silver hair is swept back from a high, smooth forehead. He remains a resolute defender of the aristocracy – 'Superiority is a dread word, but we are in very short supply of superiority because no one likes the word' – but the old hauteur has gone, replaced by humility and a kind of wonder and bafflement that he has endured so long and seen so much: a journalistic Lear, but one who is not out on the heath raging against the dying of the light.

On arrival, I am shown through to the drawing room, where Perry sits quietly near an open fire, a copy of that morning's *Times* before him. He moves to a corner armchair and passes me a copy of his book *Democracy Needs Aristocracy* (2005). 'It's all in there,' he says. 'I've always thought the English aristocracy so marvellous compared to other ruling classes. It seemed to me that we had got a ruling class of such extraordinary historical excellence, which is rooted in England almost since the Norman Conquest.

'Just read the eighteenth-century speeches – the great period – they're all Whig or Tory, but all come from that [the aristocracy]. If they didn't come directly from the aristocracy, they turned themselves very quickly into people who talk in its language. Poetic. If you read Burke, who's the best in my view, it's difficult not to be tempted to think what he says has a lot of truth in it . . .'

His voice fades. He has lost his way and asks what we were talking about. 'Oh, yes,' he says. 'It survived when others – the French and Russians and so on – were having revolutions. It was absolutely crazy to set about destroying that. There was something magical . . . the parliamentary speeches made by Burke and so on – this is a miracle! No other country has it apart from America in the early days. And I thought to get rid of it, to undermine it, was a mistake.'

I ask how exactly the aristocracy was undermined. Even today, because of the concentration of the ownership of so much land among so few and because of the enduring influence of the old families, the great schools and Oxbridge, Britain remains a peculiar hybrid: part populist hyper-democracy, and part quasi-feudal state. The Tory benches in the Commons are no longer occupied by aristocrats, but the old class structures endure.

'Equality was the order of the day after the war,' Worsthorne replies. 'And in a way, it did a lot of good, equalising people's chances in the world. But it didn't really get anywhere; the ruling class went happily on. But slowly, and I think unnecessarily dangerously, it was destroyed – and now there are no superior people around [in politics]. The Cecil family – Lord Salisbury, he was chucked out of politics. The Cecil family is being told they are not wanted. The institutions are falling apart . . .

'But there were people who had natural authority, like Denis Healey. I'm not saying it's only aristocrats – a lot of Labour people had it. But now we haven't got any Denis Healeys.'

Born in 1923, the younger son of Alexander Koch de Gooreynd, a Belgian banker, Worsthorne (the family anglicised its name) was educated at Stowe and was an undergraduate at both Cambridge (Peterhouse, where he studied under the historian Herbert Butterfield, the author of *The Whig Interpretation of History*) and Oxford (Magdalen College). 'I have always felt slightly underprivileged and de-classed by having gone to Stowe, unlike my father who went to Eton,' Worsthorne wrote in 1985.

Yet his memories of Stowe remain pellucid. There he was taught by the belletrist John Davenport, who later became a friend of Dylan Thomas. 'He was a marvellous man, a famous intellectual of the 1930s, an ex-boxer, too. But in the war he came to Stowe and he was preparing me for a scholarship to Cambridge. He told me to read three books, and find something to alleviate the boredom of an examiner, some little thing you'll pick up. And I duly did and got the scholarship.'

Can you remember which three books he recommended?

'Tawney. Something by Connolly, um . . . that's the terrible thing about getting old, extremely old - you forget. And by the time you die you can't remember your brother's name. It's a terrible shock. I used to think old age could be a joy because you'd have more time to read. But if you push your luck and get too far, and last too long, you start finding reading really quite difficult. The connections go, I suppose.'

Was the Connolly book *Enemies of Promise* (1938)?

'Yes, that's right. It was. And the other one was . . . Hang on, the writer of the book . . . What's the country invaded by Russia, next to Russia?'

Finland, I say. Edmund Wilson's *To the Finland Station* (1940)?

'Yes. Wilson. How did you get that?'

We both laugh.

Worsthorne is saddened but not surprised that so many Scots voted for independence and his preference is for Britain to remain a member of the European Union. 'What's happening is part of the hopelessness of English politics. It's horrible. I can't think why the Scots would want to be on their own but it might happen. The youth will vote [for independence]. This is part of my central theme: the Scots no longer think it's worthwhile belonging to [sic] England. The magic of England has gone - and it's the perversity of the Tory party to want to get us out of the European Union when of course we're much more than ever unlikely to be able to look after ourselves as an independent state because of the quality of our political system.

'The people who want to get us out are obviously of an undesirable kind. That the future should depend on [Nigel] Farage is part of the sickness. I mean the real horror is for him to have any influence at all. And when you think of the great days of the

Labour Party, the giants who strode the stage – famous, lasting historical figures, some of them: Healey, Attlee, who was probably the greatest, [Ernest] Bevin. I'm well aware that Labour in the good days produced people who were superior.'

He digresses to reflect on his wartime experience as a soldier – he served in Phantom, the special reconnaissance unit, alongside Michael Oakeshott, the philosopher of English conservatism who became a good friend, and the actor David Niven, their 'prize colleague'.

'I remember Harold Macmillan saying to me, after the Second World War, the British people needed their belt enlarged; they'd done their job and they deserved a reward. And that's what he set about doing. And he wasn't a right-wing, unsympathetic man at all. But he didn't – and this is what is good about conservatism – he didn't turn it into an 'ism'. It was a sympathetic feel, an instinctive feel, and of course people in the trenches felt it, too: solidarity with the rest of England and not just their own brotherhood. Of course, he didn't get on with Margaret Thatcher at all.'

Worsthorne admired Thatcher and believed that the 'Conservatives required a dictator woman' to shake things up, though he was not a Thatcherite and denounced what he called her 'bourgeois triumphalism'. He expresses regret at how the miners were treated during the strike of 1984–85. 'I quarrelled with her about the miners' strike, and the people she got around her to conduct it were a pretty ropey lot.

'I liked her as a person. I was with her that last night when she wasn't prime minister any more, but she was still in Downing Street and had everything cut off. The pressman [Bernard Ingham] got several of us to try to take her mind off her miseries that night. There's a photograph of me standing at the top of the stairs.'

In the summer of 1989, Peregrine Worsthorne was sacked as the editor of the *Sunday Telegraph* by Andrew Knight, a former journalist turned management enforcer, over breakfast at Claridge's. He wrote about the experience in an elegant diary for the *Spectator*: 'I remember well the exact moment when this thunderbolt, coming out of a blue sky, hit me. It was when the waiter had just served two perfectly poached eggs on buttered toast . . . In my mind I knew that the information just imparted was a paralysingly painful blow: pretty well a professional death sentence.'

He no longer reads the *Telegraph*.

'Politically they don't have much to say of interest. But I can't put the finger on exactly what it is I don't like about it. Boredom, I think!'

You must read Charles Moore?

'He is my favourite. Interesting fellow. He converted to Catholicism and started riding to hounds in the same week.'

He has no regrets about pursuing a long career in journalism rather than, say, as a full-time writer or academic, like his friends Cowling and Oakeshott. 'I was incredibly lucky to do journalism. What people don't realise – and perhaps you don't agree – but it's really a very easy life, compared to many others. And you have good company in other journalists and so on. I was an apprentice on the *Times*, after working [as a sub-editor] on the *Glasgow Herald*.'

How does he spend the days?

'Living, I suppose. It takes an hour to get dressed because all the muscles go. Then I read the *Times* and get bored with it halfway through. Then there's a meal to eat. The answer is, the days go. I used to go for walks but I can't do that now. But Lucy's getting me all kinds of instruments to facilitate people with no muscles, to help you walk. I'm very sceptical about it working, but then again, better than the alternative.'

He does not read as much as he would wish. He takes the

Statesman, the *Spectator* and the *Times* but no longer the *Guardian*. He is reading Niall Ferguson's biography of Kissinger; *The Maisky Diaries* by Ivan Maisky, Stalin's ambassador to London from 1932 to 1943; and *Living on Paper*, a selection of letters by Iris Murdoch, whom he knew. 'I get these massive books, thinking of a rainy day, but once I pick them up they are too heavy, physically, so they're stacked up, begging to be read.'

He watches television – the news (we speak about ISIS and the Syrian tragedy), the Marr show on Sunday mornings, and he has been enjoying *War and Peace* on BBC One. 'Andrew Marr gave my book a very good review. He's come back. He's survived [a stroke] through a degree of hard willpower to get back to that job, almost as soon as he came out of surgery. But I don't know him; he was a *Guardian* man.' (In fact, Marr is more closely associated with the *Independent*.)

Of the celebrated Peterhouse historians, both Herbert Butterfield (who was a Methodist) and Maurice Cowling were devout Christians. For High Tories, who believe in and accept natural inequalities and the organic theory of society, Christianity was a binding force that held together all social classes, as some believe was the order in late-Victorian England.

'I was a very hardened Catholic,' Worsthorne says, when I mention Cowling's book *Religion and Public Doctrine in Modern England*. 'My mother was divorced [her second marriage was to Montagu Norman, then the governor of the Bank of England] and she didn't want my brother and me to be Catholic, so she sent us to Stowe. And I used to annoy her because I read [Hilaire] Belloc. I tried to annoy the history master teaching us Queen Elizabeth I. I said to him: 'Are you covering up on her behalf: don't you know she had syphilis?'

'Once I felt very angry about not being made Catholic. But then I went to Cambridge and there was a very Catholic chaplain and he was very snobbish. And in confession I had to tell him I masturbated twice that morning or something, and so it embarrassed me when half an hour later I had to sit next to him at breakfast. I literally gave up going to Mass to get out of this embarrassing situation. But recently I've started again. I haven't actually gone to church but I've made my confessions, to a friendly bishop who came to the house.'

You *are* a believer?

'Yes. I don't know which bit I believe. But as Voltaire said: "Don't take a risk."'

He smiles and lowers his head. We are ready for lunch.

(2016)

GLOBAL SOUL:
TIGER WOODS

T HE WORLD OF professional sport thrives on exaggera-
tion and overstatement. Triumph and despair, courage and
cowardice, hero and villain, mental strength and weakness, win
and lose – these are the binary oppositions of the commonplace
sporting lexicon. So, when Hank Haney, on the second page of
this memoir, declares that Tiger Woods is the 'human being who's
fallen faster than anyone else in history', you forgive the hyperbole
because he speaks as a sportsman. More than this, he speaks as the
American golfer's former coach, from March 2004 to May 2010,
and as a man who likes to think he speaks the truth.

Not so long ago we knew Tiger Woods publicly as a golfer
of incomparable brilliance and as the world's richest and most
recognisable sportsman; one of his early ambitions was to become
sport's first billionaire, which he achieved in 2009. He was the
greatest ever to play the game, routinely expected to break Jack
Nicklaus's longstanding record of eighteen victories in 'major'
championships. (The four majors are the US Masters, the US
Open, the British Open and the US PGA, comparable in status
to the four grand slams in tennis.)

Woods turned professional in 1996. Through his dominance and because of his mixed racial heritage he quickly became an icon of globalisation, as celebrated in Asia and Africa as he was in Europe and North America: endorsed, acclaimed. Everybody wanted a piece of him and sponsors in the Gulf states or China would pay millions of dollars simply to have him put in an appearance at their tournament.

The son of an African-American former marine named Earl and an Asian mother, Kutilda, Woods was a mixed-race man in an oppressively white and often shamefully segregated game. If he mostly avoided speaking about politics and race, settling for the bland neutrality of most sports stars, his very presence on the golf courses of the elite country clubs of the American Deep South was political. That he was not only the best of his generation – Earl called his son 'golf's first athlete' – but the best ever merely underscored his significance. He was imperious. He was unignorable. Plus, he seemed to be a decent young fellow, a little intense and brooding perhaps, but a devoted son who sought to honour his parents at all times and a good husband to his ultra-blonde Nordic wife, Elin Nordegren, with whom he had two children. He also worked at his game and on his fitness like no one before: over the years the once-thin and gangly Woods transformed his body shape through relentless gym workouts, putting muscle on, bulking out. Weary of being intimidated by his supremacy and athleticism, his rivals were forced into the gym as they attempted to compete and add distance to their drives (Woods was one of the game's longest hitters).

But then, at the age of thirty-five, midway through life's journey, Woods catastrophically found himself lost in a dark wood, exposed as a serial adulterer and hypocrite – a 'sex addict', no less, with a taste for rough, dirty sex with hardcore porn performers (one hesitates to call them stars or actresses) and other women procured by his handlers for casual encounters. The carefully cultivated public image of wholesome clean-living was destroyed and the private Woods was suddenly laid bare as a monster of appetite and supreme selfishness. His fall, in a modern sporting context, is astounding, if not world-historic, as Haney in all his insularity and monomania, would wish it.

Once the first revelation was out, after Woods crashed his car into a water hydrant and tree near his Florida mansion in November 2009 following an early-hours row with his wife, the once deferential US sports media turned against him. The kiss-and-tells and lurid stories followed swiftly, one after another. Haney describes how Woods would use his smartphone to read what was being written about him, even in the comment threads.

After a period of reconciliation and therapy, Elin left and then divorced her husband. Corporate sponsors began deserting Brand Tiger. Worst of all, his golf game – his reason for being – deteriorated alarmingly and he stopped winning tournaments (he has not won a major since July 2008). In some tournaments, he has hacked around the course like a jobbing club pro, the eyes cold, the strain and suffering obvious as he rages, as if aghast at how the gods are treating him. There has been no Virgil to lead him out of the underworld.

But, for a period, there was Haney – and he has since gone about breaking all confidences. His book is the most devastating portrait yet of Woods by anyone who has worked closely with him. Haney assiduously monitored Woods's moods and frustrations, his silences and sulks. He reproduces emails that he sent to Woods and paraphrases his replies. Haney used to stay often at Woods's mansion in Florida, and yet you get the sense that he was never fully liked or trusted – sensibly, as it has turned out.

Haney is quick to say that it was not Woods but he who ended their relationship after the 2010 US Masters. He was tired of Woods's indifference and believed that his man was no longer as dedicated to refining his game as he'd once been. Woods's fascination with the military disturbed and irritated Haney, who reveals that the golfer used to attend training expeditions with the Navy SEALs and considered enlisting in the elite force. Tiger speaks in clipped, direct sentences and Haney captures well the idiom. Was he writing it all down as he went along?

Haney accepts that working so closely with Woods was the thrill of his career. After all, the Woods of old was often unbeatable and his resolve unbreakable (he won the 2008 US Open with a ruptured left knee, which meant that he could not walk without severe pain and spent hours between rounds each evening in his hotel room receiving emergency treatment). At moments of heightened on-course stress he was able to slow his pulse and operate as if at a pace entirely of his own choosing. 'Tiger was like a yogi who could level his emotions seemingly at will,' says Haney. He was the antithesis of the choker: the finest final round finisher the game has known.

He may not realise it but Haney reveals just as much about himself as he does about Woods. There are cryptic references to his struggles with alcoholism and loss of confidence as a golfer, his divorce and the various ways he felt slighted and wronged by Woods. He is thin-skinned and perhaps should have kept tight-lipped: no one in the professional game is likely to trust him again, not after what he has revealed about Tiger Woods, for whom he professes fondness even as he denounces his former pupil as a mean and unfathomable narcissist. ('Though I do hate him as I do hell's pains,' Iago says of Othello. 'Yet for necessity of present life, I must show out a flag and sign of love.')

For golfers the big miss is the rogue shot that can destroy the rhythm of a round. Too many big misses and a card and indeed a tournament are wrecked. Woods longed to build a swing that would eliminate the big miss from his game and Haney believed he could help him do it. In the event, after several notably successful years together, they separated. This book is a necessarily partial account of an often-strained partnership, as well as an enthralling record of how much it costs a man not only to dare to be the best of his generation but a champion for all the ages – until, that was, he suffered the biggest miss of all.

(2012)

THE CONTRARIAN:
CHRISTOPHER HITCHENS

IN HIS FINAL interview, conducted with Richard Dawkins and published in the *New Statesman* (and a worldwide internet hit), Christopher Hitchens, who died from cancer on 15 December 2011 at the age of sixty-two, spoke of how the one consistency for him, in his four-decade career as a writer, was in being against the totalitarian, on the left and on the right. 'The totalitarian, to me, is the enemy – the one that's absolute, the one that wants control over the inside of your head, not just your actions and your taxes.' And for him the ultimate totalitarian was God, against whom (or the notion of whom) he was raging until the end.

Hitchens himself was many things: a polemicist, reporter, author, literary critic, rhetorician, militant atheist, drinker, name-dropper and raconteur. In his own way, he too was also an absolutist. He liked a clear, defined target against which to take aim and fire; he knew what he wanted to write about and against and he did so with all the power of his formidable erudition. He was an accomplished and prolific writer, but an even better speaker: his perfectly articulated sentences cascaded and tumbled, unstoppably. He was one of our greatest debaters, taking on all-comers on all subjects, except sport, in which he professed to have no interest. 'Never be afraid of stridency,' he told Dawkins in that final interview.

Born in 1949, Hitchens remained a recognisable late-1960s archetype, radicalised by the countercultural spirit of the turbulent era of the Vietnam War and the sexual revolution. (He reminded me a little of Philip Roth's David Kepesh: celebrity journalist, upmarket talk-show star, libertine, hyper-confident scourge of bourgeois respectability and conventional behaviour.) The son of a Tory naval officer and a Jewish mother who committed suicide in a bizarre love pact, Hitchens was educated at the Leys School in Cambridge and at Oxford, where he joined the far-left, anti-Stalinist sect, the International Socialists, a forerunner of the Socialist Workers Party, agitating at demonstrations by day and romping with the daughters, and sometimes sons, of the landed classes by night.

He remained a member of the party until the late 1970s and continued, long after that, to defend the Old Man, as he and the comrades called Trotsky. If there was a parliamentary road to socialism, he didn't seem much interested in it in those early days, though towards the end of his life he claimed that the British Labour Party was 'my party'.

After university, Hitchens worked on the *New Statesman* under the editorships of Anthony Howard and Bruce Page. He was operating then very much in the shadows cast by his luminously gifted friends and fellow NS staffers Martin Amis, Julian Barnes and James Fenton. Other friends, including Salman Rushdie and Ian McEwan, were also beginning to establish themselves as successful and unusually ambitious writers of fiction. Yet there was a feeling among that group of clever young men – with their smart, rivalrous book chat and bolshie political opinions – that the Hitch, as they called him, was a powerful intellect and journalist but a mediocre stylist. 'To evolve an exalted voice appropriate to the twentieth century has been the self-imposed challenge of his work,' Amis once wrote of Saul Bellow in what served as something of a self-description and statement of ambition. Amis had his own exalted style; Hitchens, certain in his opinions but less so as a stylist, took much longer to find his.

In *Koba the Dread*, his 2002 book about Stalin and the British left's historic reluctance to condemn the crimes of the Soviet Union and its satellites, Amis suggests that his old friend began to mature as a writer, his prose gaining in 'burnish and authority', only after the fall of the Berlin Wall in 1989, as if before then he had been aesthetically restrained and compromised by a self-imposed demand to hold a fixed ideological line, even at the expense of truth-telling.

My view is different. I think Hitchens was liberated as a political writer long before the fall of the Berlin Wall – through moving, in his early thirties, first to New York and then to Washington, DC. There, after some early struggles, he found his voice and signature style, contributing to *Harper's* and the *Nation* and, later, as a well-paid deluxe contrarian, to *Vanity Fair* and the *Atlantic*.

I once had a drink with him (everyone seems to have had a drink with Hitchens) in the mid-1990s after we were introduced by the then Conservative MP George Walden. We met in the basement premises of Auberon Waugh's old Academy Club in Soho, central London, and the air was oppressive with cigarette smoke. He sat opposite me at a table, chain-smoking and drinking whisky, and he spoke in long, elaborate sentences as he recited from memory W. H. Auden's poetry. I felt battered by his erudition – can you keep up, young man! Hitchens exuded what I thought then was a superb worldliness. His voice was deep and absurdly suave – and, in manner and attitude, he closely resembled his old friend Amis, both more than half in love with their own cleverness and fluency. He was engaging, yet I found his confidence disturbing: he knew what he knew and no one could persuade him otherwise.

An absence of doubt defines his later work. His weaknesses are overstatement, especially when writing about what he despises (clericalism, God, pious moralising of all kinds), self-righteous indignation ('shameful' and 'shame', employed accusatorially, are favoured words), narcissism, and failure to acknowledge or to accept when he is wrong, as he was about the Iraq War, which he boisterously supported. His redeeming virtues are his sardonic wit, polymathic range, good literary style and his fearlessness.

Until the beginning of this century, Hitchens played the role of Keith Richards to Amis's Mick Jagger. He was the more dissolute, the heavier drinker and lesser writer, very much the junior partner in a celebrity literary double act. (Their relationship was a kind of unconsummated marriage, Amis said, though Hitchens would have happily consummated it at one stage.) Amis was a multimillionaire literary superstar, 'the most influential writer of his generation', as he liked to put it. He wrote in the High Style, after Bellow and Nabokov, and declared war on cliché. Hitchens, by contrast, wrote journalism and quick-fire columns and was not averse to using ready-made formulation and cliché. Even in his final interview, with Dawkins, he described himself as a 'jobbing hack'. 'If I was strident, it doesn't matter . . . I bang my drum.'

After the 11 September 2001 attacks, Hitchens reinvented himself as a belligerent supporter, in his writings and through public debates and his many appearances on American television, of the so-called war on terror. He supported the US-led invasions of Afghanistan and Iraq. In the arguments over dodgy dossiers, regime change and unilateral declarations of war, he sided with George W Bush, Richard Perle, Paul Wolfowitz and Tony Blair rather than with his old friends at the *Nation*.

At last, he had found his grand anti-totalitarian cause. A robust Manichaean, he denounced 'Islamofascism', a catch-all term that was so loose, generalised and opaque in its application as to be meaningless. The Taliban, Iranian Shia theocrats, Sunni al-Qaeda operatives, British Muslim jihadists, Hamas, Hezbollah – in spite of their different origins and socio-political circumstances, they were all 'Islamofascists'.

Hitchens believed his mission was comparable to that of Orwell and those who presciently warned of, and wrote against, the dangers of appeasing both communist and fascist totalitarianism in the 1930s. He became a hero to neoconservatives and the pro-war left. 'I will venture a prediction,' he wrote on a visit to Afghanistan in 2004. 'The Taliban/al-Qaeda riff-raff, as we know them, will never come back to power.' It is never wise for journalists to make predictions.

How will he be remembered? In many ways, the comparisons made between Hitchens and Orwell, to whom he returned again and again, as evangelical Christians return to Jesus ('What would George do?'), are false. He had no equivalent book to *Nineteen Eighty-Four* or *Homage to Catalonia*. He was not a philosopher or novelist and made no original contribution to intellectual thought. His anti-religious tract *God Is Not Great* is elegant but derivative. His polemical denunciations and pamphlets on powerful individuals, such as Mother Teresa, Bill Clinton, Ronald Reagan and Henry Kissinger, feel already dated, stranded in place and time.

Ultimately, I suspect, he will be remembered more for his prodigious output and for his swaggering, rhetorical style as a journalist and speaker – as well as for his lifestyle: the louche cosmopolitan and gadfly; the itinerant, sardonic man of letters and indefatigable raconteur.

In the introduction to his final book, the essay collection *Arguably*, Hitchens wrote that since being told in 2010 that he had as little as another year to live, his articles had been written with 'full consciousness that they might be my very last'. This was, he wrote: 'Sobering in one way and exhilarating in another . . . it has given me a more vivid idea of what makes life worth living, and defending.'

One is reminded here of Duke Vincentio's remark in Shakespeare's *Measure for Measure* when he urges Claudio, who has been deceived into believing that he is about to be executed:

Be absolute for death; either death or life
Shall thereby be the sweeter.

What the duke means is that through acceptance of and resignation to death we yet may find a kind of peace and a deeper knowledge of what it means to live, or to have lived, well.

Claudio replies:

To sue to live, I find I seek to die;
And, seeking death, find life: let it come on.

Hitchens has no equal in contemporary Anglo-American letters; there are followers and disciples (as well as some excellent political essayists such as Ta-Nehisi Coates and George Packer), but no heir apparent.

A. J. Liebling used to say that: 'I can write better than anybody who can write faster, and I can write faster than anybody who can write better.' He could also have been describing Hitchens, whom death may have silenced but whose essays and books will continue to be read, and who, through the internet and YouTube, will continue to be watched and listened to as he went about his business, provoking, challenging, amusing and stridently engaging with the ways of the world, always taking a position, never giving ground. Christopher Hitchens, 'the Hitch', to the last, the only one.

(2012)

THE TERROR OF
THE UNFORESEEN:
PHILIP ROTH

LATE STYLE, EDWARD Said wrote in an essay published
shortly before his death, 'has the power to render disenchantment and pleasure without realising the contradictions between
them'. Philip Roth's new novel, a counter-factual satire in which
the pioneering aviator Charles A. Lindbergh defeats Franklin
Delano Roosevelt in the 1940 presidential election and begins to
turn America, as an ally of Nazi Germany and Japan, into a qua-
si-fascist state, is an exercise in disenchantment and pleasure. In
style and tone, it is recognisably the work of a novelist entering the
final period of his writing career, peering back through the smoke
of a long, fractious but absolutely dedicated life at the person he
once was. The novel is unashamedly nostalgic – and this is the
great pleasure of it, for both writer and reader.

Roth returns once more to the mercantile neighbourhood of
his childhood in Newark, New Jersey. This time we follow him
directly into the family home as, in an act of imaginative reclamation, he introduces us to his father, Herman, an insurance agent

for Metropolitan Life, his resilient mother, Bess, and his elder brother, Sandy. The domestic detail of Roth's own lower-middle-class, war-shadowed childhood is rendered exactly in clear, plain prose. But the historical circumstances are different – and this is the true disenchantment of the novel because, as the narrator (the young Philip Roth) tells us at the outset, a 'perpetual fear' presides over these memoirs. That fear is anti-Semitism, and the precariousness of life for a minority people persecuted and menaced by their own government.

If Roth's great trilogy of novels about post-war American society – *American Pastoral* (1997), *I Married a Communist* (1998) and *The Human Stain* (2000) – as well as the novella *The Dying Animal* (2001), which served as a coda to the trilogy, have a unifying theme, it is to do with how little control the individual has over the inexorable forces of history, and is remorselessly tethered to them. In each of the three novels an aspirant everyman, buoyant on a steady stream of American optimism and expectation, is humbled and then destroyed after becoming entangled in a web of public politics and private deceit. They are destroyed by what Roth in this new book calls the 'terror of the unforeseen': the unexpected event, the chance occurrence, the unimagined catastrophe. Only in retrospect could it be said that history has a direction and meaning. The present as it is lived never feels like that; it is discontinuous, contingent. In truth, most of us live with a sense, even if only subconsciously, of the terror of the unforeseen, the event over which we have no control but which ineradicably alters the direction of our lives.

In *The Plot Against America*, the unforeseen is the election of Charles Lindbergh as president after he defeats Roosevelt. In 1927 Lindbergh, a former airmail pilot, became at the age of twenty-five the first person to fly non-stop across the Atlantic, in his single-engine monoplane, the *Spirit of St. Louis*. He flew from New

York to Paris without a radio or navigation aids, and his flight took him nearly thirty-four hours.

In many ways, he did more than cross the Atlantic on that historic flight: he flew straight into the future and became, as J. G. Ballard has written, a reluctant but authentic international celebrity of our emerging consumer and entertainment culture, 'the admired and welcome guest of kings, presidents and prime ministers'. For a period after that, Lindbergh had no peace: he was harried, pursued, adored. In 1932, his baby son was kidnapped; the story was a news sensation. The baby was later found dead, his body mauled by animals, in woods near the Lindbergh home.

In retreat, Lindbergh moved to England, from where he travelled to Germany. There he was thrilled by the pseudo-modernity and technological determinism of the Nazi state. In July 1936, Lindbergh attended a lunch hosted in his honour by Hermann Goering and was thereafter an esteemed guest at the opening ceremony of the Berlin Olympics. 'Germany,' Lindbergh wrote at the time, 'is the most interesting nation in the world today, and she is attempting to find a solution for some of our most fundamental problems.' On another trip to Germany in October 1938, Lindbergh would receive a medal of commendation from Goering, 'by order of der Führer'.

On his return to the US in 1939, Lindbergh, a determined Republican isolationist, campaigned against American intervention in what was after all, he said, a European war. At an America First Committee rally in Des Moines in 1941 (Roth moves the speech to 1940), he spoke of American Jews as 'other peoples', and warned Americans not to allow the 'natural passions and prejudices' of Jews to lead 'our country to destruction'.

You will learn very little about the true history of Charles

Lindbergh from Roth's novel. To Roth, he is less a historical figure – the 'last naive hero', as Ballard calls him – than a convenient device, a figure through which Roth can invert the founding ideal of the United States, transforming this proud vessel of migrations and new beginnings into a dystopia, the worst possible world for Jews. And Lindbergh is never more than an absent presence in the novel, someone heard on the radio or discussed in anxious conversation among senior family members.

Yet his influence on American society is all-pervasive: he flies to Iceland to sign a non-aggression pact with Hitler, he establishes a national Office of American Absorption through which he forces Jews out of the cities and into new settlements in the Midwest and the South, and he creates a society in which pogroms and politically-sponsored killings are not only possible but desirable.

In one early scene, the best in the book, Herman Roth takes his family on a trip to Washington, DC. Anti-Semitism is already biting; the Roths, despite having pre-booked their rooms, are turned away from their hotel, because they are obviously Jews – an enraging and humiliating experience for Roth *pere*, but an echo, too, of how African-Americans have been treated throughout American history. Meanwhile, out on the street, the young Roth boys look up into the sky to see a low-flying Lockheed Interceptor aircraft: it is their new president out on his daily solo flying mission, simultaneously a figure of fear and fascination.

The Plot Against America is, in many ways, an unsatisfactory book: not quite fiction and not quite believable. There are too many long, dull explicatory passages of historical narrative, too much over-elaborate scene-setting. It is Roth at his most benign and forgiving, of his parents, of his extended family, of his tormented relationship with his own Jewishness. Roth Man as hectoring raconteur, as stand-up comedian, as tyrannical monologist is absent. Instead, the tone is one of heightened resignation – and

Roth's family and their fellow Jews, following the mysterious disappearance of President Lindbergh in an unexplained aviation accident at the end of the book, are somehow redeemed by benevolent destiny as the natural order of things is, as in a fairy tale, restored.

What are we to make of all this? Indeed, what are we to make more generally of the late style of Philip Roth? Before the publication of this book, so unexpected and reflective, one would have said that it was characterised by rage against decline and death, and the realisation that, as the fallen 'Swede', the central character of *American Pastoral*, must discover, 'the worst lesson that life can teach is that life makes no sense'. But this book is different. Sparer and less exalted in style, it is Roth's homage to his family: his own black-and-white home movie, his *Radio Days*. Reading it, one thinks also of the late fictions of Saul Bellow, so elegantly reduced compared with the turbocharged exuberance of his middle years; of the pared-down austerities of late V. S. Naipaul or Muriel Spark. One thinks even of the late romances of Shakespeare, with their interconnecting themes of loss and separation, of reconciliation and forgiveness, and their belief in the redemptive capacity of art. This is a belief Roth evidently shares as he returns to wander through the rooms of the former family home in Newark, and conjures his parents into life all over again, at a time of fear.

(2004)

POSTSCRIPT

The election of Donald Trump as US president led many of us to read or re-read *The Plot Against America*. Indeed, it became one of the defining texts of the first year of the Trump presidency, not least because of Trump's isolationist America First rhetoric. David

Simon, creator of *The Wire*, is adapting the novel for a six-part television mini-series.

Reflecting on the nativist turn in American politics, Philip Roth, who died on 22 May 2018, aged eighty-five, said: 'No one I know of has foreseen an America like the one we live in today. No one could have imagined that the twenty-first-century catastrophe to befall the USA, the most debasing of disasters, would appear not, say, in the terrifying guise of an Orwellian Big Brother but in the ominously ridiculous *commedia dell'arte* figure of the boastful buffoon.'

Of his approach to fiction, Roth once commented: 'Making fake biography, false history, concocting a half-imaginary existence out of the actual drama of my life is my life.' He was fascinated by doubleness and deception, hence all those metafictional tricks he played and the alter-egos through whom he spoke. These pro-tagonists invariably shared much of his own early biography – the Newark boyhood, the conflicted Jewish identity, the troubles with women – as well as his predilections and prejudices. Several of the novels feature characters named Philip Roth, as in *The Plot Against America* – the best of them, I think, being *Operation Shylock* (1993), set partly in Israel and exploring the period when Roth was recovering from depression and a breakdown after heart surgery. Roth is adept at simultaneously asserting the veracity of the stories he tells while seeking to undermine them by drawing attention to their artificiality. Roth's strategy is one of complete disclosure interwoven with complete disavowal.

Roth has said that there is at least one significant difference between Charles Lindbergh and Trump, whom he mocked as 'the boastful buffoon'. 'It's the difference in stature between a President Lindbergh and a President Trump. Charles Lindbergh, in life as in my novel, may have been a genuine racist and an anti-Semite and a white supremacist sympathetic to fascism, but he was also

– because of the extraordinary feat of his solo transatlantic flight at the age of twenty-five – an authentic American hero thirteen years before I have him winning the presidency. Lindbergh, historically, was the courageous young pilot who in 1927, for the first time, flew non-stop across the Atlantic, from Long Island to Paris. He did it in thirty-three and a half hours in a single-seat, single-engine monoplane, thus making him a kind of twentieth-century Leif Ericson, an aeronautical Magellan, one of the earliest beacons of the age of aviation. Trump, by comparison, is a massive fraud, the evil sum of his deficiencies, devoid of everything but the hollow ideology of a megalomaniac.'

In 1960, Roth wrote about the challenge contemporary reality posed to the American writer. 'The American writer in the middle of the twentieth century has his hands full in trying to understand, describe and then make credible much of the American reality. It stupefies, it sickens, it infuriates, and finally it is even a kind of embarrassment to one's own meagre imagination. The actuality is continually outdoing our talents, and culture tosses up figures almost daily that are the envy of any novelist.' Roth met the challenge head-on – insistently, relentlessly and achieved a late-career majesty unsurpassed in modern American letters.

A POET FOR THE AGE OF
BREXIT: A. E. HOUSMAN

A. E. HOUSMAN HAS been dismissed as a minor poet and sentimentalist, and he is not currently on the school curriculum, but to read A *Shropshire Lad*, a cycle of sixty-three short interlinked poems, for the first time is, I think, to encounter one of the strangest, saddest and most affecting works in English literature. In this poetry of fond remembrance and painful loss, young men – 'lads', Housman called them – invariably die prematurely or are betrayed in love. The setting is rural Shropshire, in deepest, faraway England, but 'heartless, witless' nature does not console or redeem, even as it beguiles and tantalises. For this is a godless pastoral and the only constant in these poems, for all the pleasures of their lyric intensity and ironic refinement, is death.

The biographer and critic Peter Parker's absorbing *Housman Country* is less a formal biography than a book about legacy and about how one writer's work, specifically A *Shropshire Lad*, has resonated or 'vibrated' through the decades, acquiring new meaning and relevance for each subsequent generation. It is also a book about England and Englishness and, in the aftermath of the Brexit vote, one of deep interest and relevance.

A *Shropshire Lad* was published in 1896 after what Housman described as a period of 'continuous excitement', when the author was a thirty-six-year-old classics professor at University College London. Parker's contention is that, even if you haven't read the book, you are probably already familiar with it. You might well have heard some of the poems set to music by George Butterworth and Ralph Vaughan Williams, two composers who were fundamental to the revival of English classical music and did so much to preserve English folk songs.

You are likely to be familiar too with some of the most celebrated phrases from the poems, such as 'blue remembered hills' and 'the land of lost content'. These and others have entered the language and inspired any number of literary and popular writers and musicians, from Morrissey to Dennis Potter and Colin Dexter, the creator of the mournful *Inspector Morse*.

'It is the paradox of his life,' G. K. Chesterton wrote in a biographical study of William Cobbett, 'that he loved the past, and he alone really lived in the future.' Something similar could be said of Housman, the austere classical scholar whose outward reserve and forbidding personality disguised hurt and vulnerability that found expression only in his poetry – a poetry that was future-harrowed and death-haunted, just as his studies were backward-looking and past-fixated.

After reading A *Shropshire Lad*, the American poet Robert Lowell said that Housman 'foresaw the Somme'. How else to account for the morbid preoccupation with doomed youth? During the First World War, it was said that Housman's book was in 'every pocket', as if the young men volunteering for or sent to the Western Front saw something of themselves in Housman's lost lads.

In 'On the idle hill of summer', Housman writes, for instance, of 'Soldiers marching, all to die'. He continues: 'East and west of fields forgotten / Bleach the bones of comrades slain, / Lovely lads and dead and rotten; / None that go return again.' Housman was, says Parker, 'the supreme elegist of and for his age', which is why his poetry continues to mean so much to so many.

But it's not just the prescience of the poems that's so striking. It's something more than this, something to do with their unity of place and time and evocation of the rhythms of rural life. It is as if for Housman the true spirit of England resides in the countryside.

This is surely why his work appealed so deeply to Edward Thomas and Rupert Brooke, both young poets and patriotic volunteers killed during the First World War and both romantically concerned with what Parker calls 'dreams of England'. Fortunately, while exploring these dreams, Parker resists making too many generalisations about national identity, though he lapses when suggesting 'emotional self-denial [is] thought characteristic of the English race'. He evidently hasn't spent much time in Newcastle city centre on a Saturday night.

❧

Alfred Edward Housman was born in 1859 in Worcestershire, the eldest of seven children of a country solicitor. His mother died when Housman was only twelve and, though he grew up in a religious family, he claimed to have lost his faith at Oxford. Housman was a brilliant student and would become the outstanding classical scholar of his generation, first at University College London, and then at Trinity College, Cambridge, and yet he failed his finals.

There were suggestions that he was brought down by intellectual arrogance and was bored by the rituals of examinations, but my sense is that his failure is also likely to have been the result of emotional distress. As an undergraduate he fell desperately in love with Moses Jackson, a fellow student and champion sportsman, who was heterosexual. The experience dislocated him and destroyed his peace of mind. Many years later, in 1933, Housman delivered a public lecture at Cambridge in which, uncharacteristically, he offered some insight into his own creative process. Writing poetry was 'generally agitating and exhausting'. He discussed the effect some lines of poetry had on him and quoted from one of Keats's last letters in which he said of his beloved Fanny Brawne, from whom he was soon to be eternally separated by death, 'everything that reminds me of her goes through me like a spear'. Was Housman thinking of Moses Jackson as he cited this?

Unrequited love is of course one of the perennial themes of lyric poetry and a sense of love thwarted or love lost gives Housman's poetry much of its emotional charge. Philip Larkin called him 'the poet of unhappiness'. Certainly, Housman's poetry, with its homoerotic subtext, is fatalistic about love: it's as if sex and death are, for him, inextricable. Or, at least, there can be no true love without suffering.

We know very little about Housman's sex life: Parker is restrained on the subject. What we do know is that long after Jackson had married and emigrated with his wife first to India and then Canada, the two men continued to correspond and Housman would send him poems.

'I suppose many a man has stood at his window above a London square in April hearing a message from the lanes of England,' wrote H. V. Morton in a book titled *In Search of England* cited by Parker. The narrator of *A Shropshire Lad* has heard this calling or something like it and, from his exile in London, never ceases yearning for the 'happy highways' of his rural childhood to which he can never return, just as Housman never ceased yearning for Moses Jackson.

❧

Housman is a notable absence from Ferdinand Mount's *English Voices*, a selection of literary and political review-essays published over the past thirty years. In his introduction, Mount attempts to impose a semblance of thematic unity (the English are an 'amphibious mob' and so on) on what is, in effect, a work of miscellany. The English, Mount says, are proud of their 'mongrel heredity'. And his English voices include W. G. Sebald, a German who lived in East Anglia and wrote in German; Germaine Greer, a raucous Australian who is a long-time resident of the Essex hinterland; and V. S. Naipaul, a Trinidadian of Indian heritage who has the mannerisms of a haughty lord of the manor and is the author of some of the most distinguished books published since the war.

Mount's natural idiom is Oxbridge high table. He has an easy, unforced familiarity with the great books. He knows the history of these islands well enough. He uses the first person singular, but unostentatiously, so that he is never more than a bashful presence in these pieces. His own English voice is learned, wry, insouciant, a touch superior. He is unafraid of emotion, telling us which writers move him to tears (Keats, Wilfred Owen), and he is good on the lives of politicians – especially William Gladstone, Robert Peel, Harold Macmillan and Margaret Thatcher, for whom he worked.

Mount is a baronet, a cousin of David Cameron, and belletrist. He has laboured at the rock face of Parnassus without ascending its peaks. But he is no mere well-heeled dilettante – because, as an essayist, memoirist, novelist and polemicist (*The New Few*, his 2012 counterblast against oligarchy and runaway globalisation, was widely noticed), he is serious about the writing life. He deserves greater recognition, and these essays, best read in batches rather than in one concentrated period as I did, offer a good introduction to an urbane, if essentially old-fashioned, writer.

J. D. Taylor, who is twenty-seven and has 'no Oxbridge credentials and well-connected kin', has written an account of the four months he spent exploring Britain. *Island Story* is informed by the spirit of Cobbett's 1830 *Rural Rides*, that great work of social criticism. On his travels Taylor rides his bike, camps or stays at hostels, listens hard to those he meets and takes notes. He travels erratically but reads astutely. He is left-wing but not too preachy.

He is a good companion because he has an original mind. But he knows too that he is travelling around a country that might soon cease to exist, at least as a single polity.

Great Britain, Taylor reflects, the most successful multinational state in history, has never seemed more fragile, destabilised by its disunities. The House of Lords is outmoded. The Scots are outraged that they are being dragged out of the European Union against the will of the majority. The English are increasingly restive, especially beyond the metropolis. England and Britain were once interchangeable. No more. 'If independence means a rejection of greedy and dishonest Westminster politicians...' Taylor writes, 'then it is hard to see which regions beyond southern England might vote to remain part of the UK.'

For Taylor, 'disappointment' defines the British experience. He says it is 'the prevailing feeling I encountered in others'. For Ferdinand Mount, the dominant tone of English discourse is not disappointment but 'one of regret, of nostalgia rather than self-congratulation'. For Peter Parker, 'melancholy and nostalgia are present from the very beginnings of English literature'.

This is persuasive. Orson Welles, discussing his film *Chimes at Midnight*, said: 'There has always been an England, an older England, which was sweeter, purer ... You feel a nostalgia for it in Chaucer, and you feel it all through Shakespeare.'

You feel this nostalgia for an older, sweeter, purer England all through A *Shropshire Lad* as well. It is part of its enduring appeal, and no matter how many times you read it you cannot help but surrender to the plangent sounds of its sad music.

(2016)

MEMORY AND FORGETTING: KAZUO ISHIGURO

THE BURIED GIANT, Kazuo Ishiguro's first novel for a decade is, on one level, a complete surprise. It's set in England in the Dark Ages no less, perhaps in the fifth or early sixth century, a period about which little certain is known. The Romans have left Britain and the Saxons have arrived, built settlements, and fought wars of conquest and survival. The people Ishiguro calls 'Britons' have been forced into an uneasy accommodation with the settlers, and ogres and pixies roam a bleak, damp landscape.

Ishiguro has set novels in a parallel dystopian England in which child clones are being reared for organ donation in ignorance of their ultimate fate (*Never Let Me Go*, 2005), and in an imaginary central European city in which a concert pianist finds himself lost in a surrealist nightmare of coincidence, farce and mistaken identity (*The Unconsoled*, 1995). He is no realist. But I never expected to encounter a she-dragon in his fiction or, for that matter, the wizard Merlin, from Arthurian legend.

Yet for all its flights of fantasy and supernatural happenings – a mist has settled over the land forcing people into a condition of forgetfulness, or so they believe – *The Buried Giant* is absolutely characteristic, moving and unsettling, in the way of all Ishiguro's fiction. It's less a case of '*Game of Thrones* meets *The Hobbit*', as one wag has dubbed it, than a novel of imaginative daring that, in its subtleties of tone, mood and reflection, could be the work of no other contemporary writer. And, as ever, there is much humour.

Open it at any page and you will recognise the cadences of the restrained, meticulous sentences and paragraphs. In the manner of Cormac McCarthy's dystopian novel *The Road*, Ishiguro has created a fantastical alternate reality in which, in spite of the extremity of its setting and because of its integrity and emotional truth, you believe unhesitatingly.

The dialogue, in particular, though somewhat baffling at first, beguiles through slow accumulation. The characters address one another with elaborate courtesy and formality, even at times of stress or approaching violence. One hears echoes of the chivalric codes and vocabulary of the medieval romance tradition – one of the main characters is a knight named Sir Gawain, 'nephew of the great Arthur who once ruled these lands' – but in no way is it a work of pastiche or cod historical melodrama. And many of the themes are familiar from previous novels: the unreliability of historical memory, the way the past interacts with and disrupts the present, the regrets we nurture but never fully confront or understand, the ever-present reality of mortality.

The Buried Giant can be read as a quest narrative, rich in allusion; as an allegory about post-conflict resolution and the way nation states and their peoples cope with and recover from wars and collective trauma; and as a story that explores the meaning of love in its various manifestations. It can also be read most straightforwardly as an adventure story about the trials endured by an aged, long-time-married couple as they embark on a journey to find their missing adult son. Something disturbing in the family has happened and Axl and Beatrice, the old couple, have become inexplicably separated from their son, whom they are convinced without any evidence is living in a distant village and is waiting for them.

Axl and Beatrice are still in love, yet are confused about the origins of this love: both suffer from failing memory. They are haunted by fears of being separated from each other and by the realisation that they have forgotten much of their life together. (The novel could also be read as a parable about Alzheimer's, and about how this terrible disease devours memory and with it one's continuity of consciousness through time.)

The husband and wife face many obstacles and mortal threats on their journey. Along the way they meet Sir Gawain, whom Ishiguro transforms into a garrulous comic grotesque, as well as a Saxon warrior named Wistan, from the eastern 'fens', whose mission is to slay the she-dragon. Wistan becomes the self-appointed protector of a young Saxon boy, who is an outcast from his village. He sees in the boy something of himself – someone blessed with 'a warrior's heart'.

One of the mysteries of the book concerns the narrator. Who's in charge here? One is aware of a bashful, occasionally self-referring presence who seems directly to address the reader as if from a perspective far in the future: 'You would have searched a long time for the sort of winding lane or tranquil meadow for which England later became celebrated.' Let's call the narrator Ishiguro.

The novel is told variously from Axl's and the boy's points of view. There are also two extended first-person interjections, or 'reveries', from Sir Gawain. In the final chapter, in which we move from the past to the present tense, a Charon-like figure identified as a 'boatman' accepts the baton of narrative responsibility.

Each of the main characters is, in different ways, lost. Each is uncertain about the past, unsure of present circumstances and scared of what the future will bring – Wistan predicts there will be wars 'when ancient grievances rhyme with fresh desire for land and conquest' and this England will 'become a new land, a Saxon land'. Each is tormented by voices, dreams, visions and half-remembered episodes from their lives. Each is searching for something or someone in 'this land cursed by a mist of forgetfulness'. Even after you have finished the book, many days later, you find you can't stop thinking about it so beguiling is its effect.

※

Born in Nagasaki in 1954, Kazuo Ishiguro came with his parents to live in England at the age of five. After working as a musician and then studying creative writing under Malcolm Bradbury at the University of East Anglia, he published his first novel, A Pale View of Hills (1982), which was set in England and a war-devastated Nagasaki, when he was twenty-eight. His second, the subtle and melancholy An Artist of the Floating World (again set in Japan, just after the war), won the Whitbread Book of the Year award in 1986. Three years later The Remains of the Day won the Booker Prize and made him famous. It became a critically acclaimed international bestseller and was adapted into a film by James Ivory and Ismail Merchant.

This early success liberated Ishiguro. 'Screenplays I didn't really care about, journalism, travel books, getting my writer friends to write about their dreams or something. I was just determined to write the books I had to write,' he said in 2005.

The intervals between novels became more extended, the works themselves longer and more experimental. He moved away from the quiet, ruminative realism of his first three novels, which were written in the first person, and began to explore different forms: surrealism, the detective novel in *When We Were Orphans* (2000), science fiction.

Ishiguro's first three novels were each about the consequences of the Second World War on individuals who had not fought in it but whose lives were affected by it. In each he explores themes of culpability and collaboration, national reconciliation and personal regret. The reticent narrators – a middle-aged widow (*Pale View*), an elderly artist (*Floating World*), a repressed, buttoned-up English butler (*Remains of the Day*) – are like detectives investigating their own past lives and struggling to understand why they acted when and as they did.

Ishiguro is not a flashy or ostentatious writer, unlike several of his near-contemporaries, notably Salman Rushdie and Martin Amis, with whom he was grouped as one of *Granta's* Best of Young British Novelists in 1983 and whose achievements he has surpassed. Amis once boasted that he wanted to write sentences that 'no other guy could have written'.

One never hears such bombast from Ishiguro, and yet he is a stylist, a master of nuance, artful withholding and of making strange what can seem most familiar or habitual – the technique the Russian formalist Viktor Shklovsky called 'defamiliarisation'. One detects the influence of European modernists such as Kafka and Ford Madox Ford on his oblique, indirect methods of narration. Reading his fiction, no matter whether the setting is Japan just after the war, a country house in the 1930s or a boarding school in the bucolic English countryside of the 1970s, the reader experiences just as the characters do a sense that nothing is as it seems or should be. Ishiguro's narratives are never direct: but, to paraphrase Shakespeare's Polonius, by indirection they find directions out.

There's a deeper truth available or hinted at but, for whatever reason, it can never be fully understood – or, perhaps, it's simply too painful to contemplate or comprehend. As T. S. Eliot wrote in *Four Quartets*, and as Ishiguro reminds us again and again: 'Human kind cannot bear very much reality.'

&

Ishiguro has disavowed the influence of his Japanese heritage – he says he grew up in Surrey reading Sherlock Holmes novels and watching Hollywood Westerns – yet, in a 1985 essay, he wrote admiringly about Yasunari Kawabata, the first Japanese to win the Nobel Prize in literature. Kawabata admired the 'classical' tradition of Japanese prose-writing – a tradition, as Ishiguro wrote, 'which placed value on lyricism, mood and reflection rather than on plot and character'. Kawabata's understated, spare fictions, like Ishiguro's, especially the first three novels, leave much unexplained; there is a presiding sense of ambiguity and of sadness. Kawabata was a nostalgist and profound conservative, who declared, after the surrender and defeat of Japan in 1945, that he would write 'only elegies'.

Ishiguro ended his essay by saying that Kawabata's novels 'offer experiences unlikely to be found anywhere else in Western fiction'. Something similar could be said of Ishiguro and of the place he occupies today in English letters, because there's no one like him. His books are among the most subtle and affecting in contemporary literature. You might forget certain details about what happens in them or individual characters or entire scenes but never their mood or atmosphere.

(2016)

POSTSCRIPT

In 2017 Kazuo Ishiguro was awarded the Nobel Prize in Literature. The timing of the award – during the Brexit negotiations – was interesting. In the immediate aftermath of the vote for Brexit, Ishiguro published an essay in the *Financial Times* in which he expressed 'anger' at what had happened. He was angry that 'one of the few genuine success stories of modern history – the transforming of Europe from a slaughterhouse of total war and totalitarian regimes to a much-envied region of liberal democracies living in near-borderless friendship – should now be so profoundly undermined by such a myopic process as took place in Britain'.

It was a surprise to read his swift journalistic response to Brexit because he is not an explicitly political writer or commentator in the style of, say, Ian McEwan. But his fictions are political. They explore themes of historical amnesia and unreliable memory, of guilt and delusion, as well the untruths we tell ourselves in order to cope with disappointment and loss – personal loss, national loss.

The Remains of the Day, which won the Booker Prize in 1989, is set in the 1950s and narrated by a butler called Stevens, reflecting on a long, repressed life of service. Early in the book, Stevens muses on the question of national greatness. 'We call this land of ours *Great* Britain, and there may be those who believe this is a somewhat immodest practice. Yet I would venture that the landscape of our country alone would justify the use of this lofty adjective. And yet what precisely is this "greatness"?'

The butler, who is a reactionary, asks a pertinent question, as relevant today as it was in the 1950s, when Britain was recovering from the trauma of two world wars. The Brexiteers have a heightened sense of the greatness of Great Britain or, in their words, 'Global Britain'. But Britain will surely never have more influence than it had before the fateful decision to vote to leave the European Union.

As Ishiguro understands, nations, like people, can make historic mistakes and be in denial about their consequences. 'Global Britain' is one of the cant phrases of our times. Before the Brexit vote, Britain was already global as one of the dominant states in the EU, with enormous reserves of soft power and acting as the 'Atlantic bridge' between Europe and the United States. It already, in effect, had a soft Brexit, not being part of the eurozone or the Schengen area. It had its own currency and thus independent monetary policy. It controlled its borders. I repeat: it was *already* global.

Praising Kazuo Ishiguro, the Nobel committee said that in novels of 'great emotional force' he 'has uncovered the abyss beneath our illusory sense of connection with the world'. Was the committee also passing a comment on Brexit Britain?

THE MASTER OF
FUNERALS: YASUNARI
KAWABATA

I N 1938 YASUNARI Kawabata was commissioned by a Tokyo
newspaper to write about a championship game of Go between
the best player in Japan, the Master, and a young, gifted challenger.
It was no ordinary game of Go: the aged Master, believed to be
unbeatable, is portrayed in *The Master of Go* - Kawabata's book
based on the 1938 match - as the embodiment of a traditional and
hierarchical Japan that is threatened by the forces of change and
modernity. The Master as reimagined by Kawabata has a contem-
plative, Zen-like serenity: through Go he has learned the art of
patience and the value of silence. But he is ill, and his illness affects
the game, which keeps being interrupted and then suspended; as
such, it occupies a period of more than eight months, at the end
of which you sense the ailing Master will surely die, as indeed he
does. So, this is to be his final game, his last stand as the Master
of Go.

In the Oriental game of Go, black and white stones are moved
on a board but, unlike in chess or draughts, it is not a game of

multiple moves by the same pieces. 'Though captured stones may be taken from the board, a stone is never moved to a second position after it has been placed upon one of the three hundred and sixty-one points to which play is confined,' writes Edward Seidensticker, Kawabata's long-standing translator. 'The object is to build up positions which are invulnerable to enemy attack, meanwhile surrounding and capturing enemy stones.'

For Kawabata, Go was more than a game; at its best, and especially as played by the Master, it was an art with a certain Oriental nobility and mystery. As with Japan in the immediate post-war years, the game was changing (though begun earlier, this book was not published until 1951). 'From the way of Go the beauty of Japan and the Orient had fled,' Kawabata wrote. 'Everything had become science and regulation. The road to advancement in rank, which controlled the life of a player, had become a meticulous point system.'

So *The Master of Go* is less a celebration of a great games player or work of dramatic reportage than an elegy.

Kawabata was born in the industrial town of Osaka in 1899, the son of a doctor. His early childhood was marked by trauma and bereavement: his father died when he was one and his mother when he was two. He went to live with his grandmother, who died when he was seven. Two years later, his only sister died as well. When he was fifteen, his grandfather died, prompting Kawabata to reflect that, already at a young age, he had become a 'master of funerals'. His first important novella, *The Diary of a Sixteen-Year-Old*, offers a harrowingly realistic account of how he tended his grandfather on his deathbed.

Much later, after the atom bombs were dropped on the cities of Hiroshima and Nagasaki and Emperor Hirohito had unconditionally surrendered to end the war in the Pacific as well as the myth of his own quasi-divine provenance, Kawabata, by that time middle-aged and established as a writer, wrote, 'Since the defeat, I have gone back into the sadness that has always been with us in Japan.'

Was this sadness common to all Japanese, as he would have had us believe? Or was it something more personal, the adult expression of the traumas and loss he had suffered as a child? Whatever the origins of this sadness, Kawabata decided that, with the war's end, he would write only elegies; and so, on the whole, he did, the last major writer to work in the 'classical' Japanese tradition. Today, the Japanese writers most familiar to Western readers, from the Nobel laureate Kenzaburo Oe to Haruki Murakami, are internationalists in style, attitude and ambition, their politics largely leftist or liberal and their familiarity with popular culture – with Hollywood, the American vernacular, pop and the buzz of new technologies – apparent in their work.

Influenced by the formal austerity and sparse, fragile lyricism of haiku, Kawabata is a miniaturist. His is a fiction of extreme economy, even of emptiness: it's as if he uses language not to say something but to point at things that cannot be said. To read him is to enter into an extended act of collaboration: you are challenged to interpret and imagine, to colour in and shade the empty spaces of his stories.

Worked on and revised over many years, sometimes published as magazine extracts or episodically, Kawabata's novels do not end so much as expire, in defiance of conventional expectations of narrative resolution and closure. You know where the novels are set but never quite know when, despite the occasional oblique reference to the war and to the social and cultural changes that followed. He understands, too, the value of silence – of the precise nuance, the interval, the pause.

Much of the subtlety of his prose-poetry – the short, intricately compressed sentences and paragraphs, the tension created by juxtaposing contrasting images – is lost in translation, especially what Roy Starrs, the author of *Soundings in Time: the fictive art of Kawabata Yasunari*, calls his 'aesthetics of ma'. 'Ma', broadly, means interval or pause, and Kawabata's best sentences in Japanese are distinguished by suspensions in the action and by pauses between clauses, the equivalent of the use of white space in Japanese ink painting, or the long pause in haiku. Perhaps it is this sense of something missing that gives his work its presiding ambiguity and vagueness.

In 1968, Kawabata became the first Japanese to win the Nobel Prize for Literature. In his Nobel lecture, 'Japan, the Beautiful and Myself' (in which, addressing a Western audience, he sought perhaps too consciously to conform to stereotypes of the mysterious Orient), he described the influence of the classical poets and Zen on his work. 'The Zen disciple sits for long hours silent and motionless, with his eyes closed. Presently he enters a state of impassivity, free from all ideas and all thoughts. He departs from the self and enters the realm of nothingness. This is not the nothingness or the emptiness of the West. It is rather the reverse, a universe of the spirit in which everything communicates freely with everything, transcending bounds, limitless.'

He could have been describing the aged Master as he sits impassively at the board during a game of Go. Indeed, in his later works, the central male characters often yearn for Zen-like states of grace and harmony while remaining resolutely of this world, burdened by doubt and erotic longing. As a young man Kawabata had an intense, unfulfilled relationship with a young dancer. She became the inspiration for his novella *The Izu Dancer* (1925), and he returns again and again in later books to a certain ideal of female purity – youthful, innocent, chaste – and shows how the real must necessarily violate the ideal.

In his novella *The Lake* (1954), he describes a teacher's obsessive pursuit and stalking of an adolescent girl: he watches her from the shadows, sometimes feeling 'like dying or killing her', so tortured is he by thwarted desire. *House of the Sleeping Beauties* (1961) is about a brothel where elderly men, often impotent and close to death, go to spend the night lying beside sedated young women. The rules of the house prevent them from having sex with the women, even if they could. This does not stop Yoshi Eguchi, who is slightly younger than other visitors, from fantasising about one of the women with whom he is infatuated. Sometimes, resting beside her, he dreams of strangling her, to preserve her virginity in death; at other times, he longs to die in her arms, a rapturous surrender. The insistent linking of sex and death is powerful in these later works, and reading Kawabata one can be reminded of Othello and the tormenting desire he feels for his young wife Desdemona, her skin 'smooth as monumental alabaster', even as he prepares to murder her.

Beauty and Sadness (1965), the most gripping and tightly plotted of all Kawabata's novels, is about a successful writer called Oki who, in regretful middle age, returns to Kyoto, the old capital of Japan, to discover what became of a young woman with whom he had a relationship many years before and later wrote about in one of his novels. The woman is called Otoko; she and Oki had a child that died as an infant. In the real time of the novel she is a painter and living with a younger woman, her lover. She has never forgotten the writer or ceased to love him, and his return unsettles not only Otoko but also her lover, who is intent on avenging the unhappiness that Oki caused all those years earlier through his carelessness and arrogance. Once again, themes of male narcissism, sex, death, erotic obsession and the vulnerability of female purity are interconnected, and the preoccupation with mutability is acute: even in translation, one is moved by the delicacy of the imagery and the understated precision of the limpid prose.

As a young man, Kawabata attended Tokyo Imperial University, where he became interested in European avant-garde literature and painting. He co-edited a journal called *Literary Age*, in which, attracted by the Arnoldian idea that literature and art would one day replace religion as the pre-eminent moral force in our lives, he introduced Japanese readers to Joyce and Proust as well as the work of the surrealists, the German expressionists and Dadaists.

Slowly, however, as Kawabata moved away from European modernism and embraced cultural nationalism, his stories and novellas – with their tea ceremonies, geishas, formalities and rituals – increasingly revealed the influence of the classical Japanese tradition in style and sensibility. Perhaps his finest work is *Snow Country* (written between 1935 and 1947), set on the inaccessible and mountainous west coast of the main island of Japan, where snow settles for at least five months of the year. It is here that Shimamura, a wealthy habitué of the metropolis, travels by train through the snow to visit a hot-spring geisha called Komako. The hot-spring geisha does not have the same privileges as her city counterpart: she is condemned through social status to a life largely of servitude and isolation. The relationship between Shimamura and his geisha has a strange, formless indeterminacy. They may feel a kind of love for each other, but it is a love that imprisons rather than liberates: in seeking beauty, the jaded Shimamura discovers ultimately that he can know only sadness.

If there is a recurring motif in Kawabata's work, it is the cherry trees that bloom exquisitely for a few days each spring before shedding their flowers, and which the Japanese celebrate with hanami, cherry blossom viewing parties. In *The Old Capital* (1962), a late work praised by the Nobel committee, the cherry blossom spring in Kyoto is described with precision. 'The scarlet double flowers were blooming all the way to the tips of the slenderest weeping branches. It would be more fitting to say that the flowers were borne upon the twigs than to say they were simply blossoming there . . . The faintest touch of lavender seemed to reflect on the scarlet of the flowers.'

One understands why Kawabata would be so moved by the transience of cherry blossom: in many ways, he must have spent much of his life mourning something important – first the parents he never really knew; then his grandparents with whom he lived; and later, after the defeat, the rituals and ceremonies of the old nation that he sought to dignify in his fiction even as they were being overwhelmed by the relentless American-led forward march of technology and progress.

In 1972, at the age of seventy-two, suffering from insomnia and unsettled by the fame that the Nobel Prize had brought him, Kawabata killed himself by putting his head in a gas oven. As a practitioner of Zen, he did not believe in an afterlife. But perhaps he believed in the afterlife of art. And he chose well the month of his death – April, as the cherry blossom flowered.

(2008)

A HESITANT RADICAL
IN THE AGE OF TRUMP:
DAVID BROOKS

DAVID BROOKS IS often called the in-house conservative at the liberal *New York Times* but his writings are much more interesting than that reductive label would suggest. Unlike many Republicans, he is not an anti-government Randian. He rejects Trumpism but understands what has enabled it. In recent years, his probing twice-weekly columns have become more preoccupied with ethical, philosophical and theological questions.

'It's a matter of conviction that public conversation is over-politicised and under-moralised,' he told me when we met in London. 'That we analyse every single movement in the polls, but the big subjects about relationships and mercy and how to be a friend – these are the big subjects of life and we don't talk about them enough. Or we have our moral arguments through political means, which is a nasty way to do it because then you make politics into a culture war.'

In his 2015 book *The Road to Character*, which is about humility and moral courage, Brooks, fifty-six, writes of how the 'marketplace encourages us to live by a utilitarian calculus, to satisfy our desires and lose sight of the moral stakes involved in everyday decisions'. The competition to succeed becomes all-consuming.

So, what has gone wrong with capitalism?

'If I had to reduce it to one phrase, it would be a crisis of "social solidarity",' he says. 'Just a breakdown in social fabric, a rise in loneliness, a rise in isolation, a lot of people feeling their dignity's been assaulted; they're invisible, they're not part of the project.'

Donald Trump's supporters have a generally realistic view of his qualities as a human being but, Brooks says, 'they figured he's my shot at change'. When asked about Trump, his rule is to say that he is the wrong answer to the right question. 'We have to address the fragmentation of society. The suicide rate in the US for white men, life expectancy is dropping not rising, opioids are everywhere, so those are symptoms of the larger isolation.'

The previous evening Brooks had been the principal guest at a Legatum Institute dinner, to which I was invited but could not attend. In 2016, I'd tried without luck to speak to him when I was making a programme for BBC Radio 4's *Analysis* about the changing behaviour of young adults who, data suggested, were the most socially responsible generation since the 1960s. Brooks had written that we were entering a period of social repair and this idea was the starting point for my programme. So, it was good finally to meet him.

Like many notable American conservatives, Brooks started out on the left. 'My parents were scholars of Victorian history and house-swapped with Margaret Drabble back in the 1970s. We lived here in London and we had the *New Statesman* at home and all through my childhood.'

He was a socialist through high school and college; he was

assigned Edmund Burke in his freshman year and loathed what he read. 'But then when I became a police reporter in Chicago covering crime and social decay, I came to understand Burke's belief in epistemological modesty: the world is just super-complicated, we have to be careful how we plan. And so I became more Burkean . . . and took a wandering through American conservatism.'

Brooks has made serious mistakes as a commentator – one of which was robustly supporting the Iraq War, the kind of grand, far-reaching 'neoconservative' project to which, one would have thought, as an anti-utopian sceptic he would have been opposed. 'Well this is the great irony, of course,' he says. 'So I wrote a column arguing with Edmund Burke and Michael Oakeshott, and I said what would they make of this? And they said they would not like this, they would be very sceptical. And then at the end of the column I wrote two paragraphs about why I thought they were wrong. I wish I could take those two paragraphs back!'

American politics is even more divided and ideologically polarised than here in the UK. Brooks values moderation. 'You know I like the phrase "hesitant radicalism".'

And he is a meliorist. 'I believe in incremental change but constant change. To be a Burkean, in America these days, is to be a moderate, which is what I think I've become. It's not to be a populist right-winger, or a Reaganite-Thatcherite type.'

He believes politics, in essence, is a competition between partial truths. 'Being a moderate does not mean picking something mushy in the middle, but picking out the strong policies at either end, because politics is essentially about balance, getting the balance right.'

One of Brooks's intellectual heroes – as well as one of Barack Obama's – is the theologian-philosopher Reinhold Niebuhr. 'Nothing which is true,' Niebuhr wrote, in a passage quoted in

The Road to Character, 'or beautiful or good makes complete sense in any immediate context of history; therefore we must be saved by faith.'

Can we really be saved by faith? 'You know, it's a challenge to me,' says Brooks, who self-identifies as being 'religiously bisexual' (he is Jewish *and* profoundly influenced by Christianity). 'Faith teaches you that human beings have infinite dignity but also are greatly broken. And that's a nice balance to keep in mind, a wise anthropology. It's a source of moral wisdom that has been lost, whether you subscribe to faith or not.'

Moral wisdom: this is precisely what Donald Trump does not have.

(2017)

THE SECRET LIFE:
JOHN LE CARRÉ

I N *TINKER TAILOR* Soldier Spy (1974), George Smiley is
recalled from retirement to investigate whether there is a double
agent, or 'mole', operating at the highest level of the intelligence
service, which John le Carré calls the Circus. Melancholy and
introspective – le Carré writes of the aged spymaster's 'spiritual
exhaustion' – Smiley is drawn back reluctantly into a crepuscular
world of secrets and subterfuge, where even long-time friends and
associates cannot be trusted. Smiley, le Carré writes, 'had that art,
from miles and miles of secret life, of listening at the front of his
mind; of letting the primary incidents unroll directly before him
while another, quite separate faculty wrestled with their historical
connection'.

Making slow progress in his investigation, Smiley returns to
Oxford – his 'spiritual home' – to see a former colleague, Connie
Sachs, who is an expert in Soviet counter-intelligence and re-
nowned for her exceptional memory. In the BBC television adaptation of *Tinker Tailor*, the first episode of which was broadcast
in 1979, a few months after the election as prime minister of
Margaret Thatcher, Connie is played by Beryl Reid and Smiley

with fastidious, low-toned deliberation by Alec Guinness, in one of his most celebrated roles. Their conversation takes place in near darkness, in a room lit as if only by candles, like the setting for some venerable college feast.

Connie has experienced the post-war decline of Britain, which Mrs Thatcher came to power determined to arrest. She tells Smiley that her 'boys', as she calls the largely public school, Oxbridge-educated group with whom she used to work at the Circus, have lost their purpose: 'Trained to Empire, trained to rule the waves. All gone. All taken away.'

In many ways, le Carré is an elegist, and the major espionage novels he wrote in the 1960s and 1970s have a peculiarly sombre atmosphere – all long shadows and recessionals. Themes of conflicted loyalty and spoiled idealism recur again and again in the novels and contribute to their fascination. His protagonists seem ambivalent about what they are doing. They have been prepared for a world that no longer exists, as Connie Sachs understood, and many of them are stumbling. They remain loyal to their school, college, class and, ultimately, their Queen (if seldom their wives), yet the country they serve has ceased to be a great power.

Le Carré dramatises the loneliness of the double agent: duplicitous and loyal only to himself, he lives in a condition of acute watchfulness. His fiction, especially his espionage fiction, with its suspensions, narrative absences and aporias, leaves much unsaid and unexplained. Even when his novels reach their inevitable resolution, as the genre demands, there is nevertheless a sense of incompleteness, of uncertainty and ambiguity, as though the agents themselves are unable fully to comprehend the events that have passed, or indeed the value of what they are working for or against. Demystification leads to a greater mystification.

Inside the Circus, there is a feeling among the best that the institutions they are fighting to preserve might not be worth the struggle. And there are traitors in their ranks; reading le Carré's spy novels one is reminded of the shabby final years of the Cambridge traitor Guy Burgess, who continued to wear his Eton tie long after defecting to the Soviet Union.

If le Carré is to be believed, he did not have to search long to find his subject; the secret condition, as he has pointed out, 'was imposed on me by birth, under the influence of that monstrous father. Then that brief passage through the secret world sort of institutionalised it.'

That monstrous father was Ronnie Cornwell, an inveterate conman and recidivist whom le Carré fictionalised so memorably in his 1986 work A Perfect Spy. A wonderfully labyrinthine novel, it can be read as a complex family history, as a study in the unreliability of memory and the unstable self, as an anguished confession, and as a quasi-detective story. Le Carré uses abrupt shifts in time and perspective, as Conrad did in The Secret Agent (1907), to tell the story of Magnus Pym, an English double agent who has gone on the run after betraying secrets to the Czechs. British intelligence officers are searching for Pym, who, in turn, is hiding out in Cornwall, where he has embarked on a quest to understand fundamental questions about his father and his own motivations for betraying his country. Writing in the late 1980s, Philip Roth called A Perfect Spy the finest English novel to be published since the war.

On first impressions, David Cornwell (le Carré was a pseudonym to preserve his diplomatic cover) seems like a typical member of the English establishment. Tall, patrician and well spoken, he was educated at Sherborne and Oxford, and taught as a young man at Eton, which he called the 'spiritual home' (that phrase again) of the English upper classes.

After leaving Eton, he worked for MI5 and MI6 and, because he spoke fluent German, was posted to the British embassy in Bonn. One learns from Adam Sisman in his authorised biography that Cornwell is a brilliant raconteur and mimic, and has been fabulously wealthy for decades because of the bestselling success and film and television adaptations of the novels. But first impressions are never reliable, as any spy would know.

As Sisman tells it, David Cornwell nurtures deep resentments and class insecurities, going back to childhood. Ronnie Cornwell (1906–75) was a freewheeling chancer and conman who went to prison on several occasions. Ann, David's first wife, called Ronnie 'the only really evil person I ever met'. He had monstrous appetites – for money, women, cars, houses, always living beyond his means, never settling in one job or house for long. He hosted extravagant parties, stayed at the finest hotels (bills were mostly left unpaid), and socialised with sports stars, actors, politicians, gangsters and aristocrats. He moved from one hare-brained scheme to another, sometimes lucking out, before the inevitable fall.

One morning, when David was only five, his mother left the family home and never returned. He did not see her again until he was an adult and remained distant from her until her death. 'We were frozen children, & will always remain so,' he wrote to his elder brother decades later.

At his prep school, where he boarded and encountered the usual sadistic and perverted masters, David was still wearing a nappy at the age of seven because of an inability to control his bladder. 'He became especially sensitive to social nuance, noticing details to which boys from more secure backgrounds might be oblivious,' Sisman writes.

As a boarder at Sherborne, David felt awkward and isolated. He was embarrassed by Ronnie, who inevitably defaulted on the fees, and by his humble relatives. He has since complained about

'the indelible scars that a neo-fascist regime of corporal punishment and single-sex confinement inflicts upon its wards'. Yet,
when the time came, he chose to send his sons away to boarding
schools, a decision he regards as a 'tragic mistake'.

After leaving Sherborne prematurely (he was sixteen), David
went to live in Bern, Switzerland. There he read Goethe, studied
German and was in tentative contact with the British security services. He completed his national service and, assisted by a contact
from Sherborne (the old boy network doing its thing), won a place
to study modern languages at Oxford, where he mixed with the
privileged sons of inherited wealth without being one of them.

Before long he was also serving as an informer for MI5, betraying the confidences of many left-wing university friends and
acquaintances. 'He had chosen loyalty to his country over loyalty
to his friends,' his biographer writes.

Adam Sisman has written a curious biography. It's at its best
when recounting the amoral behaviour of Ronnie Cornwell and
his son David's struggles to escape from his monstrous father's
malign influence and find purpose in life, which he did when the
worldwide success of his third novel, *The Spy Who Came in from
the Cold* (1963), liberated him to write full-time.

As the author of distinguished biographies of historians
A. J. P. Taylor and Hugh Trevor-Roper, Sisman is familiar with
the mores and machinations of the high English establishment.
He understands the interconnections that existed (and still exist)
between the great schools, Oxbridge, Whitehall, Westminster, the
Inns of Court, the BBC and the press, the gentlemen's clubs and
the City. He knows the codes and can speak the language – all of
which has helped in his appreciation of the textures and intricacies
of what le Carré calls the 'clandestine world'.

There is, however, something missing. It's as if Sisman is, or
feels, constrained: he seems unwilling to pass judgment on le

Carré as he follows him on his journey through life or properly evaluate the novels. When his research contradicts something le Carré has written or told him, he simply puts it down to an instance of 'false memory' and moves on. In his introduction Sisman says that his subject read the manuscript in advance of publication and that it will be revised, presumably when he is dead.

But in the book we have now, as it stands, Sisman does not really come close to capturing the inner life of the man we know as John le Carré, always the hardest task for any biographer, especially when his subject is alive. Le Carré is a man and writer of multiple contradictions. He is of and for the establishment but simultaneously estranged from it. A patriot who at university put country before friends, he has refused all official honours, including a knighthood. He has had close friendships with strident right-wingers such as Alan Clark, the late Conservative MP and diarist, and William Shawcross, but claims to have been a long-time Labour voter (though he loathed Tony Blair). He has certainly become angrier with age, raging against the Iraq War and condemning the iniquities of 'extraordinary rendition' and the rapacity of multinational pharmaceutical companies.

Le Carré has been accused of being anti-American and anti-Israeli, and has feuded publicly with Salman Rushdie, Christopher Hitchens and Tina Brown (when she was editor of the *New Yorker*). He frequently changes agent, as if always restlessly seeking self-validation and a better deal ('how much am I worth?') He refuses to allow his novels to be entered for literary prizes such as the Man Booker, perhaps because he fears the humiliation of rejection by the London literati.

Sisman hints that le Carré has considered suicide but does not elaborate or explain how close he came. Similarly, we know that his marriage to Ann was destroyed by his long absences and affairs, and that his second wife has tolerated his adulteries. In particular, Ann, who had literary ambitions, emerges from the book as a wounded, pleading woman. What does David think about her hurt and failures and what does Sisman think about how she was treated? We are not told.

An outstanding absence – especially curious in a book about a major writer – is literary criticism. Sisman writes at length about the business of books: about the rights deals, agents, royalty cheques, publishers, reviews and so on. But when it comes to the novels he offers little beyond perfunctory plot summaries. He tells us repeatedly that le Carré is a great novelist, but does not attempt to explain how he achieves his effects. Who are le Carré's precursors? What are his stylistic and technical innovations? Is he a conventional realist or a more experimental novelist? How did the spy genre evolve? What of the influence of Graham Greene or novels such as Conrad's *The Secret Agent* and *Under Western Eyes* (1911)? Sisman has nothing to say.

In the end, one suspects, John le Carré remains an enigma even to himself. But whatever his private turmoil, his considerable public achievement has been to chronicle and interrogate the history of our times. More than this, he invented his own lexicon of espionage – the Circus, tradecraft, lamplighters, moles, scalphunters, pavement artists, the honey trap – that will surely endure as a permanent part of the language.

Conrad said he wrote *Under Western Eyes*, his great novel of espionage and revolutionaries in pre-First World War Europe, 'to render not so much the political style as the psychology of Russia itself'. Conrad's Russia is a 'monstrous blank page awaiting the record of an inconceivable history'. It's a country on the edge of complete moral breakdown. In his different way, Le Carré has provided a valuable psychological portrait of the relationship between Russia and the West during the decades of the Cold War. And through reading his books we can better understand something of the failings and complacency of an English ruling class that was once trained for empire and to rule the waves, as Connie Sachs said, but has ended up scrambling even to preserve the unity of the United Kingdom itself.

(2015)

POSTSCRIPT

In 2017, at the age of eighty-five, John le Carré published *A Legacy of Spies*, returning to the period of the Cold War and some of his most enduring characters, including Smiley and the spymaster's former colleague and ally Peter Guillam. The book is a prequel as well as a coda to the 1963 novel *The Spy Who Came in from the Cold*. It's also a political book about current events – notably Britain's unhappy relationship with Europe.

In the penultimate chapter, Guillam visits Smiley, who is now an old man and living in exile in Freiburg. They reflect on what they got right and wrong when they worked together in the secret world. Guillam asks whether it had been worth the struggle and sacrifice. What was it all for, he asks, was it for England?

Smiley considers the question and then replies:

'There was a time, of course there was. But *whose* England [le Carré's italics]? Which England? England all alone, a citizen of nowhere? I'm a European, Peter. If I had a mission – if I was ever aware of one beyond our business with the enemy, it was to Europe. If I was heartless, I was heartless for Europe. If I had an unattainable ideal, it was of leading Europe out of her darkness towards a new age of reason. I have it still.'

Smiley – whose allusion to Theresa May's 2016 Conservative party conference speech will be noted by the alert reader – is not alone in yearning for a new age of reason. But these are unreasonable times. Darkness is visible wherever one looks: Trump's United States, Vladimir Putin's Russia, the former Eastern Bloc states of Poland and Hungary, the Middle East . . .

'It was terribly hard to write A *Legacy of Spies* during the period of Brexit and the ascendancy of Trump,' le Carré told the BBC. 'And I'd like to think that Smiley was aware of the sense of aimlessness which has entered into all of our minds – we seem to be joined by nothing but fear.'

He continued, 'Smiley, who has spent his life defending the flag in one way or another, feels alienated from it, feels a stranger in his own country, and that's why we find him and indeed leave him in a foreign place.'

ACKNOWLEDGEMENTS

I wish to express my gratitude to Jen Hamilton-Emery and Chris Hamilton-Emery for their commitment to and enthusiasm for this book. They are admirable champions of independent literary publishing.

I am grateful to Lorien Kite, Neil O'Sullivan, Sigrid Rausing and Jane Ferguson for their commissions.

Phil Whitaker, doctor and novelist, introduced me to Chris and Jen. Emma Dowson, publicist extraordinaire, has sent me all over the country to speak about this age of upheaval.

I would particularly like to thank my colleagues on the New Statesman, especially those who assisted in the preparation of this book: George Eaton, India Bourke, Peter Williams and Xan Rice.

Mike Danson, businessman, philanthropist and owner of the New Statesman, appointed me to my job and has been unstinting in his support.

Above all, I would like to thank my wife Sarah, our son Edward, and my mother Lilian for their love and support as well as my late father Tony for his guidance and humanity.

Earlier versions of pieces in this book appeared in the *New Statesman*, the *Financial Times*, the *Observer* and *Granta*.

I would like to thank Faber for their permission to quote from Philip Larkin's poem "An Arundel Tomb".

This book has been typeset by
SALT PUBLISHING LIMITED
using Neacademia, a font designed by Sergei Egorov
for the Rosetta Type Foundry in the Czech Republic.
It is manufactured using Creamy 70gsm, a Forest
Stewardship Council™ certified paper from Stora Enso's
Anjala Mill in Finland. It was printed and bound by
Clays Limited in Bungay, Suffolk, Great Britain.

CROMER
GREAT BRITAIN
MMXVIII